Archbishop Demetrios of America

Primate of the Greek Orthodox Church in America
Exarch of the Ecumenical Patriarchate

A Call to Faith
Addresses and Lectures 1999-2003

Edited by
Rev. Father Nektarios Morrow

Greek Orthodox Archdiocese of America
New York, New York 10021
2004

The Greek Orthodox Archdiocese of America wishes to acknowledge the generosity of Mr. Michael Jaharis in the publication of this book.

Greek Orthodox Archdiocese of America
8 East 79th Street, New York, NY 10021

ISBN 1-58438-028-4
ISBN 1-58438-029-2 (pbk.)

Printed in the United States of America

To the Noble and Beloved Clergy and Laity
of the
Holy Greek Orthodox Archdiocese
of America

Table of Contents

Introduction

On September 18, 1999, His Eminence Archbishop Demetrios was enthroned as the sixth Archbishop of the Greek Orthodox Archdiocese of America. Certainly, this historic and majestic event was the beginning of a new era for the Church in America. It was also the inauguration of an archpastoral ministry that would be both an embodiment and a bearer of *a call to faith*.

Archbishop Demetrios' election and enthronement as the Primate of the Greek Orthodox Church in America was not his first offering of service to the Archdiocese. During his Ph.D. studies at Harvard University from 1965 to 1971, and as the Distinguished Professor of Biblical Studies at Holy Cross Greek Orthodox School of Theology from 1983-1993, His Eminence made numerous pastoral visits throughout the United States, conducting services, offering lectures, and providing guidance and leadership drawn from his many years of faithful service to the Church.

In the almost five years since his enthronement, he has labored together with the Hierarchs, clergy, and laity of the Greek Orthodox Archdiocese in an intense effort to strengthen conditions of unity and peace and to advance the administrative and ecclesiastical stability of the work of the Church in America. He has traveled extensively throughout the Archdiocese leading services, consecrating churches, ordaining clergy, and extending the scope of the work of the Church, while concurrently experiencing the vitality and accomplishments of the Orthodox faithful and their parishes.

The Archbishop's ministry has been a clear witness of his life-long commitment to the sacred work of God and to offering his gifts and abilities *for the work of ministry and for building up the body of Christ* (Ephesians 4:12). But his labors in the vineyard of the Lord have also been a reflection of his response to God's call to faith. His faith in God through Christ has shaped his life and guided his service to the Church. It has also empowered him to meet the numerous challenges and obstacles that arise when God's people strive to do His holy will in this world. Essentially, his life and work has been, by the grace of God, his answer to the call of the Gospel, a call to respond to Christ in faith and to allow that faith to transform, renew, guide, and save.

This same call to faith has been a distinctive element of all aspects of the Archbishop's ministry and message. It is very evident in the addresses and lectures that comprise this volume. While each text is distinct in terms of topic, place, time, manner, and occasion, individually and collectively they are characterized by a call to seek God, to know God, and to have faith in His divine work and will. From his enthronement address to scholarly presentations in the halls of major universities, from conference keynotes to speeches of an ecclesiastical nature, all are imbued with a recognition of God's presence in our world and in our lives, His call for us to respond to His grace, and our divinely created abilities to ascribe to higher levels of understanding and existence that are ultimately rooted in faith.

This collection of addresses certainly represents a call to faith issued to Orthodox Christians in America, as the clergy and laity of our Holy Archdiocese have been the Archbishop's primary concern since his election. However, given the unique settings and opportunities offered to His Eminence, this volume is also representative of his commitment to the divine commission to preach and teach the Gospel to all people. Both in parishes, universities, conferences, banquets, and even in the halls of governments, His Eminence has consistently issued a call to faith by directing hearts and minds to our Creator and our Savior.

It is the significance and priority of this call to faith that has led to the collection and publication of the major address and lectures given during the first four years of His Eminence's service as Archbishop. It is also significant to note that this volume, at the request of the Archbishop, has been dedicated to the "Noble and Beloved Clergy and Laity of the Holy Greek Orthodox Archdiocese of America." As the Archbishop has responded to and issued a call to faith in all aspects of his pastoral ministry, he has joyfully witnessed the response of faith and the great endeavors of faith offered by the clergy and laity of the Church in America. In all of his journeys to parishes both small and large, to national, metropolitan, and local events he has beheld how the vitality of faith has both perpetuated our Church and broadened the offering of our Orthodox faith in America. This volume and its dedication is a firm recognition of the essential role of each and every member of the clergy and each and every layperson in the function and growth of the Church.

In conclusion, I want to thank and recognize those who have made this publication possible. On behalf of all who have contributed to this significant endeavor, I offer our deepest gratitude to Mr. Michael Jaharis, the esteemed benefactor of this book. His offering is but one of many that have marked his faithful support and distinguished service to the Church in America. Also, I wish to thank the Archdiocesan staff members who participated in the editorial process: Alice Keurian, the Director of the Office of the Archbishop, Christine Athanasopoulos, Marissa Costidis, and Paul Zamora. Their kind and patient assistance made this an enjoyable and edifying process. In addition, I would also like to thank Rev. Father Mark Sietsema, the Archbishop's first deacon upon his election and enthronement. Father Mark began the processing of editing and compiling some of the texts that are included in this volume. Finally, but most importantly, I offer my sincere gratitude to His Eminence for the opportunity to serve for over two years as his deacon and for the responsibility of editing this volume. For me, it is the culmination of the blessings received from being at many of these addresses, knowing their impact upon the hearers, and sharing a recognition that a collected work of this type will be a tremendous resource for fulfilling our sacred work and calling as Orthodox Christians.

It is thus in the spirit of the feast and season of Pentecost that we must hear God's call to greater and deeper faith; we must each respond with all of our heart, soul, mind, and body; and we, in continuing the work of His Church and His holy Apostles, must offer to our families, to our communities, and to our world a genuine call to faith, a call to believe in the truth, salvation, hope, and love offered to us by God through our Lord Jesus Christ.

Rev. Father Nektarios Morrow
On the Holy Feast of Pentecost
May 30, 2004

A Call to Faith

Enthronement Address

Archdiocesan Cathedral of the Holy Trinity

New York, NY
September 18, 1999

Blessing and glory and wisdom and thanksgiving and honor and power and might be to our God forever and ever. Amen (Revelation 7:12).

This beautiful Biblical hymn from the book of the Revelation of John expresses my feelings at this solemn hour: feelings of fervent worship and adoration offered to the Triune God, and, at the same time, intense prayer to have His mercy, love, and power supporting me in the sacred task in which He has called me, to serve as Archbishop, His selected and beloved people of the Greek Orthodox Archdiocese of America.

My adoring reference to God is accompanied by feelings of the warmest thanks to His All Holiness Ecumenical Patriarch Bartholomew and to the Holy and Sacred Synod of the Ecumenical Patriarchate for the supreme honor of bestowing upon me the awesome responsibility of tending the bright and high promising flock of the Greek Orthodox faithful in this great country.

I am thinking, also very thankfully, of my distinguished and holy predecessors, the Archbishops Alexander, Athenagoras and Michael of blessed memory, and the Archbishops Iakovos and Spyridon. They have served with all their power the very same people whom I am going to serve, thus continuing their work. I extend my particular thanks to His Eminence Archbishop Iakovos for the very gracious words he offered me as representative of the Ecumenical Patriarch and for his truly inspiring and edifying address.

I should like to extend my sincere thanks to my precious Brothers, the Metropolitans and Bishops, the pious clergy and the faithful lay people for the warm reception and the plentiful love they have shown me. My wholehearted thanks also extend to the Church of Greece and to the Greek Government for their support and their presence here through distinguished representatives. Last but not least, I express my warm thanks to the honorable representatives of the American governmental and political leadership and to all my distinguished friends, the religious, civil, academic, and business leaders, who were kind enough to participate in this ceremony.

On this solemn occasion, please allow me, in a spirit of love and honor for all of you, to bring to our attention a few basic issues that are significant for our work in the years to follow. Three of them, in particular, seem to be the most significant and constitute fundamental priorities in the life of the Church.

The first is the issue of the cultivation and growth of our Orthodox faith which our Ecumenical Patriarchate has preserved intact and immaculate. This is a faith by which our Church lives and has functioned for twenty centuries; a faith which gave to the world millions of true Christians faithful to the Gospel of Christ, millions of saints and martyrs; a faith which the great and genius Fathers and Ecumenical Teachers of the Church defended, safeguarded and delivered to us whole, clear, and undistorted; and a faith which created a wonderful tradition in which elements from the Greek cultural heritage have been used and incorporated with utter discretion and control.

This Orthodox faith has been always and is still today a basic priority for us. This is the reason why a number of serious questions are raised at this crucial moment. How intense and deep is our consciousness of this Orthodox faith? How much do we feel bound as individuals and as a community to our Orthodox Christian beliefs? How much do we know the substance of this faith as power and knowledge, as a power capable of changing human beings and the world, as capable of moving even the mountains and of rendering the impossible possible (Matthew 17:20-21), as a knowledge which offers the saving truth of God concerning humanity and the entire creation? Finally, how much does our Orthodox faith constitute our real and genuine identity within the pluralistic and multidimensional world of contemporary American society?

The questions are many and so are the answers, as we contemplate the past and look towards the future which the love of God has granted to us. Regardless of the answers, however, one thing is certain: Here, a remarkably wide field of a truly great work is open to us, a work with immense possibilities and huge perspectives, a work aiming at the invigoration, cultivation and growth of a dynamic and illumined faith within the clergy and the lay people of the blessed *Omogenia* which constitutes the flock of our Holy Archdiocese.

To this superb work, to this wonderful effort, I should like to invite today all of you, my beloved brothers and sisters. We have to be the Church that gives a whole, powerful and genuine witness of faith to this great country of America where God has planted us. All of us, without exception, have been called by the Lord to become conscious, true, dynamic and illumined people of faith, who, as the Apostle Peter underscores, are ready and *prepared to make a defense to any one who calls us to account for the hope that is in us* (I Peter 3:15).

There is no doubt, that such a work, such an orientation, necessitates an emphasis and an intensification of the didactic, educational, and cultural activities and programs of our Church. Within this perspective, it becomes imperative that we revitalize and further develop our theological and educational centers, specifically our Holy Cross School of Theology and our Hellenic College. They must be given the resources to attain the greatest levels of educational dynamism and become brilliant centers of cultivation and promotion of the values of the Orthodox faith and Greek *paideia* and culture.

Within the same perspective, all the Dioceses and communities of our Holy Archdiocese are called to make the work of the cultivation and development of the Orthodox faith a substantive part of their activities and programs by using all possible available means, from the traditional educational processes to advanced communication technologies. Our target is the growth and preservation of a robust and illumined Orthodox identity as a basic characteristic of the members of our Greek Orthodox Church, particularly of our young generation, our beloved and very promising children. This Greek Orthodox identity will enable our Greek-American faithful to stand with dignity and pride in the midst of our American fellow-citizens, respecting their religious and political beliefs within the large scheme of pluralism and globalization but, at the same time, insisting in the effort to safeguard the unique treasure which is our Orthodox faith, and to cherish our precious asset which we all acknowledge to be our Greek heritage.

The second major issue that deserves special attention is the issue of love, charity, and care for the human being. Our Orthodox Church, faithful to the Gospel of her

Founder, is the Church that loves each and every human person without any limitation, discrimination or reservation, especially when he or she is in a condition of need, pain and ordeal.

At the center of our faith is a God Who is love, the Son of God who became man in order to serve man, in order to redeem humanity and the whole of creation from evil, decay, and death. Our Church, following the steps of this God Who is a serving God, is permanently dedicated to the care of man, serving man not only within the limits of the possible, but beyond all limits. Simply, our Church loves beyond any measure.

All of our communities in the Archdiocese are invited to intensify and to continually optimize this excellent spirit of love and *diakonia*. Let our living, mutual love and the eagerness to transcend ourselves for the sake of the other who is in need be the distinctive signs of our Orthodox ethos. Here, we are not talking only about philanthropy or offering of material help to our suffering brothers and sisters; here, we are talking about an attitude of life that encompasses our whole existence. This attitude, in turn, manifests itself in initiative, dynamism, and avant-garde programs which cover conditions of sorrow, isolation and loneliness, sickness, despair, poverty, and all sorts of ordeals. Of course, for many years, our Church in America has given plenty of palpable evidence for her philanthropic ethos and disposition. Today, however, we emphasize the need to intensify such an offering in all directions. Here, there is an outstanding human dynamic and in addition tremendous possibilities due to the astonishing progress and the very impressive growth of the *Omogenia* on all levels. Here, there appears the bright opportunity for the Greek Orthodox Church in America to be, with the blessings and the grace of God Who is love, a Church that is truly a model in terms of offering love to man, a Church which embraces every human being, especially those who suffer, and that offers, on a continuous basis, love, care, and tenderness to a world tormented by cruelty, violence, alienation and selfishness.

Limitless love translated into service of the suffering human being is a basic priority which we have as members of the Church of Christ, especially in view of the dawning third millennium, a millennium which in all probability may have in store serious ordeals for humanity. It seems that people will need strong support in order to survive and progress in the midst of huge changes in the environment, the economy, social transformations, biotechnology, the population explosion, ideological confusion and the continuous technological revolution. Our Church here in the United States, as a Church of limitless love and philanthropy, as a Church destined to serve and to give, can play a significant role in the sacred effort to support man and his right to life, and to contribute in the task of resolving pressing problems which humanity will face in the years to come. Here, the limitless, wise and inexhaustible love of the Church becomes a strong element when faced with its future, no matter what this future might be.

At this point, please allow me to close with a third important issue, which in addition to the two previous ones, constitutes a basic priority for us. This is the issue of unity, concord, and unanimity of our ecclesiastical body, and of our Greek Orthodox community in general.

Let us remember what the Lord, immediately before His Passion, requested from the Father concerning the believers: "*Keep them in Your name, which You have given me, so that they may be one like us* (John 17:11)... *that they may all be one; even as You, Father, are in me and I in You, that they may also be one in us, so that the world may believe that You have sent me*" (John 17:21). And Paul, the Apostle to the nations, pleads with the believers to live *forbearing one another in love, eager to maintain the unity of the Spirit in the bond of peace.* Why? Because we are *one body and one Spirit, just as we are called to the one hope that belongs to our call, one Lord, one faith, one baptism, one God and Father of us all, Who is above all and through all and in all of us* (Ephesians 4:2-6).

This is precisely the reason why we feel it our duty to stress the need for unity and peace among us. Without fear or hesitation we are invited, beloved brothers and sisters, to set aside differences, misunderstandings or conflicts that could create distances among us, distances that shake unity and drive away the peace of God. Nothing should jeopardize the great and divine gifts of unity and harmony, of unanimity and communal accord. We have all the presuppositions, as people and as Church, to build in the highest and strongest possible degree a unity that is dynamic and unbreakable, so that we could be and stay one body, one soul, one mind, one will. In our case, the continuation and intensification of the task for unity and peace is the wonderful work into which God calls us today. He calls us in view of the great objectives which are being set in front of us. The future is our superb destination, and the future can be built only on the basis of our unity.

Our unity and harmony must be cultivated and pursued on many levels and in many forms within our Greek Orthodox Archdiocese and our Greek-American community in general. It must be cultivated among all generations, young, middle aged and old; it must be cultivated between the clergy and the laity; it must be cultivated between new Greek-American immigrants and the Greek Americans of the third and fourth generations; it must be cultivated as an unbreakable bond between the people of the *Omogenia* and the people of Mother Greece.

Such multidimensional unity and concord is not exhausted within the area of our Archdiocese, but is supported and treasured as a unity integrally connected to the

Mother Church, our Ecumenical Patriarchate. This unity is extended through our Ecumenical Patriarchate to the larger circle of the Orthodox Churches in the United States and the world.

Today, all of us under the wings of God are called to continue our creative march, to continue in the bright avenues in which the love and the wisdom of our God leads us. This is a march of a dynamic faith, of an unlimited love, and of an unbreakable unity, a march in which we will feel in every step the need to repeat the beautiful hymn from the Book of Revelation with which we started: *Blessing and glory and wisdom and thanksgiving and honor and power and might be to our God for ever and ever. Amen.*

ΕΝΘΡΟΝΙΣΤΗΡΙΟΣ ΛΟΓΟΣ

ARCHDIOCESAN CATHEDRAL OF THE HOLY TRINITY

NEW YORK, NY
SEPTEMBER 18, 1999

Ἡ εὐλογία καί ἡ δόξα καί ἡ σοφία καί ἡ εὐχαριστία καί ἡ τιμή καί ἡ δύναμις καί ἡ ἰσχύς τῷ Θεῷ ἡμῶν εἰς τούς αἰῶνας τῶν αἰώνων· Ἀμήν (Ἀποκ. Ἰωάννου. 7, 12).

Ὁ ὑπέροχος αὐτός βιβλικός ὕμνος ἀπό τήν Ἀποκάλυψη τοῦ Ἰωάννου, ἐκφράζει τά αἰσθήματα τά ὁποῖα κυριαρχοῦν εἰς τήν ψυχήν μου κατά τήν σημαντικήν αὐτήν ὥραν. Αἰσθήματα ἀπεριορίστου λατρείας τοῦ ἐν Τριάδι Θεοῦ, καί ταυτοχρόνως θερμῆς δεήσεως, τό ἔλεος, ἡ ἀγάπη καί ἡ δύναμίς Του νά μέ συνοδεύουν καί νά μέ ἐνισχύουν εἰς τήν ἱερωτάτην προσπάθειαν τήν ὁποίαν ἐν τῷ ὀνόματί Του ἀναλαμβάνω. Νά μέ ἐνισχύουν εἰς τό μεγάλο ἔργον εἰς τό ὁποῖον Ἐκεῖνος μέ ἐκάλεσε: νά διακονήσω ὡς Ἀρχιεπίσκοπος τόν ἐκλεκτόν καί προσφιλέστατον λαόν Του τῆς Ἑλληνικῆς Ὀρθοδόξου Ἀρχιεπισκοπῆς Ἀμερικῆς.

Τήν λατρευτικήν μου ἀναφοράν πρός τόν Θεόν συνοδεύουν αἰσθήματα θερμοτάτης εὐχαριστίας πρός τόν Παναγιώτατον Οἰκουμενικόν Πατριάρχην Κύριον Βαρθολομαῖον καί τήν Ἁγίαν καί Ἱεράν Σύνοδον τοῦ Οἰκουμενικοῦ Πατριαρχείου μας διότι μοῦ ἔκαμαν τήν μεγίστην τιμήν νά μοῦ ἀναθέσουν τήν εὐθύνην τῆς διαποιμάνσεως τοῦ ἐν Ἀμερικῇ λαμπροῦ ὁμογενειακοῦ ποιμνίου τῆς Ἐκκλησίας καί νά μέ στηρίξουν μέ κάθε τρόπον.

Σκέπτομαι ἐπίσης μετά πολλῶν εὐχαριστιῶν τούς ἁγίους προκατόχους μου, τόσον τούς κεκοιμημένους Ἀρχιεπισκόπους Ἀλέξανδρον, Ἀθηναγόραν καί Μιχαήλ, ὅσον καί τούς ζῶντας Ἀρχιεπισκόπους Ἰάκωβον καί Σπυρίδωνα, διότι ὑπηρέτησαν μέ ὅλας των τάς δυνάμεις τόν εὐγενῆ καί φιλοπρόοδον αὐτόν λαόν τόν ὁποῖον καλοῦμαι καί ἐγώ νά ὑπηρετήσω, συνεχίζων τό ἔργον των. Ἰδιαιτέρως εὐχαριστῶ τόν Σεβασμιώτατον Γέροντα Ἀρχιεπίσκοπον πρώην Ἀμερικῆς Κύριον Ἰάκωβον διά τά ἐξαιρετικῶς εὐμενῆ λόγια τά ὁποῖα μοῦ ἀπηύθυνε ἐκ προσώπου τοῦ Παναγιωτάτου Οἰκουμενικοῦ Πατριάρχου καί διά τήν ἄκρως ἐνισχυτικήν προσφώνησίν του.

Θά ἤθελα ἐπί πλέον νά εὐχαριστήσω ἐκ βάθους καρδίας τούς πολυτίμους ἀδελφούς μου ἁγίους Ἀρχιερεῖς, τόν εὐσεβῆ κλῆρον καί τόν πιστόν λαόν διά τήν θερμοτάτην ὑποδοχήν πού μοῦ ἐπεφύλαξαν καί τήν περίσσειαν ἀγάπην πού μοῦ ἐπεδαψίλευσαν. Ἐπίσης θά ἤθελα νά ἐκφράσω ἐγκαρδίους εὐχαριστίας καί πρός τήν Ἐκκλησίαν τῆς Ἑλλάδος καθώς καί πρός τήν Ἑλληνικήν Πολιτείαν διά τήν ὅλην θερμήν συμπαράστασιν καί διά τήν ἐδῶ παρουσίαν των δι᾽ ἐκλεκτῶν ἀντιπροσώπων. Τέλος αἱ εὐχαριστίαι μου ἐπεκτείνονται καί εἰς ὅλους τούς ἐκλεκτούς ἐκπροσώπους τῆς πολιτικῆς ἡγεσίας τῶν Ἡνωμένων Πολιτειῶν τῆς Ἀμερικῆς πού μέ τιμοῦν μέ τήν παρουσίαν των, καθώς καί ὅλους τούς φίλους πού συμμετέχουν εἰς τήν ἱεράν αὐτήν τελετήν, τούς ἐπισήμους θρησκευτικούς, πολιτικούς, κρατικούς, ἀκαδημαϊκούς καί λοιπούς ἡγέτας.

Μέ τήν εὐκαιρίαν τῆς σημερινῆς ἀναλήψεως τῶν καθηκόντων μου, θά ἤθελα μέ ὅλην μου τήν ἀγάπην καί τήν τιμήν πού αἰσθάνομαι ἀπέναντί σας, νά ὑπενθυμίσω ἐν συντομίᾳ ὡρισμένα βασικά θέματα, τά ὁποῖα ἔχουν σημασίαν διά τήν πορείαν μας εἰς τά ἔτη πού ἀκολουθοῦν. Θά περιορισθῶ εἰς τρία τά ὁποῖα εἶναι ἴσως τά πλέον σημαντικά καί ἀποτελοῦν θεμελιώδεις προτεραιότητας τῆς ζωῆς τῆς Ἐκκλησίας μας.

Τό πρῶτον εἶναι τό θέμα καλλιεργείας καί ἀναπτύξεως τῆς Ὀρθοδόξου πίστεώς μας, τήν ὁποίαν ὡς κόρην ὀφθαλμοῦ διατηρεῖ ἀπαραχάρακτον τό Οἰκουμενικόν Πατριαρχεῖον μας. Ἐδῶ πρόκειται διά μίαν πίστιν μέ τήν ὁποίαν ἡ Ἐκκλησία μας ζεῖ καί ἐργάζεται ἐπί εἴκοσιν ὁλοκλήρους αἰῶνας. Μίαν πίστιν ἡ ὁποία ἔδωκε εἰς τόν κόσμον ἑκατομμύρια ἀληθινῶν χριστιανῶν, ἑκατομμύρια ἁγίων καί μαρτύρων. Μίαν πίστιν, τήν ὁποίαν ὑπερήσπισαν μέχρι θανάτου, διεφύλαξαν καί μᾶς παρέδωκαν ἀκεραίαν καί καθαράν οἱ μεγαλοφυεῖς Πατέρες καί Οἰκουμενικοί Διδάσκαλοι τῆς Ἐκκλησίας. Μίαν πίστιν, ἡ ὁποία ἐδημιούργησε μίαν θαυμαστήν παράδοσιν, εἰς τήν ὁποίαν μέ ἄκραν διάκρισιν καί πλήρη ἔλεγχον ἐχρησιμοποιήθησαν καί ἐνεσωματώθησαν στοιχεῖα καί ἀπό τήν Ἑλληνικήν πολιτιστικήν κληρονομίαν.

Αὐτή ἡ Ὀρθόδοξος πίστις ὑπῆρξε πάντοτε καί εἶναι καί σήμερα βασική προτεραιότης μας. Διά τόν λόγον αὐτόν καί τά ἐρωτήματα τά ὁποῖα τίθενται ἐνώπιόν μας κατ᾽ αὐτήν τήν ἱεράν στιγμήν εἶναι πολλά: Πόσον ἔντονα καί βαθειά ἔχομεν συνείδησιν αὐτῆς τῆς Ὀρθοδόξου πίστεως; Πόσον ἔχομεν δεσμευθῆ ὡς ἄτομα καί ὡς σύνολον εἰς τό Ὀρθόδοξον χριστιανικόν πιστεύω μας; Πόσον γνωρίζομε τήν οὐσίαν αὐτῆς τῆς πίστεως ὡς δυνάμεως ἀλλά καί ὡς γνώσεως; Ὡς δυνάμεως ζωῆς ἱκανῆς νά ἀλλάξῃ τόν ἄνθρωπον καί τόν κόσμον, ἱκανῆς νά μετακινήσῃ ὄρη καί νά κάνῃ τά ἀδύνατα δυνατά (Ματθαίου 17, 20-21). Ὡς γνώσεως ἡ ὁποία μᾶς προσφέρει τήν σώζουσαν ἀλήθειαν διά τόν Θεόν, τόν ἄνθρωπον καί τήν ὅλην δημιουργίαν. Τέλος, πόσον ἡ Ὀρθόδοξος πίστις μας ἀποτελεῖ τήν ἀληθινήν ταυτότητά μας μέσα εἰς τόν πλουραλιστικόν καί πολυδιάστατον κόσμον τῆς συγχρόνου Ἀμερικανικῆς κοινωνίας.

Τά ἐρωτήματα εἶναι πολλά καί πολύ περισσότεραι αἱ ἀπαντήσεις εἰς μίαν ὥραν ὅπως ἡ παροῦσα κατά τήν ὁποίαν ἀναθεωροῦμεν τό παρελθόν καί ἀτενίζομεν τό μέλλον τό ὁποῖον μᾶς χαρίζει ἡ ἀγάπη τοῦ Θεοῦ. Ἀσχέτως ὅμως ἀπαντήσεων, ἕνα πρᾶγμα εἶναι βέβαιον: Ἐδῶ ἀνοίγεται ἐμπρός μας ἕνα τεράστιον πεδίον ἑνός πράγματι μεγάλου ἔργου. Ἑνός ἔργου μέ ἀπεράντους δυνατότητας καί εὐρυτάτην προοπτικήν, Ἑνός ἔργου πού θά ἀποβλέπῃ εἰς τήν ἀναζωογόνησιν, καλλιέργειαν καί ἀνάπτυξιν μιᾶς φωτισμένης καί δυναμικῆς Ὀρθοδόξου πίστεως ἐντός τοῦ κλήρου καί τοῦ λαοῦ τῆς εὐλογημένης Ὁμογενείας πού ἀποτελεῖ καί τό πλήρωμα τῆς Ἱερᾶς μας Ἀρχιεπισκοπῆς.

Εἰς αὐτό τό ἔργον, εἰς αὐτήν τήν εὐλογημένην προσπάθειαν νά εἴμεθα ἡ Ἐκκλησία ἡ ὁποία θά καταθέτῃ ἀκεραίαν καί ἄσπιλον τήν μαρτυρίαν τῆς πίστεως εἰς τήν μεγάλην χώραν εἰς τήν ὁποίαν μᾶς ἐφύτευσεν ὁ Θεός, τήν Ἀμερικήν, θά ἤθελα νά καλέσω σήμερα ὅλους τούς ἀδελφούς. Ὅλοι ἀνεξαιρέτως καλούμεθα νά γίνωμε καί νά εἴμεθα οἱ συνειδητοί, ἀληθινοί, δυναμικοί καί φωτισμένοι πιστοί, οἱ ὁποῖοι ὅπως τονίζει ὁ Ἀπόστολος Πέτρος εἶναι *ἕτοιμοι ἀεί πρός ἀπολογίαν παντί τῷ αἰτοῦντι ἡμᾶς λόγον περί τῆς ἐν ἡμῖν ἐλπίδος* (1 Πέτρου 3, 15).

Χωρίς ἀμφιβολίαν, ἕνα τέτοιο ἔργον, ἕνας παρόμοιος προσανατολισμός σημαίνει ἔμφασιν καί ἐντατικοποίησιν τῶν διδακτικῶν, ἐκπαιδευτικῶν καί μορφωτικῶν δραστηριοτήτων καί προγραμμάτων τῆς Ἐκκλησίας μας. Ἐντός αὐτῆς τῆς προοπτικῆς ἀποκτᾶ ἀποφασιστικήν σημασίαν ἡ ἀνασυγκρότησις καί ἀνάπτυξις τῶν θεολογικῶν καί ἐκπαιδευτικῶν μας κέντρων ὅπως εἶναι ἡ Θεολογική μας Σχολή τοῦ Τιμίου Σταυροῦ καί τό Ἑλληνικόν Κολλέγιον, ὥστε νά μεγιστοποιήσουν τόν μορφωτικόν δυναμισμόν των καί νά μεγαλουργήσουν ὡς κέντρα μελέτης, καλλιεργείας καί ἀκτινοβολίας τῶν ἀξιῶν τῆς Ὀρθοδόξου πίστεως καί τῆς Ἑλληνικῆς παιδείας.

Μέ τήν ἰδίαν προοπτικήν, αἱ Ἐπισκοπαί καί Κοινότητες τῆς Ἱερᾶς Ἀρχιεπισκοπῆς καλοῦνται νά ἐντείνουν τό ἔργον τῆς καλλιεργείας καί ἀναπτύξεως τῆς Ὀρθοδόξου πίστεως, καί νά τό κάμουν οὐσιῶδες μέρος τῆς ζωῆς, τῶν δραστηριοτήτων, καί τῶν προγραμμάτων των. Νά τό κάμουν μέ τήν χρησιμοποίησιν καί ἀξιοποίησιν ὅλων τῶν μέσων πού προσφέρονται τόσον ἀπό τήν παραδοσιακήν παιδείαν ὅσον καί ἀπό τήν σύγχρονον προηγμένην ἐπικοινωνιακήν τεχνολογίαν. Σκοπός μας εἶναι ἡ ἀνάπτυξις καί διατήρησις μιᾶς ρωμαλαίας καί φωτισμένης ταυτότητος Ὀρθοδόξου πίστεως ὡς βασικοῦ χαρακτηριστικοῦ τῶν μελῶν τῆς Ἑλληνορθοδόξου Ἐκκλησίας μας, ἰδιαιτέρως τῆς νέας γενεᾶς, τῶν παιδιῶν μας. Ἡ Ἑλληνορθόδοξος αὐτή ταυτότης καθιστᾶ τούς Ἑλληνοαμερικανούς πιστούς μας ἱκανούς νά σταθοῦν μέ ἀξιοπρέπειαν καί ὑπερηφάνειαν μεταξύ τῶν Ἀμερικανῶν συμπολιτῶν μας, σεβομένους τάς θρησκευτικάς καί πολιτικάς πεποιθήσεις των μέσα εἰς τό εὐρύ σχῆμα τοῦ πλουραλισμοῦ καί τῆς παγκοσμιοποιήσεως, ἀλλά καί ἐπιμένοντας εἰς τήν διατήρησιν τοῦ μοναδικοῦ θησαυροῦ πού ὀνομάζεται Ὀρθόδοξος χριστιανική πίστις καί τοῦ πολυτίμου κεφαλαίου πού ὀνομάζεται Ἑλληνική πολιτιστική κληρονομία.

Τό δεύτερον μεῖζον θέμα, τό ὁποῖον θά ἤθελα νά παρακαλέσω νά προσεχθῇ ἰδιαιτέρως, εἶναι τό θέμα τῆς ἐντονοποιήσεως τῆς ἀγάπης, τῆς στοργῆς καί τῆς φροντίδος διά τόν ἄνθρωπον. Ἡ Ὀρθόδοξος Ἐκκλησία μας, πιστή εἰς τό Εὐαγγέλιον τοῦ Ἱδρυτοῦ της τοῦ Κυρίου Ἰησοῦ Χριστοῦ, εἶναι ἡ Ἐκκλησία πού ἀγαπᾶ χωρίς μέτρον, χωρίς διακρίσεις καί χωρίς ἐπιφυλάξεις τόν ἄνθρωπον. Ἰδιαιτέρως τόν ἄνθρωπον, ὁ ὁποῖος εὑρίσκεται εἰς κατάστασιν ἀνάγκης, θλίψεως καί δοκιμασίας.

Κέντρον τῆς πίστεώς μας εἶναι ἕνας Θεός, ὁ Ὁποῖος εἶναι ἀγάπη, εἶναι ὁ Υἱός τοῦ Θεοῦ πού ἔγινε ἄνθρωπος διά νά ὑπηρετήσῃ τόν ἄνθρωπον διά νά λυτρώσῃ τήν ἀνθρωπότητα καί τήν κτίσιν ἀπό τό κακόν, τήν φθοράν καί τόν θάνατον. Ἡ Ἐκκλησία μας πού ἀκολουθεῖ τά βήματα αὐτοῦ τοῦ Θεοῦ, πού εἶναι "ὁ διακονῶν Θεός," εἶναι μονίμως εἰς τήν ὑπηρεσίαν τοῦ ἀνθρώπου, διακονεῖ τόν ἄνθρωπον, ὄχι ἁπλῶς εἰς τά μέτρα τοῦ δυνατοῦ, ἀλλά καί πέραν οἱουδήποτε ὁρίου. Ἁπλούστατα ἀγαπᾶ χωρίς μέτρον.

Εἰς τήν ἐντονοποίησιν καί συνεχῆ ἀνάπτυξιν τοῦ γνησίου χριστιανικοῦ αὐτοῦ πνεύματος τῆς ἀγάπης καί διακονίας ἀξίζει νά ἐπιδοθοῦν ὅλαι αἱ κοινότητές μας τῆς Ἱερᾶς Ἀρχιεπισκοπῆς. Μόνιμον χαρακτηριστικόν τῶν ἐνοριῶν μας καί διακριτικόν σημεῖον τοῦ Ὀρθοδόξου ἤθους μας, ἄς εἶναι ἡ ζωντανή πρός ἀλλήλους ἀγάπη, καί ἡ ἑτοιμότης ὑπερβάσεως τοῦ ἑαυτοῦ μας χάριν τῶν ἄλλων. Ἐδῶ δέν πρόκειται μόνον διά τήν φιλανθρωπίαν ἤ διά τήν προσφοράν ὑλικῆς βοηθείας πρός τούς πάσχοντας ἀδελφούς μας. Ἐδῶ πρόκειται διά μίαν στάσιν ζωῆς ἡ ὁποία σημαίνει πρωτοβουλίαν καί δυναμισμόν καί πρωτοπορεακά προγράμματα πού καλύπτουν καταστάσεις θλίψεως, μοναξιᾶς, ἀρρώστειας, ἀπελπισίας, φτώχειας, καί κάθε μορφῆς δοκιμασίας. Βεβαίως, ἡ ἐν Ἀμερικῇ Ἐκκλησία μας ἔχει δώσει ἐπί μακράν σειράν ἐτῶν πολλά δείγματα τοῦ ἀληθινά φιλανθρώπου ἤθους της. Σήμερα τονίζομεν τήν ἀνάγκην νά μεγιστοποιηθῇ ἡ προσφορά αὐτή πρός πᾶσαν κατεύθυνσιν. Ἐδῶ ὑπάρχει ἕνα ἔξοχον ἀνθρώπινον δυναμικόν καί ἐπί πλέον τεράστιαι δυνατότητες πού ὀφείλονται εἰς τήν ἐκπληκτικήν πρόοδον καί τήν ἐντυπωσιακήν ἀνάπτυξιν τῆς Ὁμογενείας. Ἐδῶ ὑπάρχει ἡ λαμπρά εὐκαιρία, ἡ Ἑλληνική Ὀρθόδοξος Ἐκκλησία τῆς Ἀμερικῆς, νά εἶναι μέ τήν εὐλογίαν τοῦ Θεοῦ τῆς ἀγάπης, μία Ἐκκλησία πρότυπον προσφορᾶς ἀγάπης εἰς τόν ἄνθρωπον. Μία Ἐκκλησία, ἡ ὁποία ἀγκαλιάζει κάθε ἀνθρώπινον πλᾶσμα, ἡ ὁποία προσφέρει ἐπί συνεχοῦς βάσεως στοργήν, φροντίδα καί τρυφερότητα εἰς ἕνα κόσμον πού βασανίζεται ἀπό τήν σκληρότητα, τήν βίαν, τήν ἀποξένωσιν καί τόν ἐγωκεντρισμόν.

Ἡ ἀπεριόριστη ἀγάπη, μεταφρασμένη εἰς διακονίαν τοῦ ἀνθρώπου, πρέπει νά εἶναι ἡ προτεραιότης μας ὡς πιστῶν καί ὡς Ἐκκλησία τοῦ Χριστοῦ, ἰδιαιτέρως εἰς τήν χιλιετίαν πού ἀνατέλλει. Μίαν χιλιετίαν, ἡ ὁποία πιθανόν νά ἐπιφυλάσσῃ μεγάλας δοκιμασίας διά τήν ἀνθρωπότητα. Οἱ ἄνθρωποι φαίνεται ὅτι θά χρειασθοῦν ἰσχυρά στηρίγματα διά νά ἐπιβιώσουν καί νά προοδεύσουν ἐν μέσῳ τῶν τεραστίων ἀλλαγῶν εἰς τό περιβάλλον, τήν οἰκονομίαν, τήν κοινωνικήν συγκρότησιν, τήν βιοτεχνολογίαν, τήν πληθυσμιακήν ἔκρηξιν, τήν σύγχυσιν τῶν ἰδεῶν καί τήν συνεχῆ τεχνολογικήν ἐπανάστασιν. Ἡ Ἑλληνική Ὀρθόδοξος Ἐκκλησία μας ἐδῶ εἰς τάς Ἡνωμένας Πολιτείας, ὡς Ἐκκλησία ἀγάπης καί φιλανθρωπίας χωρίς ὅρια, ὡς Ἐκκλησία διακονοῦσα τόν ἄνθρωπον, δύναται νά παίξῃ σημαντικόν ρόλον εἰς τήν ἱερωτάτην προσπάθειαν ὑποστηρίξεως τοῦ ἀνθρώπου καί συμβολῆς εἰς τήν ἐπίλυσιν τῶν πιεστικῶν προβλημάτων τά ὁποῖα θά ὀρθωθοῦν ἐνώπιόν του εἰς τά χρόνια πού ἔρχονται. Ἐδῶ ἡ ἀπεριόριστη, σοφή καί ἀστείρευτη ἀγάπη τῆς Ἐκκλησίας γίνεται ἰσχυρότατον στοιχεῖον ἀντιμετωπίσεως τοῦ μέλλοντος, ὅ,τι καί ἄν ἐπιφυλάσσει τό μέλλον αὐτό.

Ἐπιτρέψατέ μου νά ἐπισημάνω, καί νά κατακλείσω μέ αὐτό, ἕνα τρίτον σπουδαιότατον θέμα, τό ὁποῖον ἐν συνδυασμῷ πρός τά δύο προηγούμενα πρέπει νά ἀποτελῇ ἐπίσης ἄμεσον προτεραιότητά μας. Πρόκειται διά τό θέμα τῆς ἑνότητος καί ὁμοψυχίας τοῦ Ἐκκλησιαστικοῦ ἀλλά καί τοῦ Ὁμογενειακοῦ μας σώματος.

Ἄς ἐνθυμηθοῦμε τί ἐζήτησεν ὁ Κύριος εἰς τήν περίφημον ἀρχιερατικήν προσευχήν πρό τοῦ Πάθους Του ἀπό τόν Πατέρα του διά τούς πιστούς: "*Τήρησον αὐτούς ἐν τῷ ὀνόματί σου οὕς δέδωκάς μοι ἵνα ὦσιν ἕν καθώς ἡμεῖς* (Ἰωάν. 17, 11), ...*ἵνα πάντες ἕν ὦσι, καθώς σύ, Πάτερ, ἐν ἐμοί κἀγώ ἐν σοί, ἵνα καί αὐτοί ἐν ἡμῖν ἕν ὦσιν, ἵνα ὁ κόσμος πιστεύσῃ ὅτι σύ με ἀπέστειλας*" (Ἰωάν. 17, 21). Καί ὁ Ἀπόστολος Παῦλος, παρεκάλεσεν ἐντόνως τούς πιστούς νά ζοῦν *ἀνεχόμενοι ἀλλήλων ἐν ἀγάπῃ, σπουδάζοντες τηρεῖν τήν ἑνότητα τοῦ Πνεύματος ἐν τῷ συνδέσμῳ τῆς εἰρήνης*. Διατί; Διότι εἴμεθα *ἕν σῶμα καί ἕν Πνεῦμα, καθώς καί ἐκλήθητε ἐν μιᾷ ἐλπίδι τῆς κλήσεως ὑμῶν· εἷς Κύριος, μία πίστις, ἕν βάπτισμα, εἷς Θεός καί Πατήρ πάντων, ὁ ἐπί πάντων, καί διά πάντων, καί ἐν πᾶσιν ἡμῖν* (Πρός Ἐφεσίους 4, 2-6).

Αὐτήν ἀκριβῶς τήν ἐπιτακτικήν ἀνάγκην τῆς ἑνότητος καί τῆς μεταξύ μας εἰρήνης αἰσθανόμεθα χρέος νά τονίσωμεν. Χωρίς φόβον καί δειλίαν, καλούμεθα ἀδελφοί μου, νά παραμερίσωμεν οἱανδήποτε διαφοράν, παρεξήγησιν ἤ σύγκρουσιν πού ἐνδέχεται νά δημιουργοῦν ἀποστάσεις μεταξύ μας. Ἀποστάσεις πού κλονίζουν τήν ἑνότητα καί φυγαδεύουν τήν εἰρήνην τοῦ Θεοῦ. Τίποτε δέν πρέπει νά θέτῃ εἰς κίνδυνον τό θεῖον δῶρον τῆς ἑνότητος καί ἁρμονίας τῆς ὁμοψυχίας καί τῆς κοινοτικῆς μας εἰρήνης. Ὡς λαός ὡς Ἐκκλησία ἔχομεν ὅλας τάς προϋποθέσεις διά νά οἰκοδομήσωμεν εἰς τό μέγιστον δυνατόν μίαν ἑνότητα δυναμικήν καί ἀκλόνητον, διά νά εἴμεθα καί νά μείνωμεν ἕν σῶμα, ἕν πνεῦμα, μία ψυχή, μία θέλησις. Εἰς τήν περίπτωσίν μας ἡ συνέχισις τῆς προσπαθείας διά τήν ἑνότητα καί τήν εἰρήνην εἶναι τό θαυμάσιον ἔργον εἰς τό ὁποῖον μᾶς καλεῖ σήμερα ὁ Θεός. Μᾶς καλεῖ ἐν ὄψει τῶν μεγάλων στόχων πού διανοίγονται ἐνώπιόν μας. Τό μέλλον, τό ἐγγύς καί τό ἀπώτερον εἶναι ὁ μεγάλος προορισμός μας καί τό μέλλον οἰκοδομεῖται ἐπί τῆς ἑνότητος μας.

Μιᾶς ἑνότητος καί ἁρμονίας, ἡ ὁποία πρέπει νά καλλιεργηθῇ εἰς πολλά ἐπίπεδα καί διαφόρους μορφάς ἐντός τῆς Ἱερᾶς Ἀρχιεπισκοπῆς καί τῆς Ὁμογενείας γενικώτερον. Πρέπει νά καλλιεργηθῇ ὡς ἑνότης καί ἀμοιβαία κατανόησις καί συνεργασία μεταξύ τῶν γενεῶν, δηλαδή μεταξύ τῶν νέων, τῶν ὡρίμων καί τῶν ἡλικιωμένων. Πρέπει νά καλλιεργηθῇ ὡς ἑνότης καί ἁρμονική συνεργασία μεταξύ κλήρου καί λαοῦ. Πρέπει νά καλλιεργηθῇ ὡς ἑνότης μεταξύ τῶν νεοφερμένων Ἑλληνοαμερικανῶν μεταναστῶν καί τῶν Ἑλληνοαμερικανῶν τῆς τρίτης ἤ καί τῆς τετάρτης γενεᾶς. Πρέπει νά καλλιεργηθῇ ὡς ἑνότης καί δεσμός ἀδιάσπαστος καί δημιουργικός μεταξύ τοῦ λαοῦ τῆς Ὁμογενείας καί τοῦ λαοῦ τῆς Μητρός Ἑλλάδος.

Ἡ πολυδιάστατος αὐτή ἑνότης δέν ἐξαντλεῖται εἰς τό πλήρωμα τῆς Ἱερᾶς Ἀρχιεπισκοπῆς μας, ἀλλά στηρίζεται καί διασφαλίζεται ὀργανικά ὡς ἑνότης ἀδιάσπαστος καί ζωογόνος μέ τήν Μητέρα Ἐκκλησίαν, τό Οἰκουμενικόν μας Πατριαρχεῖον. Ὡς ἑνότης, ἡ ὁποία διά τοῦ Οἰκουμενικοῦ μας Πατριαρχείου ἐπεκτείνεται καί εἰς τόν εὐρύτερον κύκλον τῶν ἐδῶ Ὀρθοδόξων Ἐκκλησιῶν διά νά ἐναγκαλισθῇ τελικῶς ὅλον τόν κόσμον.

Ὅλοι μαζί, ὑπό τήν πνοήν καί δύναμιν τοῦ Θεοῦ, καλούμεθα σήμερα νά συνεχίσωμεν τήν δημιουργικήν πορείαν μας. Νά τήν συνεχίσωμεν εἰς τάς φωτεινάς λεωφόρους εἰς τάς ὁποίας μᾶς ὁδηγεῖ ἡ ἀγάπη καί ἡ σοφία τοῦ Θεοῦ. Πρόκειται διά μίαν πορείαν δυναμικῆς πίστεως, ἀπεριορίστου ἀγάπης καί ἀκλονήτου ἑνότητος, ἡ ὁποία εἰς κάθε βῆμα θά μᾶς κάνῃ νά ἐπαναλαμβάνωμεν τόν ἐξαίσιον ὕμνον τῆς Ἀποκαλύψεως μέ τόν ὁποῖον ἀρχίσαμεν: *Ἡ εὐλογία καί ἡ δόξα καί ἡ σοφία καί ἡ εὐχαριστία καί ἡ τιμή καί ἡ δύναμις καί ἡ ἰσχύς τῷ Θεῷ ἡμῶν εἰς τούς αἰῶνας τῶν αἰώνων. Ἀμήν.*

Aspects of the Legacy of the Classical and The Christian Hellenic Tradition

Richard Stockton College of New Jersey*

Pomona, NJ
October 31, 1999

Esteemed President, Deans, Faculty, Students, and Friends:

It is a heartfelt joy for me to be here at Stockton College today and to address you at this Celebration of Greek Letters. On this special occasion, I first would like to express my deep thanks to you for this invitation and for the great honor of conferring upon me an honorary degree of Doctor of Letters. Indeed, simply being in a college with such a vibrant faculty and with a student body that is so eager to learn, constitutes in itself an honor.

These are not impressions that I have of Stockton College based upon the particular moment. I happen to know of the dynamic nature of the faculty and students of Stockton through the many conversations that I have had with my good friend the Very Reverend Professor Demetrios Constantelos. In the past twenty-five to thirty years, he would speak to me about his wonderful experiences as a

*This address was delivered on the occasion of receiving an honorary Doctor of Letters degree from the Richard Stockton College of New Jersey, Pomona, NJ, October 1999.

professor at Stockton College every time we met, never failing to praise the dynamism, indeed, the beauty of this wonderful place of learning.

The development of programs related to Greek Letters and to Greek civilization at Stockton College has arrived at a point where this College could compete with larger universities on an equal level. Occasions such as this one today are indicative of this fact, in that they constitute an expression of a continuous love and appreciation of the legacy of classical Greek. This is seen through the honoring of Greek Letters, Greek *paideia* and Greek culture. It is also witnessed by the impressive pertinent lectures that continue to be offered at Stockton.

For me, the celebration of the legacy of classical Greek in general, and the celebration of Greek Letters in particular, is a deeply personal event. Growing up in Greece, I remember playing with my friends through miles of ancient city streets, near ancient houses and temples which served as our playgrounds, so to speak. But beyond my Greek origins, as a child I remember having long exposure to ancient Greek texts. From the age of ten, for eight years in high school alone, we were exposed for two hours per day, six days a week to various philosophical, poetic, theatrical, and scientific texts in ancient Greek.

Today's event, however, is a personal event for me not only because of my origins or because of my continuous exposure to ancient Greek texts, to Greek *paideia*, and to the classical works of the Fathers of the Church, but also because it honors the classical Hellenic heritage in a totally contemporary setting. It should not pass unnoticed that today's celebration takes place in a modern American university situated in Pomona, New Jersey, and honors a culture at least 3000 years old. Obviously, this culture is worthy of exceptional honor for many reasons, which could be elaborated upon at length. Allow me to present, very briefly, some of them.

The first reason for honoring the Hellenic classical tradition is the concept that it offers concerning the immensity and manifold nuances of knowledge. There exists within the classical Greek mind an amazing openness to all possibilities and forms of knowledge: science, philosophy, literature, and a tremendous diversity of fields, from cosmology to anthropology, zoology, geology, and language. In such a vast framework, knowledge is understood as occupying immense proportions, having nuances that are indicated by a rich, pertinent terminology offered to us by the classical Greek language. Note, for example, some of the words which describe the unlimited and subtly differentiated aspects of knowledge:

Knowledge – Γνῶσις
Deep Knowledge – Ἐπίγνωσις
Science – Ἐπιστήμη
Wisdom – Σοφία
Understanding – Κατανόησις
Intuition – Διαίσθησις
Thinking – Διανόησις

It is important to note that these aspects of knowledge are, for the classical Hellenic mind, accompanied by a deep joy and a true amazement. In this condition of joy, awe, and wonder resides the essence of the classical Greek spirit: to be in a perpetual state of amazement, to face knowledge as something truly wonderful, inspiring, and even leading to ecstasy.

A second and related reason for honoring the classical Greek culture is its strong concept of the priority of beauty. There exists a tremendous sensitivity in the ancient Hellenic culture for the beautiful. This sensitivity is not limited to the affirmation of the beautiful or the praise of the handsome; rather, the classical Greek mind was committed to an outward rejection of the ugly, to a rejection of the amorphous. It saw a horror in view of the chaotic and monstrous. The creation of the beautiful in all fields was the chief concern in classical Hellenism. Fields such as literature, be it prose or poetry, music, sculpture, architecture, and theatre were vivid displays of beauty. Today, all over the world, we can behold thousands of statues, pieces of architecture, vases and other artifacts related to daily life, all coming from classical Greece. All these art forms were accorded a deliberate association with all things beautiful. There could not be, for example, such a concept as ugly music, ugly poetry, ugly sculpture, or ugly drama; music, poetry, sculpture and drama were by definition things of beauty, intimately related to the highest reaches of truth, knowledge, and wisdom.

In this sense, beauty also concerned the overcoming of all things chaotic, disproportioned, and otherwise not harmonious. Here, we note the close and deliberate association of beauty with form and order; we note the almost automatic propensity of the classical Greek mind toward structure, purpose and balance, in other words, toward the arrangement of all things into carefully defined categories of beauty.

The two aforementioned contributions to our world that we owe to classical Hellenism, namely the immensity and diversity of knowledge and the unyielding adherence to beauty, are indeed essential contributions, pointing to an integration of these two concepts. To these two fields, however, we must now add a third, namely, ethics–ethics as an expression of life and daily existence. Here, we can see the tremendous contribution of classical Hellenism, which is the presentation of the ideal ethical character under the phrase "καλός κἀγαθός" [beautiful and good].

Ancient Greeks seemed to be always asking: "What is good; what is ethical perfection; what is virtue?" For the classical Greek mind, the very *identity* of a human being was rooted in concepts of honor, beauty, and virtue, and society was geared, in a total and comprehensive way, toward the support and formation of this identity. Such a legacy presents an extraordinary contribution for our contemporary times, where the formation of human identity is all too often influenced by a variety of uncontrollable external, social, and technological pressures. These pressures place the acquisition of virtue, the achievement of the ideal of "καλός κἀγαθός," unfortunately, at the bottom of the list as to what a human being should be aiming at obtaining.

Something, however, is still missing from this list of the immense contributions of classical Hellenism to our contemporary age. This is the unique legacy of Christian Hellenism, namely the legacy of love, philanthropy, and humanism. On this subject, I would refer you especially to Fr. Constantelos' several works, true masterpieces on the theme of Christian Hellenism as a tradition of love and care and of intense philanthropy, particularly at the time of Byzantium.

These four themes, the immensity and diversity of knowledge, the priority of beauty, the priority of ethics, and the indispensability of love and philanthropy, are hallmarks of the classical and the Christian Hellenic spirit to which our world owes a considerable deal of gratitude. Today, this legacy of Hellenism lives on in places of learning, in halls of governments, in museums and libraries, in concert halls and art galleries. It is a spirit that teems with life, begging us to consider and to grow in all that which is good and beautiful in the human race. It is in this legacy that I stand before you today, and offer my thanks and commendation. You, the faculty, students, and administrators of Stockton College, are indeed worthy of thanks and commendation for your noble preservation and communication of the importance of the vital legacy of classical and Christian Hellenism, a legacy that is exemplary and eternal in its quest for knowledge, beauty, virtue, and love.

Technology, Information, Communication and the Mystery and Wisdom of Faith

Commencement Address
Hellenic College
Holy Cross Greek Orthodox School of Theology

Brookline, MA
May 20, 2000

Beloved Graduates of the Class of 2000:

I address you today with great joy, thankfulness to God, and genuine pride in your accomplishments over the past years that culminate in this joyous event of today. I speak for all who have gathered here in saying, we applaud you for your hard work; we congratulate you for your success; and we anticipate even greater accomplishments from you in the future under the dynamic guidance of the Holy Spirit.

I also want to recognize and congratulate those who accompanied you in your long and sometimes difficult journey to this high point in your life—namely, your families, your parents, your spouses, your children, and all those who stood by you and supported you through the time of your studies. This day is their day too, and they are worthy of our recognition and congratulations.

In fact, not just for those of us who attend this commencement exercise, but for our entire Church today, your graduation is an occasion for great rejoicing and thanksgiving, because in academic terms at least, you, the Class of 2000 of Hellenic College and Holy Cross Greek Orthodox School of Theology, *you* are the first-fruits of the new millennium that lies ahead of us. In your faces we see the face of the future—the future both of our Church and of our society. And beholding your faces today, we are made glad, for we see the promise of God's immeasurable blessings in the years and decades to come.

And so this day is a special blessing for all of us who have gathered for this solemn ceremony, to honor you and to rejoice with you in the completion of your scholastic work here at Hellenic College and Holy Cross.

But this occasion is also a double blessing for you, the graduates, as well. To be a member of the Class of 2000 is an honor not to be received lightly, for it is an honor bestowed by the providence of God, whose guiding hand has brought you to this place and time today.

There is something special about being a graduate of the Class of 2000, not because 2000 is a conveniently round number, or because of the association with all of the many "Y2K" activities and celebrations. Rather, the year 2000 is a significant symbolic entity in and of itself, as a benchmark of a new era in the history of humanity. With the turn of the new century and the new millennium, the final three digits of 2000, the "zero-zero-zero" all in a row, gives the world a real sense that as a single community of humankind, we begin together a new stage in our common life—more than a new chapter of history, but in fact a whole new volume.

This sense of a fresh beginning is more than simply a symbolic concept. In very real terms we stand at the threshold of a new era. As human beings we find ourselves at the portal of a truly momentous time in the life of the world, with ramifications and consequences more sweeping and more far-reaching than we can presently imagine or predict. I speak, of course, of the new age of technology and information that we have entered.

The real significance of the Information Age, however, is not to be found in silicon chips, glass-fiber cables, or virtual reality software and the like, anymore than the significance of the Industrial Revolution could be assigned to the steam engines that powered the factories and assembly lines of previous centuries.

The real significance of the Information Age lies in the new possibilities that have opened up before us to *communicate* with one another, to share the wealth of experience of past and present generations of people in every land of every continent across the globe. The Information Age is an era of heightened consciousness and renewed awareness of the world in which we live, of the human family of which we are members, and of the God whose image and likeness we bear.

Through the new modes of communication made available by technology, there is in the world around us a renewed fascination with the priority of the human person in the minds and hearts of the citizens of this planet. The twentieth century, for its part, was an age for discovering and conquering the wonders of nature, from the infinite depths of space to the infinitesimal parts of the atom. The twenty-first century, however, because of previously unheard-of possibilities for communication, promises to be an age for rediscovering the mystery of our humanity. The phenomenon of man and the uniqueness, dignity, and inestimable value of each individual human being are once again dominating the thoughts and the consciousness of humankind with renewed interest.

We are, therefore, at a defining moment in the history of our race. We have an unparalleled potential to observe, to communicate, and to record information about ourselves, about the world in which we live, and about our God who created us. But these new potentialities also raise new challenges: will there be any real progress if we receive this knowledge without wisdom, if we absorb this information without understanding?

Our newfound abilities as humans to analyze, to quantify, to digitize, could become nothing more than a spiritual and intellectual "Midas touch," that is, a touch turning everything to gold. But if everything becomes gold, then there is simply no possibility for life anymore. If we are unable to control these newly discovered potentialities, to use them with discernment and to exercise them for the benefit of our world, then our strength becomes our weakness, and we as humans succumb to the temptation of reductionism, in which the value of any given thing is understood merely in terms of our ability to encode it in the bytes and bits of computerization.

Let me illustrate a telling example of this point. Our understanding of the breadth and variety of human cultures has expanded exponentially in recent years. This is a wonderful thing and a most welcome situation. But if multicultural studies become "information for the sake of information" and for the monolithic glory of cultures, then everything in life is reduced to a matter of culture. If we are tempted—as I believe we are nowadays, because of the vast amount of information that is available—to conceive of all differences in faith, morality, and values as mere differences in culture, then we suffer from the stifling dominion of the Information Age, where all things are relative and nothing is meaningful except as an interesting matter of statistical analysis. The technology of information, if it becomes the supreme deity within our world, by necessity renders all things useful only insofar as they are comprehensible and appropriate for feeding into the computer;

this leaves no possibility in the world for the sense of mystery, transcendence, and awe that we cherish as Orthodox Christians.

And this, beloved graduates of the Class of 2000, brings me back to you. I ask you plainly, who will be the spiritual and intellectual leaders of this new era of human advancement, if not you?

Who will guide our world so that it becomes an age, not just of information, but also of wisdom and understanding, especially of the wisdom and understanding of Jesus Christ, *in Whom are hid all the treasures of wisdom and knowledge* (Colossians 2:3)?

You are the ones who have inherited the legacy of our ageless Orthodox Christian Tradition, which you have acquired by living it and studying it, especially in your education here at Hellenic College and Holy Cross. You are also the generation which has grown up with the latest innovations and advancements of the Information Age, the generation that can use in the best possible ways the advantages of our technological era that are developing and proliferating around us.

You, the Class of 2000 of Hellenic College and Holy Cross, are the ones who have been uniquely blessed with the tools and the skills to communicate the fundamental spiritual and intellectual values that the world needs at this time in every field of human endeavor. Whether your training is in theology, education, the sciences, or the humanities, your fellow human beings need the timeless grounding and orientation that you have to offer as an Orthodox Christian. Your ministry—and you are all called to ministry, whether as clergymen or as laypeople—extends both to those within the Church and without, as the great ideological wave of the Information Age sweeps over us all.

In whatever enterprise or field of inquiry that you find yourself in the future, it falls to you to have the boldness and the intellectual courage to ask the deep questions of life: "Who are we?" "Where do we come from?" "Where are we going?"

It will be your mission in the twenty-first century, Class of 2000, to raise the consciousness of those around you to true human values. Above all, it will be your task to communicate to others the profound *mysteries* of our humanity, of our world, and of the God who called all things into being. In this task, the Fathers of the Church will be your guide and inspiration, for they stood where you now stand, at the watershed of a new age in human affairs. They were, as you must be, accomplished scholars of the learning of their own age, as well as beholders of the mysteries of the world of God through devotion and spiritual discipline.

Having a double exposure to the Information Age and the technological explosion on the one hand, and to the mystery of Faith and the wealth of our Orthodox Tradition on the other, you are called by God to be His special agents and His powerful witnesses in the years to come.

In this day and age of technology and information, your task will be to master the new and evolving modes of communication and to use them to the fullest possible advantage as you project the unchanging Truth of Jesus Christ to a world in constant change.

Class of 2000, please keep constantly in mind that this is an extremely critical time in the life of our world and in the life of the people of God in the world. The Church of Jesus Christ needs you; the Church needs *every one* of you, for we know you to be a remarkable and diverse group of talented people, each one with particular gifts and charismata for the building up of the body of Christ.

Looking at all of you sitting now before me, I am reminded of the Old Testament story of Esther. Esther was a young Jewish woman who became the queen and wife of Ahasuerus, the king of the Medes and the Persians. Esther's people were living at a critical juncture of time, a time of great promise for them and a time of great peril. Queen Esther was in a position to accomplish amazing things for the people of God, but only at the risk of her own life and freedom and welfare. Her commitment to act on behalf of her people came at great personal cost, but offered tremendous benefits to her entire community.

At this critical moment, Esther was told by her wise uncle Mordecai that she had to act immediately and drastically. He asked her, *"Who knows whether you have come to the kingdom* [of Persia and Media] *for such a time as this?"* (Esther 4:14) In other words, who knows whether, in the providence of God, your very reason for existing at this precise time and in this specific place was in order to commit yourself to this self-sacrificial act for the sake of the people of God? That is to say, how could she *not* trust that the gracious God who had brought her to this critical moment in her life would neither abandon her nor forsake her, but would be with her always, especially when she offered herself completely for the sake of His people?

Mordecai also reminded her that if she refused to act, help and deliverance for her people would arise from some other quarter, but she herself would lose the privilege of this great opportunity and responsibility.

This is something that you, the class of 2000, must seriously consider. For you might have been chosen by God to live at this juncture of time in order to be the agents of a mighty action, the decisive protagonists in fashioning a future determined by God and His word. Especially you, the graduates of Holy Cross, *you* might have been chosen by God in order to offer to the Church a priesthood of new dimensions, new special qualities and characteristics, a genuine Orthodox priesthood for the twenty-first century and the new millennium. Who knows whether you have come through difficult times and arduous trials to the completion of your priestly studies for such a time as this? Before you lies the possibility of a tremendous ministry, an open door (Acts 14:27, Revelation 3:8) for communicating the Good News of Jesus Christ in unprecedented ways. Our gracious God who has led you to the joy of this graduation day will indeed be with you always as you commit yourselves and offer your lives to His glorious service.

For the Class of 2000 of Hellenic College and Holy Cross, I can think of no more fitting exhortation than that which comes from the pen of the Apostle Paul in his first letter to the Thessalonians (1 Thessalonians 5:20): *Πάντα δὲ δοκιμάζετε, τὸ καλὸν κατέχετε—Examine all things, hold fast to that which is good.*

This is a principle of life which is basic to our Scriptural, Patristic and Hellenic heritage. *We examine all things,* rejoicing in the vastness and variety of the created world, of things visible and invisible, of the world of men and angels, of the order of things infinite and infinitesimal. And having examined all things, with discernment and wisdom we supply our souls, as Saint Basil advises (*To the Youths,* IX), with those things that are best, *holding fast to that which is good.*

In the Information Age, a time when the learning of a thousand generations of humanity is literally at your fingertips, you have an awesome responsibility through this Apostolic exhortation, to examine all things and to hold fast to the good; but you also have an experience of untold *joy* ahead of you as you put to use the intellectual tools that you have acquired in your studies here. Yours will be the thrill of constant discovery, the joy of thinking, creating, and comprehending this fascinating work of God that is ourselves and our world. Reach out and seize all the joy that is yours as thinkers, scholars, and communicators. Cherish the beauty of understanding and wisdom, and you will be true sons and daughters of God in Jesus Christ. And remember that you have been called to be the apostles of the true faith and Orthodox wisdom in the new age of technology, of the explosion of information and the possibilities for communication. May the blessings and the joy of this moment shine forth in your hearts forevermore.

And may the Lord bless you and keep you; may the Lord make His face shine upon you and be gracious to you; may the Lord lift up the light of His presence upon you always, and give you peace. Amen.

Saint John Chrysostom: Anthropological Insights for Our Times

Bampton Lecture[1]
Columbia University

New York, NY
March 8, 2001

Introduction

It constitutes a truly high honor for me to have been invited by the great Columbia University to deliver the prestigious Bampton Lecture of this year. I express my deepest thanks to President Rupp, a distinguished old friend and colleague from our years at Harvard University in the late sixties, to Dean Cole, to Dean Awn, and to all colleagues responsible for this great honor. I feel at home, here tonight, addressing esteemed friends and colleagues and beloved students of a renown academic institution as this, recognized for its long tradition of dedication to research, teaching, and learning.

As announced, the topic of tonight's lecture is "Saint John Chrysostom: Anthropological Insights for Our Times."

[1]This lecture was the 33rd Bampton Lecture. The Bampton Lectures were established at Columbia University through a bequest of Ada Byron Bampton Tremaine and were modeled after a similar series at Oxford University. The address will be published by Columbia University in the Bampton Lecture series.

It is well known that Saint John Chrysostom's work is huge and highly diversified, including biblical commentaries on the books of Genesis, Psalms, the Prophet Isaiah, the Gospels of Matthew and John, the book of Acts, and the extensive corpus of the Pauline Letters; homilies, panegyrics, essays, treatises, liturgical texts, and epistles. Here we have thousands of pages, bursting with life, combining brilliance and tenderness, rigorous intellectual involvement and strong emotional coloration, mighty admonitions and eloquently presented teachings. From these pages emerges a strong, exceedingly complex and fascinating anthropology, which has a value extending far beyond the time of its creation and reaching our own times as well.

During the presentation of my lecture today, I will make an effort to offer a few aspects of Chrysostom's anthropology that seem to be insightful and certainly worth considering.[2] My selection is, of course, not exhaustive, definitely fragmentary and limited, and rather anthological in nature.

Chrysostom's anthropological insights will be presented in three main groups. The first is comprised of two basic and interrelated attitudes that have an immediate bearing on dealing with human beings and consequently have anthropological significance. The second group aims at showing two fundamental and truly insightful Chrysostomic ideas related to human nature. Finally, the third group of Chrysostom's anthropological ideas that we will present deals with three human models. These three models constitute for him types of human excellence to which he frequently returns.

[2]I have already made references to some of the ideas presented in this lecture in my paper "Being Transformed: Chrysostom's Exegesis of the Epistle to the Romans" published in the *Greek Orthodox Theological Review* 36 (1991) 211-229.

Two Basic Anthropological Attitudes

a) Here we encounter two basic Chrysostomic attitudes or positions. The first is *the tremendous passion of Chrysostom for the human being as such* and for every human being. The original Greek term for human being in Chrysostom's works, the word ἄνθρωπος, is never used by him in a distant, neutral or indifferent way. The context within which the term ἄνθρωπος, human being, appears is almost always a context of intensity, vibrancy, and passionate language. It is characteristic that Chrysostom's cherished motto and constant slogan to his people is expressed in the phrase: "Come and become human being" ['Ελθὲ, καὶ γενοῦ ἄνθρωπος]. His formulation is strong and clear: "These I say and I will not cease saying, 'Come and become human being.'"[3] He did not say "come and become a holy, righteous, pure, saintly ἄνθρωπος, man." He said, just come and become ἄνθρωπος, human being, thus revealing his understanding of the human being as such in its human, existential essence.

Chrysostom's anthropology, as we can easily see, is not a theoretical construction conceived and developed at a distance from its object, which is the human being. Chrysostom does not think in general and abstract terms about man. He is not interested in suggesting handsome anthropological theories in the quietness of his study. He suffers for man; he feels his agony, he shares the tragedy of man's situation. At the same time he is ecstatic with the human potential. The sight of human beings sets in movement all his spiritual faculties. Here is a sheer and an

[3]Chrysostom, *On the Saying of Prophet David* in Psalm 49:16 (Migne Patrologia Graeca 55, 500): "Ταῦτα δὲ λέγω, καὶ λέγων οὐ παύσομαι. Ἐλθὲ, καὶ γενοῦ ἄνθρωπος."

all-consuming passion for the human being, a total commitment to people, which is perhaps an interpretive key for understanding Chrysostom's anthropology.

This passion may well constitute a remarkable anthropological insight for us living in the twenty-first century. In our times, we encounter innumerable anthropologies or anthropological theories related to philosophical, ideological, scientific, or political principles. How many of them are the result of a passion for human beings? How many of them are characterized by a deep, unrestricted and committed love for the inhabitants of the planet Earth who are the truly invaluable object of any anthropology?

b) The second anthropological attitude displayed by Chrysostom and comprised in this group is the orientation and focus of Chrysostom's passion for the human being. The orientation is theocentric. Chrysostom's passion for ἄνθρωπος is a theocentric anthropological passion. It is not merely the passion of a great humanist, of an exceptionally gifted scholar, or an extraordinary thinker. It is something above and beyond this. His is the passion of someone who lives, moves, and who has his being entirely in the reality above the material, residing instead in the supernatural sphere, seeing everything in a vision centered in God. Indeed, Saint John Chrysostom sees, feels, lives, and praises or laments man not as a being belonging only to this world, but as a being rooted in God, essentially linked with God.[4] His attitude towards the human being is an attitude not simply intellectual but truly existential, wholistic, and passionate, constantly focused on God. For Chrysostom, human beings are unique entities, intensely loved but totally transparent, so that he is always able to see God through them.

[4]This explains why Chrysostom urges every human being to become angel and ἄνθρωπος: "Γενοῦ ἄγγελος καὶ ἄνθρωπος" (*Ibid.* 55, 500).

Such an attitude offers again an anthropological insight worth studying. It serves as an enriching component for those contemporary anthropologies that do not go beyond the material, the visible, or the scientifically verifiable as far as human existence is concerned. But what, then, happens to the possible bond of human beings with the divine, the link to the transcendent, the likely reality of the sacred, the holy, the numinous to which humanity is invited, to say the least? Chrysostom's theocentric anthropology issues a call to revisit this idea by any anthropology.

Two Fundamental Ideas

In this group we deal again with two important anthropological contributions by John Chrysostom.

a) The first relates to the very dark, very evil reality in which human beings may find themselves. Chrysostom is not a romantic, utopian, and idealistic anthropologist. His theocentric passion for ἄνθρωπος, his total commitment to the human race, does not lead him to a naïve and beautifying view of what people are in reality. He is aware of the extremely bad and fully negative characteristics of human beings. He speaks constantly about his daily confrontations with malice, criminality, evil, moral decay, perversion, and sheer bestiality. His anthropology is very realistic and extremely practical, even to the point of being provocative in its usage of a strong, graphic language in describing human depravity.

An example would be useful here. In his comments on Psalm 49:16, he addresses a person who is representative of a condition of moral decay with the following words: "When I see you living against the rules of reason, how shall I call you a human being (ἄνθρωπος) and not an ox?

When I see you grasping and snatching unjustly from others, how shall I call you man (ἄνθρωπος) and not a wolf? When I see you impure and lascivious, how shall I call you a human person (ἄνθρωπος) and not a pig? When I see you sly and deceitful, how shall I call you man (ἄνθρωπος) and not a serpent? When I see you stupid or foolish, how shall I call you man (ἄνθρωπος) and not an ass? . . . When I see you disobedient and unwise, how shall I call you man (ἄνθρωπος) and not a stone?"[5] "I cannot count you among human beings," he remarks elsewhere. "If I did, I should be in danger of not finding any difference between man (ἄνθρωπος) and the wild beasts; although the latter have only one of these defects each, whereas you have gathered in you all of them, going thus beyond the wild beasts' animality and lack of reason."[6]

Chrysostom does not hesitate to use a sharp and uninhibited language when revealing the degree of malice and depravity even among his own flock. In his *Homily 8* on the Epistle of Saint Paul to the Romans he states: "I am mourning (πενθῶ), that living as we do among brethren, we need be on our guard to avoid being harmed; and we light up so many fires, and set guards and outposts! The reason is the prevalence of falsehood, the prevalence of deceit, the prevailing secession of love, and ruthless, un-

[5]*Ibid.* (MPG 55, 500-01). "Ὅταν γὰρ ἴδω σε ἀλόγως βιοῦντα, πῶς σε καλέσω ἄνθρωπον, ἀλλ᾿ οὐχὶ βοῦν; Ὅταν ἴδω σε ἁρπάζοντα, πῶς σε καλέσω ἄνθρωπον, ἀλλ᾿ οὐχὶ λύκον; Ὅταν ἴδω σε πορνεύοντα, πῶς σε καλέσω ἄνθρωπον, ἀλλ᾿ οὐχὶ χοῖρον; Ὅταν ἴδω σε δολερόν, πῶς σε καλέσω ἄνθρωπον, ἀλλ᾿ οὐχὶ ὄφιν; Ὅταν ἴδω σε ἀνόητον, πῶς σε καλέσω ἄνθρωπον, ἀλλ᾿ οὐχὶ ὄνον; Ὅταν ἴδω σε ἀπειθῆ καὶ ἀσύνετον, πῶς σε καλέσω ἄνθρωπον, ἀλλ᾿ οὐχὶ λίθον;"

[6]Chrysostom, *Homilies on the Gospel of Saint Matthew*, Homily 4 (MPG 57, 48): "Πῶς δυνήσομαι σε μετὰ τῶν ἀριθμεῖν; ...κινδυνεύω μηδὲ ἀνδρὸς καὶ θηρίου εὑρεῖν διαφοράν. Τί γάρ σε εἴπω; Θηρίον; Ἀλλὰ τὰ θηρία ἑνὶ τούτων τῶν ἐλαττωμάτων κατέχεται· σὺ δὲ ὁμοῦ συμφορήσας πάντα, πоῤῥωτέρω τῆς ἐκείνων ἀλογίας ὁδεύεις."

ceasing war. As a result, one may find people who feel more confidence in Gentiles than in Christians!"[7] "We are cruel and savage," he will add at the conclusion of his *Homily 23* on Romans.[8]

The tragedy, according to Chrysostom, is that people, although they fall in the categories described above, do not realize their absolutely miserable condition. He painfully concludes, "The worst is that being in such a dreadful state, we do not think of the formlessness of our soul, nor do we realize its ugliness."[9]

This conclusion adds something significant. For Chrysostom the condition of being enslaved to evil and sin is a condition of formlessness and ugliness. Here we encounter the introduction to anthropology of categories of aesthetics. Chrysostom wants to draw attention to a situation which is not only morally but also aesthetically unacceptable and tragic. This is why he speaks about the ugly and deformed face of the soul subjugated to evil, sin, and depravity.

There is a double anthropological insight in this case: first, the acute and painful awareness of the tragic condition of the human being enslaved to evil and sin, and second, the description of such a condition in a language of aesthetics. The first insight is significant for our times because of the often encountered tendency not to face the given human negative reality and name it by its real dark name, but

[7]Chrysostom, *Homilies on Romans*, Homily 8 (MPG 60, 465): "Πολὺ τὸ ψεῦδος, πολὺς ὁ δόλος, πολλὴ τῆς ἀγάπης ἡ ἀναίρεσις, καὶ πόλεμος ἄσπονδος. Διά τοι τοῦτο πολλοὺς εὕροι τις ἂν Ἕλλησι θαῤῥοῦτας μᾶλλον ἢ Χριστιανοῖς."

[8]*Ibid.* Homily 23 (MPG 60, 622): "...'Αλλ' ἡμεῖς ἀπηνεῖς, καὶ ὠμοί."

[9]Chrysostom, *Homilies on the Gospel of Saint Matthew*, Homily 4 (MPG 57, 49): "Καὶ τὸ δὴ χαλεπώτερον, ὅτι οὕτω διακείμενοι κακῶς, οὐδὲ ἐννοοῦμεν τῆς ψυχῆς ἡμῶν τὴν ἀμορφίαν, οὐδὲ καταμανθάνομεν αὐτῆς τὸ δυσειδές."

rather to cover it or just passively accept it and even try to justify it, thus creating anthropologies of full accommodation and rather unconditional surrendering to current voguish trends.

The second insight is equally important for contemporary people who are extremely sensitive to the categories of aesthetics and who try by all means to acquire what is beautiful: beautiful faces, beautiful bodies, smart dresses, handsome homes. Beauty seems to be a prevailing concept that plays a crucial role in our understanding of what the true human being should be in today's world, the world of the third millennium. Under these circumstances Chrysostom would certainly have asked: What happened to the need for the beauty of the soul? How much do contemporary anthropologies directly and indirectly contribute to an extended awareness of beauty including the beauty of the soul, the handsomeness of the inner self of every human being?

b) The second major anthropological insight in this group is John Chrysostom's insistence on a very special human attribute that he calls προαίρεσις. Προαίρεσις is a classical Greek word used already by Plato and Aristotle[10] and then by some early ecclesiastical authors like Justin Martyr, Clement of Alexandria, Tatian, Origen, Saint Athanasios, and Gregory of Nyssa.[11] In Chrysostom, however, and particularly in his Commentary on Paul's Epistle to the Romans, the term προαίρεσις appears with high frequency in a meaning which goes beyond the concept of free will and combines the concepts of free choice, deliber-

[10]Plato, *Parmenides*, 143C. Aristotle, *Politica*, 1280a, 34.

[11]Justin Martyr, *Dialogue with Trypho*, 88, 5; Clement of Alexandria, *Stromata*, 4, 6; Tatian, *Discourse to the Greeks*, 7; Origen, *On Principles*, 3.1.24; Saint Athanasios, *On the Incarnation*, MPG 25, 101C; and Gregory of Nyssa, *Catechetical Oration*, MPG 45, 77A.

ate decision, free decision. The word obviously implies a combination of volitional, intellectual, and emotional elements, and constitutes according to Chrysostom the real essence of every human being, the genuine human self. Προαίρεσις provides the decisive factor for any transforming processes, i.e. processes enhancing our human identity and quality. This is a fundamental anthropological idea of Chrysostom. The intention, the will of man, and the freedom of decision, the προαίρεσις, is such a powerful factor that it can overcome and subdue human nature itself. Chrysostom goes so far as to ask, "What difference is there between nature and προαίρεσις,"[12] thus making προαίρεσις equal to nature in terms of power. This emphasis on the προαίρεσις, on the will and the decision power of human beings, is a favorite theme of Chrysostom, around which he develops a series of fascinating thoughts. By the προαίρεσις, which we submit to God, the realization of immense steps in the domain of the transformation of human beings is made possible. Chrysostom is not afraid of the ugliness and corruption of human nature, for he believes that "by rectifying our προαίρεσις, our will, free choice, and intention, we can correct the defects of our nature and overcome its infirmities."[13]

Nothing is impossible for this προαίρεσις. Thanks to it, human beings who were previously fallen can now begin to follow the way to change, the route leading to a radical enhancement. "Let us not think that it is impossible to acquire such a great and good thing," Chrysostom says. "It is possible, provided that we have the will to be sober and vigilant. And not only this, but it is possible for

[12]Chrysostom, *Homilies on Saint Paul*, Homily 6 (MPG 50, 505): "Τί γὰρ διαφέρει τοῦτο φύσει, ἢ προαιρέσει εἶναι;"

[13]*Ibid.* (MPG 50, 504): "Τῆς προαιρέσεως διορθουμένης τὸ τῆς φύσεως ἐλάττωμα, καὶ κρατούσης τῆς ἀσθενείας ἐκείνης."

us to achieve every virtue; for we are ruled not by the necessity of a blind destiny, but by προαίρεσις, by free will and deliberate choice, being free to want or not to want, to acquire good things and bad things."[14]

In many instances and in support of his strong idea about προαίρεσις, Chrysostom uses the example of Paul the Apostle. Here is an eloquent passage from his sermons on Paul's first Epistle to the Corinthians: "Even if you are slanderers, even if you are mean and grasping, even if you are anything, bear always in mind that Paul too was a blasphemer, a persecutor, an insulter, the greatest of sinners and suddenly he rose to the very top of virtue without any of his previous defects being an obstacle to it."[15] "Because for him who has the will to become good, nothing can be an obstacle, not even the worst things he has committed before."[16] Chrysostom connects προαίρεσις with desire (πόθος) showing that desire, especially desire for God as a component of προαίρεσις, makes it a terrific dynamic factor. He writes on this subject: "There is nothing, absolutely nothing, that desire cannot overcome. And when the desire is the desire for God then it proves to be stronger than anything else. Neither fire nor sword, neither poverty nor

[14]Chrysostom, *Sermon on Perfect Love*, (MPG 56, 282): "Μὴ τοίνυν ἀδυνατον εἶναι νομίσωμεν τὸ τοιοῦτον ἀγαθὸν κτήσασθαι. Δυνατὸν γάρ, ὄντως δυνατόν, εἴ γε βουλόμεθα νήφειν· οὐ τοῦτο δὲ μόνον, ἀλλὰ καὶ πᾶσαν κατορθῶσαι τὴν ἀρετήν. Αὐτεξουσίῳ γὰρ προαιρέσει κυβερνώμεθα, καὶ οὐχ εἱμαρμένης ἀνάγκῃ, κατά τινας, ὑποκείμεθα, ἐν τῷ θέλειν καὶ μὴ θέλειν ὁριζόμενοι καὶ τὰ καλὰ κεῖσθαι καὶ τὰ κακά."

[15]Chrysostom, *Homilies on 1 Corinthians*, Homily 22 (MPG 61, 185): "Μὴ τοίνυν ἀπογνῶμεν, ἀλλά, κἂν λοίδορος ἦς, κἂν πλεονέκτης, κἄν ὁτιοῦν, ἐννόησον ὅτι Παῦλος βλάσφημος ἦν καὶ διώκτης καὶ ὑβριστής, καὶ τῶν ἁμαρτωλῶν πρῶτος, καὶ ἐξαίφνης πρὸς αὐτὴν ἀνέβη τὴν κορυφὴν τῆς ἀρετῆς, καὶ οὐδὲν αὐτῷ κώλυμα τὰ πρότερα γέγονε."

[16]*Ibid.* (MPG 61, 186): "Τὸν γὰρ βουλόμενον γενέσθαι ἀγαθὸν οὐδέν ἐστι τὸ κωλύον, κἄν τῶν πονηροτάτων ἔμποσθεν ἦ."

disease, neither death nor anything else will seem dreadful to him who is possessed by such desire, such love. But deriding all else he will wing upwards to heaven, and will lack none of the things that those have who live there. He is indifferent to everything, to heaven and earth and sea, he will tend to the one and only beauty."[17]

Chrysostom is aware and speaks continuously about the need for assistance from God in order to obtain a real human transformation. He is clear about faith in and love for Christ as a decisive factor in any transformational process; but he is also clear in constantly emphasizing the absolute significance of προαίρεσις in such an awesome process. He would even go so far as to use the telling example of the diamond: "Look at the precious stone diamond. While it receives blows, it hits the item which hits it. Well, you probably object, this happens because of the very nature of the diamond. But you too have the possibility through your προαίρεσις to acquire the power which diamond has by nature."[18] When such a man as Chrysostom speaks about the possibilities of human προαίρεσις, of human will, desire, and the power of decision, what he says is of the greatest importance, and his words are worthy of serious attention on our part; for this is a man who during his whole life breathed an air full of the poison of human misery and perversity, and who saw a great part of his pastoral efforts rendered useless because of human weakness.

[17]Chrysostom, *Homilies on Romans*, Homily 9 (MPG 60, 474): "Οὐ γὰρ ἔστιν. Οὐκ ἔστιν οὐδέν, ὃ μὴ νικᾷ πόθος· ὅταν δὲ καὶ Θεοῦ πόθος ᾖ, πάντων ἐστὶν ὑψηλότερος, καὶ οὔτε πῦρ, οὐ σίδηρος, οὐ πενία, οὐκ ἀῤῥωστία, οὐ θάνατος, οὐκ ἄλλο τι τῶν τοιούτων φανεῖται δεινὸν τῷ τοιοῦτον κεκτημένῳ τὸν ἔρωτα."

[18]*Ibid*. Homily 2, (MPG 60, 416): "Οὐχ ὁρᾷς τὸν ἀδάμαντα ἐν τῷ παίεσθαι πλήττοντα. Ἀλλ' ἡ φύσις, φησὶ τοῦτο ἔχει. Ἀλλ' καὶ σοὶ δυνατὸν ἐν τῇ προαιρέσει γενέσθαι τοιοῦτον, ὅπερ ἀπὸ φύσεως ἐκείνῳ συμβαίνει."

Here, again, we have an excellent anthropological insight for our times. Where modern authors, thinkers, and artists often speak about a bleeding of the will, a loss of nerve, a submission to inexorable fate, Chrysostom raises his voice and reminds us of the huge power of volitional, intellectual, and emotional properties inherent in our true and inalienable self, in our προαίρεσις.

Three Superb Human Models

The third group of anthropological insights offered by Saint John Chrysostom consists of three human models. Knowing very well the power of example, Chrysostom knew that in order to be practical and effective with the people with whom he was constantly dealing, he had to present concrete, human models. He did this with every homily, bringing in the midst of theoretical arguments specific human types either from the biblical field, from history, or from contemporary times.

However, he was very particular with three human models, three types of human excellence, two of them embodied in historical personalities, the third being a special human category. In this case, Chrysostom eventually creates advanced anthropological models which constitute an insightful contribution to anthropology.

a) The first of the three Chrysostomic models is Abraham, the great Patriarch. We are impressed by the deep love and immense admiration Chrysostom had for Abraham. This was perhaps due to the same reason for which fifteen hundred years later the Danish existentialist philosopher Sören Kierkegaard was so much interested in Abraham, namely, for his faith as faithfulness, as fidelity. It is characteristic that Chrysostom, besides numerous places in which he speaks about Abraham, consecrated a whole series of nineteen long, complete homilies to the great Patriarch. Hundreds of pages burst with the huge amount of material he uses in order to draw the picture of Abraham. "And don't be astonished," he says, "if speaking for so many days, we have been unable to complete Abraham's story."[19]

Chrysostom does not tire of stressing Abraham's everyday fidelity, his astonishing ability to remain steadfastly and unshakably faithful in a most difficult daily life. Chrysostom's Abraham is one of the best and most beautiful human models expressive of a faithfulness that is consistent and operative at any moment, in any condition, at any cost. On this point Chrysostom insists much. He does not hesitate to speak in great detail using the most dangerous elements of Abraham's life in order to show the immense beauty of his fidelity that is without limits or reservations. We can easily verify this by simply reading his *Homily 32* or his *Homily 38* on the book of Genesis. In these homilies, we have an admirable anthropological presentation of Abraham remaining faithful under the worst possible conditions.

Here we have an insightful description of an anthropological model exhibiting faithfulness as a superb human quality. Modern family, social, national, and international experiences tell us how vital and indispensable is such an anthropological quality. It remains questionable, however, just how much this quality is part of contemporary studies dealing with desirable human behavior.

[19]Chrysostom, *Homilies on Genesis*, Homily 38 (MPG 53, 350): "καὶ μὴ θαυμάσητε εἰ ἐπὶ τοσαύταις ἡμέραις τὴν κατ' αὐτὸν ἱστορίαν εἰς μέσον παραγαγόντες, οὐδέπω καὶ τήμερον αὐτὴν ἀπαρτίσαι δεδυνήμεθα. Πολλὴ γὰρ ἡ περιουσία τῆς τοῦ δικαίου ἀρετῆς, καὶ τῶν τούτου κατορθωμάτων τὸ μέγεθος ἅπασαν ἀνθρωπίνην νικᾷ γλῶτταν."

b) The second anthropological model of this group belongs to a special category of human beings, namely the priest. In his famous work *On the Priesthood*, but in other cases too, Chrysostom presents an ingenious picture of the priestly identity. This picture is a true anthropological creation, springing from a brilliant mind and a soul imbued with the light and the wisdom of theology. In essence, this picture is an eloquent description of the immense possibilities for astonishing advancements available to human creatures.

Chrysostom speaks extensively about the honor and the awesome authority given to priests; he even makes a bold comparison between priests and angels. "The priests who live on earth have received the right to rule what is in heaven and have been given by God a power that was given neither the angels nor the archangels.... They are as if they were already elevated into heaven and had transcended the limits of human nature, as if they were already free from our passions; so great is their authority."[20] In this passage, we ought to note two things. First, we may note the comparison between priest and angel, and second, the statement that priests are "as if they were already elevated into heaven and had transcended the limits of human nature." This is not a rhetorical exaggeration. Chrysostom speaks of the priest as if he were a special kind of human being, a being possessing a different sort of nature and not that of man. The very important insight in this case is the terrific poten-

[20]Chrysostom, *On the Priesthood*, Homily 3 (MPG 48, 643): "Οἱ γὰρ τὴν γῆν οἰκοῦντες, καὶ ἐν ταύτῃ ποιούμενοι τὴν διατριβήν, τὰ ἐν οὐρανοῖς διοικεῖν ἐπετράπησαν, καὶ ἐξουσίαν ἔλαβον ἣν οὔτε ἀγγέλοις οὔτε ἀρχαγγέλοις ἔδωκεν ὁ Θεός.... Ὥσπερ γὰρ εἰς οὐρανοὺς ἤδη μετατεθέντες, καὶ τὴν ἀνθρωπείαν ὑπερβάντες φύσιν, καὶ τῶν ἡμετέρων ἀπαλλαγέντες παθῶν, οὕτως εἰς ταύτην ἤχθησαν τὴν ἀρχήν."

tial opened to human nature to transcend even itself, to go beyond its natural bodily limits. Through the priest, Chrysostom advocates an anthropology of immense possibilities.

It should be noted here again, that Chrysostom says what he says in full awareness of the difficulties, the weaknesses, and the dangers that are related to priestly function. A characteristic passage will indicate such a truly painful awareness: "More waves than all the waves of the sea afflict the soul of the priest.... Anger, discouragement, envy, strife, slander, accusations, lies, hypocrisy, jealousy, wrath against the innocent, pleasure of talking about the defects of others, sorrow for their success, love of praises, desire of honors, flattery inspired by interest, indecent gestures, indifference for the poor, interest for the rich and the mighty."[21] In spite of all these elements of possible deficiency, the priest in essence remains a very special human being. Chrysostom's realism about the negative aspects surrounding the priest as human being is coupled with his realism about the anthropologically unique status of the priest as priest, to the point that he exclaims: "Tell me in what order must I classify such a being?"[22] This question, which Chrysostom leaves without an answer, is of particular importance because it implies the existence of an anthropological model of an unlimited potential.

c) The third and final anthropological model is Saint Paul the Apostle. In Paul, Chrysostom sees the wholeness, the perfection of the human being regarded not as

[21]*Ibid.* (MPG 48, 646): "Πλείονα γὰρ τῶν τὴν θάλατταν ταραττόντων πνευμάτων χειμάζει κύματα τὴν τοῦ ἱερωμένου ψυχήν.... Τίνα δὲ ἐστι τὰ θηρία; Θυμός, ἀθυμία, φθόνος, ἔρις, διαβολαί, κατηγορίαι, ψεῦδος, ὑπόκρισις, ἐπιβουλαί, ὀργαὶ κατὰ τῶν ἠδικηκότων οὐδέν, ἡδοναὶ ἐπὶ ταῖς τῶν λειτουργούντων ἀσχημοσύναις, πένθος ἐπὶ ταῖς εὐημερίαις, ἐπαίνων ἔρως, τιμῆς πόθος, διδασκαλίαι πρὸς ἡδονήν, ἀνελεύθεροι κολακεῖαι, θωπεῖαι ἀγεννεῖς, καταφρονήσεις πενήτων, θεραπεῖαι πλουσίων."

[22]*Ibid.* Homily 6 MPG 48, 681: "ποῦ τάξομεν αὐτόν, εἰπέ μοι;"

a particular, isolated case but as a representative model, a guiding human type. He states this idea in no uncertain terms: "What a human being truly is, how great the dignity of his nature, and how far can he advance in virtue, has been shown to us by Paul more than by any other human being."[23] Chrysostom is aware that Paul's elevated status is significantly due to his connection with Jesus; but he is also aware of Paul's own amazing achievement. He says, "When a soul, like the soul of a human being (i.e. Paul), richly and abundantly possesses not only all the qualities which belong to a human being, but also those which belong to the angels, how can we justly and worthily praise it?"[24] In order to show Paul's superb anthropological status, Chrysostom proceeds with a comparison between him and the great biblical figures. "Whatever great qualities characterized the patriarchs and the prophets and the just men of old, the apostles and the martyrs and the saints, all this together, and in a more perfect and excellent way, characterized the Apostle Paul. Did Abel once offer a holy and most pleasing sacrifice? Paul offered every day of his life a sacrifice which differed from that as heaven differs from earth.... Was Abel killed by Cain? Paul suffered a thousand deaths. Was Noah the only just man in his generation? Paul's justice excels the justice of every one.... We all admire Abraham because when he heard the voice of the Lord saying, 'Get thee out of thy country and from thy kindred, and from thy father's house, unto a land that I

[23]Chrysostom, *Homilies on Saint Paul*, Homily 2 (MPG 50, 477-9): "Τί ποτέ ἔστιν ἄνθρωπος, καὶ ὅση τῆς φύσεως τῆς ἡμετέρας ἡ εὐγένεια, καὶ ὅσης ἐστὶ δεκτικὸν ἀρετῆς τουτὶ τὸ ζῶον, ἔδειξε μάλιστα πάντων ἀνθρώπων ὁ Παῦλος."

[24]*Ibid*. Homily 1 MPG 50, 473: "Ὅταν γὰρ ἅπαντα τὰ ἐν ἀνθρώποις καλὰ συλλαβοῦσα ἔχῃ ψυχὴ μία, καὶ πάντα μεθ' ὑπερβολῆς, οὐ μόνον δὲ τὰ τῶν ἀνθρώπων, ἀλλὰ καὶ τὰ τῶν ἀγγέλων, πῶς περιεσόμεθα τοῦ μεγέθους τῶν ἐγκωμίων;"

will show thee,' he immediately obeyed. But what admiration must one have for Paul who not only left his country, his house, his family, but sacrificed the whole world and held for nothing heaven itself? ...There is no man who is not astonished by Job's patience and persevering struggle and final victory. But what must our astonishment be when we see Paul living and fighting under similar conditions not for a few months but for many years, struggling alike against foe and friend and finally earning as a crown of victory a most costly martyrdom?"[25] Chrysostom hastens to indicate that Paul by nature was a man like all of us. "He loved his life very much and all that he could get from it,"[26] "his weak and ill body trembled at the idea of punishment,"[27] and "he was afraid of death."[28] However, Chrysostom hastens to say, "the obvious weakness of his nature was the best proof of his virtue. He was not free of the necessities to which we are all enslaved. And because of the number and the greatness of the dangers he so successfully faced could create in us the impression that he was being different and superior from us, he was allowed to suffer so that we can understand that, from the point of view of nature, he was one like us, though from the point of view of eager willingness (προθυμία), he was not only superior to us, but was like one of the angels."[29]

[25]*Ibid.* Homily 1 (MPG 50, 473-4).

[26]*Ibid.* Homily 5 (MPG 50, 497): "Σφόδρα τῆς παρούσης ἤρα ζωῆς διὰ τὸ κέρδος τὸ ἐξ αὐτῆς."

[27]*Ibid.* Homily 6 (MPG 50, 503): "[Paul having] σῶμα οὕτως εἶκον πληγαῖς καὶ μάστιγας."

[28]*Ibid.* (MPG 50, 504): "Οὕτω καὶ Παῦλος φοβούμενος θάνατον."

[29]*Ibid.* (MPG 50, 503): "Αὐτὴ γὰρ ἡ δοκοῦσα τῆς φύσεως εἶναι ἀσθένεια, αὐτὴ μέγιστον δεῖγμα τῆς ἀρετῆς ἐστι τῆς ἐκείνου, ὅτι οὐκ ἀπηλλαγμένος τῆς τῶν πολλῶν ἀνάγκης τοιοῦτος ἦν. Ἐπειδὴ γὰρ ἡ τῶν κινδύνων ὑπερβολὴ πολλοῖς ἂν ταύτην παρέσχε τὴν

For Chrysostom, the greatness of Paul and his anthropological significance as a model, lies in his absolute dedication to his mission dictated by an enormous love. Here is one of the most telling passages of Chrysostom: "Paul, being great in the greatest of goods, which is love, was more burning than a flame of fire; and as the iron when it falls into the fire, becomes itself all fire, so Paul, having been set on fire by the fire of love, became himself all love.... Being like a common father to the whole universe he imitated all his ancestors and overcame all his forefathers in love by his bodily and spiritual cares for his children, sacrificing things and words, body and soul for the sake of his beloved."[30] Chrysostom's Paul is the anthropological model of an outstanding human being in a permanent condition of mission that is motivated by a burning love.

Here is the precise anthropological insight: the condition of a human life that has a mission motivated by love—human beings in mission, in movement serving high purposes and ideals. Is this not an attitude proper to our times, behooving human beings?

ὑπόληψιν, καὶ ὑποπτεύειν ἴσως ἐποίησεν, ὅτι ἀνώτερος τῶν ἀνθρωπίνων γενόμενος, τοιοῦτος ἦν. Διὰ ταῦτα συνεχεπεῖτο πάσχειν, ἵνα μάθης ὅτι εἷς τῶν πολλῶν ὥν κατὰ τὴν φύσιν, κατὰ τὴν προθυμίαν, οὐ μόνον ὑπὲρ τοὺς πολλοὺς ἦν, ἀλλὰ καὶ τῶν ἀγγέλων εἷς ἦν."

[30]*Ibid.* Homily 3, (MPG 50, 486): "Καὶ ὢν μέγας, ἐν τῷ κεφαλαίῳ τῶν ἀγαθῶν, τῇ ἀγάπῃ, φλογὸς πάσης σφοδρότερος ἦν· καὶ καθάπερ σίδηρος εἰς πῦρ ἐμπεσὼν, ὅλος γίνεται πῦρ, οὕτω καὶ αὐτὸς τῷ πυρὶ τῆς ἀγάπης ἀναφθεὶς, ὅλος γέγονεν ἀγάπη· καὶ ὥσπερ κοινὸς πατὴρ τῆς οἰκουμένης ἁπάσης ὤν, οὕτω τοὺς γεγεννηκότας αὐτοὺς ἐμιμεῖτο· μᾶλλον δὲ καὶ πάντας ὑπερηκόντισε πατέρας, καὶ σωματικῶν καὶ πνευματικῶν ἕνεκεν φροντίδων, καὶ χρήματα, καὶ ῥήματα, καὶ σῶμα, καὶ ψυχὴν, καὶ πάντα ἐπιδιδοὺς ὑπὲρ τῶν ἠγαπημένων."

Conclusion

At this point the present lecture comes to a close, having displayed a limited number of Saint John Chrysostom's anthropological ideas and attitudes.

As you have noticed throughout my presentation, I made only a few references to the role that God and His mighty grace plays in Chrysostom's anthropology. Of course, Chrysostom's fundamental theocentric orientation was emphasized, but I did not elaborate on its concrete and decisive anthropological applications.

You also must have noticed that limited references were made to Jesus Christ as an indispensable factor, as a truly integral and a *sine qua non* agent in Chrysostom's anthropology.

My lack of frequent references to God and to Christ was the result of a deliberate methodological approach adopted for this specific lecture. The intent was to show that John Chrysostom's anthropological insights, their theological and Christological references notwithstanding, have an undeniable validity by themselves and could be stimulating for any anthropology regardless of its specific faith or metaphysical orientation. In other words, I intended to draw attention to Chrysostom's anthropological universality, which goes beyond any limitations of time, geography, and culture.

In the final analysis, Chrysostom's anthropological legacy is the fundamental idea of the human potential for a radical transformation, for a change from the dark abyss of humiliation to the luminous heights of an unheard of exaltation. The astonishing fact is that this unheard of exaltation is described by Chrysostom by his simple phrase "just become human being" [γενοῦ ἄνθρωπος]. Leave behind what you are and become human being.

It is really refreshing and stimulating to allow the echo of Chrysostom's voice to linger longer and longer in the halls of our anthropological research centers: "These I say and I will not cease saying, come and become human being." [Ταῦτα δὲ λέγω, καὶ λέγων οὐ παύσομαι. Ἐλθὲ, καὶ γενοῦ ἄνθρωπος.]

Six Challenges Confronting Orthodoxy In the Twenty-First Century

A Context for Discussion of the Pastoral Letter "And the Word Became Flesh and Dwelt Among Us"

Conference of the
Standing Conference of Canonical Orthodox Bishops
In the Americas (SCOBA)

Washington, D.C.
May 1, 2001

Introduction

Most Reverend and truly Beloved Brothers, Christ is Risen! I greet you with a heart full of joy as we meet today in this solemn conference of all canonical Orthodox Bishops in the Americas.

This is a particular event of great significance that happens under handsome circumstances. This conference takes place during the Paschal period, hence, it is permeated by the joy, the peace, and the love radiating from the Resurrection of the Lord. He, being God, the Son and Logos, Word, not only *became flesh and dwelt among us* (John 1:14), *but he humbled himself and became obedient unto death, even death on a cross* (Philippians 2:8), in order to eventually offer to us His astonishing, triumphant, live-giving Resurrection on the third day (1 Corinthians 15:4).

A meeting like ours, occurring in the time and the spirit of Christ's Resurrection, obviously takes on a special significance, for this is the first conference of the canonical Orthodox Bishops in the Americas in the new millennium and in the twenty-first century. We celebrated the ending of the second Christian millennium with the important pastoral letter *And the Word Became Flesh and Dwelt Among Us,* issued last Christmas by SCOBA. We celebrate today the beginning of the third Christian millennium by gathering together as a sacred body of Hierarchs on the first Easter of the new era—quite an opportune time in the history of humanity.

There is another element of importance related to our conference. We meet in Washington, the capital of this nation, in essence the capital of the most advanced and powerful nation on earth. And we meet here, aiming at offering in this remarkable place the genuine witness of Orthodoxy, a witness full of truth, love, hope, and faith, a witness desperately needed in our contemporary world. This meeting place adds importance to our conference and accentuates our responsibility as carriers of the unique Gospel message.

All of us, especially as Hierarchs of SCOBA, are grateful to God for granting us the opportunity of convening the present conference. We are thankful also to all the Hierarchs, Priests, Deacons and lay people who contributed to the preparation and realization of this brotherly meeting. Their reward comes from the Lord, since we are in no position to know the tremendous amount of work that both known and unknown people have offered in this instance.

As you know, SCOBA intended and planned the present conference as a God-sent opportunity for achieving two major objectives, for promoting and enhancing two vital and eminent issues. The first is the issue of mutual acquaintance and fellowship, a spirit of cooperation, love, and appreciation among the Orthodox Bishops in this country, the possibility to enhance the sacred bond, to increase brotherly love, so that as the great Apostle said, *our love may abound more and more, with knowledge and all discernment* (Philippians 1:9). This is a central objective for our conference, a witness of strong love and fellowship as a fact, as an event, as a creative act on behalf of Orthodoxy, manifested here in Washington, D.C.

The second major issue and objective of our meeting is to study together and in-depth the theological and pastoral dimensions and implications of the milestone encyclical letter *And the Word Became Flesh and Dwelt Among Us*. In essence, this is a declaration of the Orthodox faith in contemporary language; this letter is a clear and strong witness to the invaluable, salvific and eternal Gospel tradition of our Church. Just the titles of the main parts of the encyclical immediately show its importance:

God's Plan for our Salvation
The Sin that Separates us from God
The Joy of Our Witness
Preaching the Gospel in a Pluralistic Society
A Community of Healing and Reconciliation
The Community that Remembers
A Community of Hope and Joy

We shall proceed with the responsible and God-fearing study and analysis of the document in the two lectures and the ensuing group discussions tomorrow. It is obvious that the proper approach in achieving such a lofty goal is to remain focused upon the content of the SCOBA pastoral letter unto the very end of our deliberations.

The two objectives, namely, the enhancing of fellowship and love and the thorough study of the outstanding

Christological content of the SCOBA document, have a common characteristic. They are both witnesses of our Orthodox faith, and they should be kept in the forefront of our conference at every moment and at every step.

Thus, the two basic objectives of our conference converge into one and the same point: witnessing our faith by being faithful to the superb declaration of our Lord to his Apostles and to the immense grace God has also shown to us, *As the Father has sent me, even so I send you* (John 20:21). We are being sent. As the one who became flesh and dwelt among us (John 1:14), so we are in a constant condition of mission. Our *modus vivendi* is witnessing.

We will have the opportunity to discuss this in conjunction with the two objectives of our meeting. In order to do that more effectively, however, we should perhaps also keep in mind that our witness is not produced and placed in a vacuum or timeless situation. Our witness is (a) presented to our specific concrete world living in modernity, or rather post-modernity, and (b) being proffered in a concrete and precise time, namely, the twenty-first century.

This twenty-first century, however, and this world we live in, present us with a number of challenges that we must address in conjunction with our mission to proclaim the Gospel. Allow me, please, to point out some of them, which are mentioned also in the SCOBA pastoral letter and which may facilitate our discussions tomorrow.

The Bioethical Challenge

The first of these challenges is the challenge related to the area of bioethics, biomedical engineering, and scientific and technological advances pertaining to living organisms, humans, animals, or plants. Cloning, interfering with the genome, i.e. the genetic material of organisms, and manipulating DNA are some of the results of such astonishing technological advances.

What happens in this crucial area of scientific endeavor is the potential for truly revolutionary steps that will drastically affect not only human life, but human beings in their essence, in their God-created humanness. Prospects for huge anthropological changes are looming on the horizon. The pertinent processes are already in place; they are in function, following an inexorable way that no one seems to be able to control completely.

Obviously, a considerable part of this effort deals with the strong need for coping effectively with diseases and illnesses, especially the incurable ones, and for improving health in general. The employment of advances in scientific technology also deals with the desire to be able to produce food which will be abundant and cheaper, hence adequate for large populations that are presently undernourished and starving.

There are, however, parts of the bioengineering enterprise, such as cloning, for example, which will have a gigantic and direct impact on human beings. To phrase it differently, bioengineering will have the potential to produce radical anthropological changes, real permutations in human beings, by rearranging existing biological elements or by inventing new ones.

Here is a serious challenge for Christianity in general and, in particular, for the Orthodox Church in the twenty-first century. We unyieldingly adhere to the fundamental anthropological belief that human beings have been created by God *in His image and after His likeness* (Genesis 1:26). We also unyieldingly adhere to the other fundamental anthropological and Christological belief that God *became flesh and dwelt among us* (John 1:14), that God became a human being, assuming our very human nature in its sinless status, and that we are united with Him in His death and Resurrection. Where should we place, anthropologically speaking, a hypothetical being created by cloning procedures? Where do we stand on the potential radical anthropological permutations resulting from scientific interference with the human genome? What can we do in order not to remain passive spectators of uncontrollable developments? What can we do in order to offer some basic principles or possible guidelines in the field of bioengineering concerning such critical matters as the respect for human life, the sanctity of human existence, the uniqueness of each and every human person living on earth, and the decisive interconnection between a human organism and any other living organism?

The Changing Institutions Challenge

The second major challenge comes from the area of important institutions that seem to be undergoing a deteriorating change with enormous implications for society and for the Church. I would like to focus on one of them, namely, the sacred institution of marriage and family. Changes of an easily discernible nature are on the increase, and no one can predict what will happen during the course of the twenty-first century.

What we experience is a general phenomenon with multiple aspects. The phenomenon may be summarily described by the phrase "the erosion of the family." A central aspect of such an erosion is the desacralization of the institution of marriage. People do not talk or even think of Holy Matrimony as the sacred union of two people. Rather, they think of temporary relationships, of an understanding of marriage as a contract, as a social convenience or routine, or as a conventional agreement to live together and so on. They even think of the "one parent family!" The change from the sacred and holy to the conventional, the contractual, and the arbitrary is certainly detrimental, if not fatal.

Another aspect of the erosion is the rearing of children. With the father and the mother working, children in the critical, early years of their lives are left for hours and hours every day in the care of baby sitters or child-care centers. We do not have to describe the consequences of such a condition, which recently became the center of controversial studies and debates both in academia and the media.

Due to socioeconomic conditions, especially in large cities, and to other factors, the family does not cultivate a reality and spirit of people being together, living together, growing together, simply said, living as a family. This is another aspect of erosion that affects the unity of the family.

We do not need to speak about the alarming divorce rate and the ease of the relevant procedures of divorce in order to point out yet one more aspect of familial erosion.

The ongoing erosion of the institution of marriage and family constitutes a huge problem for us as the Church, with a strong belief in the sacredness and paramount importance of the sacrament of Holy Matrimony. Here is a real, immediate challenge for us. The challenge is greater, because in addition to all other factors which interfere with the family, we also have the phenomenon of interfaith marriages. Such a phenomenon, which is extensive and prevailing, adds difficulties to an already difficult and complicated situation.

The challenge related to the family is truly inescapable and inexorable. The issue of the family should become a high priority for our Church if we intend to be a living, dynamic, and well-functioning Church. An ecclesiastical community without strong, well-functioning families cannot be a witness to the Gospel. Perhaps it is necessary to go beyond a minimalistic approach that says, "Let us be satisfied just with the survival of the family as such." No! The family in our Orthodox understanding is a "κατ' οἶκον Εκκλησία" [a Church in the house] in the way Saint Paul speaks about in his Epistles (Romans 16:5, 1 Corinthians 16:19, Colossians 4:15, Philemon 2). This kind of family is not only a blessed, joyful entity; it is a mighty witness to the faith. Here is a challenge opening magnificent vistas to our mission as the Orthodox Church.

The Relativization Challenge

A third significant challenge for us living in twenty-first century America is the increasing relativization of everything. Language becomes more and more a relative entity, susceptible to manipulation, limited, and ever-changing. Perception is a subjective understanding of reality, hence it is relative by its very nature. Communication aided by technology is in a state of inflation, therefore it suffers the fate of relativization.

The realm of absolutes seems to be rapidly shrinking, whereas relativizing processes seem to be quickly encompassing more and more spheres of human life and activity. Moral principles, ethical behaviors, ideological positions, metaphysical ideas, and, finally, religious beliefs are constantly being made relative. The very existence of many religions in one place, the contemporary attractiveness of syncretistic religions, sects, and cults, and the fact that you can pick and choose whatever suits you from any religion, are clear indications of a prevailing relativistic tendency *vis-à-vis* religion. This phenomenon projects the tacit assumption that there is no absolute truth, there is no absolute religion.

Such an underlying principle, paradoxically absolute in and of itself because it states that there is only one absolute, i.e. the fact that everything is relative, leads many people to positions that we would call compromising religious positions, but which they themselves consider natural, based on the premise of a relativized understanding of religion.

We do not need prophetic foresight to predict an increasing relativizing process in the years ahead. Our people, especially the younger generations, will live in a world dominated by a relativistic understanding of everything, including, of course, religion and, ultimately, truth.

In this case we could remember the dramatic dialog in the praetorium of Jerusalem between Jesus Christ and Pontius Pilate: *Jesus answered* [to Pilate]...*"For this I was born, and for this I have come into the world, to bear witness to the truth. Everyone who is of the truth hears my voice." Pilate said to him, "What is truth?"* (John 18:37-38). The answer by the Roman governor of Judaea could be interpreted as an outright cynical rejection of any possibility for reaching the truth. It could also be interpreted, however, as a concise definition of the truth as something fully relative and in no way whatsoever absolute.

But the answer by the Lord—*"for this I was born, and for this I have come into the world, to bear witness to the truth,"* and His declaration, *"I am the way and the truth and the life"* (John 14:6)—makes perfectly clear that His revealed truth, His Gospel, His Church are absolute in nature. Just read again the Gospel of John and see the absolute position and nature of the truth. In that Gospel there is an impressive number of twenty-four passages in which Jesus Christ speaks about "doing the truth," "worshipping in truth," "staying in the truth," "being of the truth," "declaring the truth," "revealing the truth," "being sanctified in the truth," "being liberated by the truth," "witnessing the truth," and finally making known that the Holy Spirit, the Comforter, is "the Spirit of the truth." There is no room here for any relativization. The truth of the faith, of which we have the supreme honor to be witnesses, is not susceptible to any relativization or compromise or manipulative handling.

But how do we cope with the relativizing process around us? How do we combine faithful adherence to the absolute nature of our witness with a genuine openness to and respect for the religious and other beliefs of millions of people who constitute the overwhelming majority of our society? The challenge remains, and it requires viable responses.

The Technological Challenge

The galloping developments in the area of information technologies constitute one more challenge, the fourth in this list, that the twenty-first century presents to the Church.

The challenge in this case comes in many forms and in diversified areas. Here, we are struck by the immediate availability of huge amounts of information pertaining to all fields of knowledge from the most trivial daily notes to sophisticated, advanced, scientific knowledge. Human brains are flooded with data to the point of saturation, where no room, disposition, or tolerance for anything more exists. How are we going to promote the knowledge related to our Orthodox faith when we have to operate under the massive pressure of the information producing media? Of course, one might say, by using the very same media. Things are not so simple. Just think about the space and time that is available to us for declaring our faith through the dissemination of information in contemporary forms of media! Thousands upon thousands of hours are being used by

TV and radio stations, web sites, and Internet connections, and yet a fraction of a fraction of this time is used by us.

This is not a problem of intellectual and artistic inability, or a lack of talent on our part. It is a problem that has to do with sheer difference in numbers and resources as far as population, political power, marketing tactics, and global economic strategies are concerned. It is a question of who controls the media, who controls the information technologies both as tools and carriers of ideas, and as contents of ideas.

One might argue that most of the large amounts of information are not related at all to subjects that affect our faith. Yes! But the extraordinary proportions of information leave plenty of room for the dissemination of ideas that are directly or indirectly related to matters of faith in all its manifestations. Blatant religious or antireligious propaganda, diversified reports on Church affairs, promotion of religious books, and matters concerning ethical issues that are supported or opposed by religious communities circulate in abundance and with the utmost comfort through amazing technological innovations on a twenty-four hour basis.

This is not the proper time and place to offer suggestions for solutions to the problems and challenges presented by such technologies. It is, however, the proper time to increase our awareness of the magnitude and significance of the technological challenge. It is time to remember that the Church has been, from her initial phase to modern times, an avant-guard entity and a primary agent in using the oral and the printed word in abundance as a means for extensive communication and dissemination of the Gospel. Today, next to the oral and the printed word, we have the all-pervasive electronic word. How are we doing with this word? Having been the principle producers of speeches, manuscripts, and books for centuries, are we going to be insignificant partners in the vast array of electronic textual productions?

The Social and Environmental Challenge

The fifth challenge confronting Orthodoxy in the twenty-first century relates to social and environmental issues. We declare that we are the Church, which has philanthropy in its real sense, i.e. as a strong love and care for human beings in their environment, in the center of her life. Throughout the twenty centuries of our existence, Orthodoxy has shown, even under the worst circumstances, her uncompromising adherence to philanthropy, her sharp sensitivity to social issues or to issues in general affecting the life of people. Injustices, violence, poverty, diseases, exiles, captivities, imprisonments, wars, to mention a few indicative issues, have been permanent daily concerns dominating the action of our Church. Saint John Chrysostom on his way to exile, being seriously ill and on the verge of his death which soon followed, wrote passionate letters to his flock in Constantinople asking them to send food to specific areas heavily affected by famine, arguing that this would be the best medicine and comfort for him under the excruciating circumstances he was experiencing. This is the true spirit of Orthodox philanthropy—a consuming, all-absorbing spirit.

We try to be faithful to this vital tradition; we have to be faithful. But we must be aware of and prepared for the demanding tasks ahead. The world we live in and the twenty-first century confront us with strong challenges on two levels.

The first is the entire range of social issues. The distance between the people who have plenty of everything and the people who have almost nothing appears to be increasing dangerously, as the SCOBA letter eloquently presents. Injustices of all kinds are rapidly spreading. More and more people seem to suffer from unfair practices and discrimination in the areas of health and employment. We do not have to go to well-known particular cases which create grave social problems related to drug addiction, sexual abuse, homelessness, incurable diseases, adolescent criminality, and increasing violence, in order to indicate the magnitude and the seriousness of the pertinent issues.

Are we ready to face the challenge and be participants in the effort to resolve these painful issues? Are we ready to continue the two thousand year tradition of the Church and offer a strong and generous hand in healing wounds and ills related to social diseases and deficiencies?

And then, there is another level of challenges in front of us as we begin the twenty-first century. These challenges are related to environmental problems. Our natural world appears to be deteriorating constantly. Air and water pollution, exhaustion of natural resources, and nonreversible damages to the habitat of people and animals are the main components of something that seems to take the shape of a nightmare. Elementary sources of life, like water, seem to be seriously threatened. Analyses offered by UNESCO (Jerome Binde of the UNESCO Office of Analyses) point out that the twenty-first century may be the century of wars related to water supplies, as it is already happening in some strategic areas of our planet.

What is our role in this ongoing environmental deterioration? How are we to translate into action Orthodoxy's strong commitment to the sanctity of the natural environment created by God for the benefit of humanity?

The Spirituality Challenge

The sixth challenge, with which I would like to close the list, by no means exhausting it, of course, is the challenge related to the issue of spirituality.

In a recent discussion with a group of distinguished Protestant theologians at Columbia University, I asked them to tell me, frankly and clearly, what they really thought the Orthodox Church could offer to American society, specifically to the American religious scene in the twenty-first century. They answered with one word: spirituality—spirituality as a fundamental expression of the prayer and the liturgical life, of the theological activity, of the pastoral care, and of the essential Christian ethos of the Orthodox Church.

I further asked them, "Could you please be more specific about what you mean by the word *spirituality*?" They answered: The emphasis on the absolute priority and presence of God in all aspects of Church thinking, speaking, and operating; the constant projection that He truly is first, that He is the constant focus; the reality of the Holy Spirit as the prime, decisive, and all-encompassing factor in ecclesiastical life and witness.

This is exactly how we are perceived by many non-Orthodox theologians. This is what they expect from us: spirituality in all possible expressions and manifestations. But how are we to respond to such a lofty expectation, to such a challenge, a challenge which is highlighted by the cover story in the current issue of *Newsweek* magazine (May 7, 2001, p. 50) entitled "God and the Brain: How we're wired for Spirituality"?

We live in an advanced, technological environment. We live more and more under pressures from powerful economic, social, and political agents. We encounter on a daily basis a relentless attack of diverse priorities, some of them blatantly materialistic and secular. How can we offer the treasure of the spirituality that has been an ageless characteristic of Orthodoxy?

Here is a challenge. Here is the potential for a tremendous contribution by Orthodox generations to twenty-first century America: Offering full and genuine Orthodox spirituality to the most advanced technological society that has ever existed on earth. Offering the mysterious yet accessible presence of God in large metropolitan cities and small towns, in the hospitals, laboratories, and schools; offering the reality of the holy and the sacred to environments dominated by the secular, the profane, and the materialistic; offering the aroma of holiness and saintly presence in places where sin, evil, guilt, and corruption seem to abound; offering the immensity and the eternity of Orthodox spirituality to people captive to the ephemeral, the limited, the perishable.

Epilogue

In a sketchy, telegraphic way, we have seen 6 major challenges that confront us as we face the new millennium and the first year of the twenty-first century in America. They are:

The Bioethical Challenge
The Changing Institutions Challenge
The Relativization Challenge
The Information Technologies Challenge
The Social and Environmental Challenge
The Spirituality Challenge

Certainly, these are formidable challenges. But we, as Hierarchs of the Orthodox Church, are under God, with God, and for God. Therefore all things are possible to us, because *all things are possible with God* (Matthew 19:26) and *all things are possible to him who believes* (Mark 9:23).

There is, however, more. During his farewell speech to the disciples, the Lord made an amazing declaration. He said, *"Truly, truly, I say to you, he who believes in me will also do the works that I do; and greater works than these will he do, because I go to the Father"* (John 14:12). Greater works than Jesus Christ did? Are we offered this unbelievable possibility? Perhaps we could forget any other challenge we have been talking about and think that this is the challenge for us in view of the twenty-first century: To be able through our faith to do greater works than the works of Christ.

Paideia, Wisdom and Priesthood

Commencement Address
Hellenic College
Holy Cross Greek Orthodox School of Theology

Brookline, MA
May 19, 2001

Beloved Graduates of the Class of 2001:

As we gather on this day we offer praise and thanksgiving to God our Creator and Redeemer who has brought us out of darkness and guides us into the radiant light of His eternal glory.

This first commencement of the new millennium is a momentous occasion that brings us together for several reasons: we are here to recognize the achievements of these men and women who are soon to be graduates of Hellenic College and Holy Cross; we are here to honor and remember those who have contributed to the life and work of this vital institution of our Holy Archdiocese; and we are here to acknowledge the continuous service and provision to the Church that has come from a school and a community that is now embracing a renewed vision for the future of ministry and mission in our parishes, in the broader society, and throughout the world.

Today, our hope and prayer is that such a vision has been established and will be perpetuated in the hearts and minds of you, our graduates. May the knowledge, wisdom, deep insights, and the spiritual and intellectual resources that you have acquired here be an invaluable guide and a firm foundation for the tasks that God will give to you. In affirmation of your future role in our parishes and communities and of your witness to the transformative power and presence of our Risen Lord, it is not enough to say that you represent the struggle for ideals, the love of learning, the endeavor for truth, and the cultivation of faith that we seek to manifest in this place; rather, you are the embodiment of these labors. You are the fruit of the true vine, who have been nurtured and strengthened by being members of this sacred community.

Such an image of our graduates and of all those who have preceded them directs us to consider our God-given task and responsibility to remain constantly in a mode of progress, advancement, and achievement. The lives of these men and women and of the generations to come, their ministry that will bring honor and glory to God, the challenges and turmoil of our contemporary world, the needs of our parishes, all of these require us to examine carefully our goals for this school and the means by which they are accomplished. We must affirm that our rich cultural and spiritual heritage does not lead us to accept the status quo or to be satisfied and limited by the parameters of excellence determined by the society around us. We must progress further; we must advance beyond; we must strive for the highest level of achievement that can be conceived.

The validity and necessity of this task is magnified by our cherished understanding of παιδεία and by the biblical conception of wisdom. First, παιδεία—namely, education, learning, the shaping of character, of mind and body—is not focused on a fixed or final standard, a stagnant mark that can be easily determined or influenced by the world around us. On the contrary, true παιδεία has as its focus ever-expanding goals, ideals, and concepts that challenge our intellectual abilities, transform our perceptions, and lead us in directions we never knew existed.

Second, passages from the books of Proverbs and The Wisdom of Solomon portray divine wisdom as having incomprehensible limits and inexhaustible knowledge, truly a gift from God for our perfection and salvation. From The Wisdom of Solomon let me quote the following:

> *For wisdom is more mobile than any motion; because of her purity she pervades and penetrates all things. For she is a breath of the power of God, and a pure emanation of the glory of the Almighty; therefore nothing defiled gains entrance into her. For she is a reflection of eternal light, a spotless mirror of the working of God, and an image of his goodness. Although she is but one, she can do all things, and while remaining in herself, she renews all things; in every generation she passes into holy souls and makes them friends of God, and prophets; for God loves nothing so much as the person who lives with wisdom. She is more beautiful than the sun, and excels every constellation of the stars. Compared with the light she is found to be superior, for it is succeeded by the night; but against wisdom evil does not prevail. She reaches mightily from one end of the earth to the other, and she orders all things well* (The Wisdom of Solomon 7:24-8:1).

These brief references to παιδεία and to divine wisdom are further exemplified by Christ and the labors of the martyrs, saints, and great theologians of the Church. They collectively present to us a mind-set, a method, a mode of shaping our work so that we are constantly progressing and offering ourselves to God, to the Church, and to others at the highest levels of achievement.

Thus, we are presented with a challenge that speaks directly to our work here at Hellenic College and Holy Cross. How do we progress? What are the practical steps that will move us toward the goals and levels of achievement we so desire? Certainly, these are issues that are being discussed by the leadership of this institution. However, allow me to speak specifically concerning the task before us if we are to be good stewards of what has been granted to us by God.

First, I will address the role of Hellenic College. Those among us who are Greeks and Greek Americans have a mandate from our own history and from the needs of our contemporary world to foster an awareness of the value and worthiness of Hellenic ideals. These ideals are exemplified in our culture, language, literature, art, and our understanding of the sciences. It is redundant to say that these ideals, associated modes of thought, and established principles have shaped and permeated societies and cultures throughout history. Here exists an understanding of excellence and achievement that has tremendous potential in revitalizing aspects of modern life and further transforming the world around us. This is our heritage; this is our inheritance to offer to others in a substantive way. This means that Hellenic College should not simply *be* a place to study history, language, and literature related to Greece and Hellenism; Hellenic College should be *the* place to study, a distinguished center of learning and research. Our ambition should be to offer the best in these areas and related fields so that the name Hellenic College will be associated with a thorough and intensive education in our rich heritage that has so much to offer to our modern world.

Second, allow me to address the role of Holy Cross Greek Orthodox School of Theology. First and foremost we have a mandate issued by our parishes, by our faithful laity and clergy, and by our beloved Hierarchs. We have an urgent need for a dramatic increase in the number of clergy in our Holy Archdiocese. Allow me to offer a personal experience. After a Liturgy in one of our parishes, the church having been filled to capacity, I asked the priest and the parish council how many families belonged to the community. They said, "Approximately five hundred." I asked them, "Are there other Greek Orthodox people in the specific geographical area of the parish who are not involved?" They said, "Yes." I said, "Have you any idea how many?" They answered, "Five hundred at least, maybe seven hundred." I almost fell from my chair. We speak of five hundred families connected to the church, while at least another five hundred are not. Then the members of the parish council added, "You know, if an additional priest were here we could gather many of the unchurched."

These comments point to a genuine need to cultivate and to prepare an adequate number of priests in order to minister effectively. Another experience is from a trip to an area of our country that has experienced a tremendous growth in population. In less than a decade one established parish has expanded to four parishes and two missions, without diminishing the size of the first parish. Further, throughout our Archdiocese there exists an extensive activity of building and expansion to accommodate worship, Sunday schools, day schools, youth activities, social ministries, and camp and recreational programs. In addition, opportunities arise on an almost daily basis throughout America for mission and service in unique and meaningful ways. At this moment we lack a sufficient number of clergy *to equip the saints for the work of ministry* (Ephesians 4:12). Certainly, this is a challenge to our parishes to nurture and motivate our young men toward the priesthood. However, it also a challenge to us in evaluating, affirming, and extending the program of Holy Cross to provide a spiritual and intellectual environment, and to foster a deep experience of κοινωνία, of community and fellowship. We are also challenged to edify and nourish faith and love for God that not only affirms the divine calling placed upon the life of a man, but transforms that calling into a life-long vocation of priestly ministry to the body of Christ.

In accepting this mandate and in our efforts to meet the needs of our parishes, our School of Theology has an additional role of being an invaluable resource, a vital center for addressing the challenges of twenty-first century American society. At the recent Conference of the Canonical Orthodox Bishops in the Americas held in Washington, D.C., the following list was offered of the most pressing challenges of our time that we must be able to address in conjunction with our mission to proclaim the Gospel: 1) the bioethical challenge, 2) the challenge of the changing structure of the family and altered conceptions of marriage, 3) the relativization challenge, 4) the technological challenge, 5) the social and environmental challenge, and 6) the spirituality challenge. Certainly, these challenges are formidable ones for our society, our communities, and our people. In the face of these challenges, we must have the resources and the persons to address the challenges in knowledgeable and insightful ways that manifest the spiritual wealth of Orthodoxy and the ability of our faith to guide us in life and relationships in these modern times. Thus, this school must expand its role as a place for theological consultation, a place for dialog and quality interaction, and a place where we gather those who can contribute to the life and ministry of the Orthodox Church in North America and beyond.

Today, we seek to renew our awareness of the task that lies before us. From our religious tradition and cultural heritage we have the proper orientation in striving for excellence and unlimited achievement. From the needs of our parishes and the challenges of our contemporary society, we have a mandate to cultivate the priestly vocation and to equip our Orthodox faithful in the work of ministry. Our commission and motivation for accomplishing these things is rooted in the transformation that is being affected in each of our lives. Our faith and experience of the Risen Lord animates and imbues with life all that we do, for in these days we have celebrated and affirmed that faith and life, and ministry and mission are centered on the Resurrection of Christ. The ultimate power manifested in His victory over evil, sin, and death is the same magnificent power given to us through the amazing love of God for our salvation, for our ministry to one another, and for our service through this sacred institution to our parishes and the world. The affirmation of this bond of love and its transformative and unifying power is sung triumphantly by the Apostle Paul: *If God is for us, who is against us? He who did not spare his own Son but gave him up for us all, will he not also give us all things with him? ...For I am sure that neither death, nor life, nor angels, nor principalities, nor things present, nor things to come, nor powers, nor height, nor depth, nor anything else in all creation, will be able to separate us from the love of God in Christ Jesus our Lord* (Romans 8:31-32,38-39).

In the joy and light of this blessed Paschal season we affirm that we are empowered in love *to do all things through Christ, to move mountains, to do greater works than these,* and to do the work of God; for His blessings are unlimited, His mercy is boundless, and His love endures forever.

Voices from the Past Addressing Our Present

Harvard Divinity School[1]

Cambridge, MA
March 12, 2002

Introduction

In September of the year 1965, thirty-seven years ago, I found myself sitting in a class in this precise building. It was the New Testament doctoral seminar dealing with Saint Paul's Epistle to the Romans, and it was directed by Professor Krister Stendahl. Since then, and through various handsome occasions, including my six years of Ph.D. study in the field of New Testament and Christian origins, my participation in the Seminars for New Testament Archaeology in the Aegean area conducted by Professor Helmut Koester, and through the visiting professorships at Harvard Divinity School in the 80's, I have been the happy and honored captive of this extraordinary institution. For such a blessed captivity, I am deeply grateful to God and thankful to all of the people of this University and this School throughout the past thirty-seven years.

Of course, back in 1965, I could not have even dreamed or imagined that one day, in the spring semester of the year 2002, a year of a new century and a new millennium,

[1]The text of the address at Harvard University was originally published in the *Harvard Divinity Bulletin*, Vol. 30 No. 4 (Spring 2002), 12-14.

I would be invited, as Archbishop of the Greek Orthodox Archdiocese of America, to give a lecture at Harvard Divinity School. The honor is truly great; the audience is overwhelmingly awesome; the ways of the Lord are absolutely and amazingly unpredictable and mysterious. And here I am tremendously enjoying your friendship and company, deeply thankful for the present occasion to former Dean Hehir, the Acting Dean Graham, Professor Bovon and the Associate Dean for Development, Ms. Susan Sherwin; and I am prepared to offer a simple, humble presentation of a few thoughts.

My presentation has as its title "Voices From the Past Addressing Our Present." The title does not define the exact past. It could have been the past around the years 1963 or 1968 when two important papers were published in the *Harvard Theological Review*. One by Krister Stendahl entitled "The Apostle Paul and the Introspective Conscience of the West," and the other by Helmut Koester under the title "One Jesus and Four Primitive Gospels." They could very well be the subject of my presentation because of their seminal nature and importance.

Today, however, I should like to travel a bit more and go way back into the past, reaching the time of the Early Church, and selecting among the many voices just three: the voices of Ignatius of Antioch, Justin the Philosopher and Martyr, and Basil the Great of Caesarea. These are voices which are relevant to our times and which could help us in addressing questions and issues of today.

Ignatius of Antioch:
The Theocentric Principle and Attitude

The first voice from the past relevant to our present is the voice of Ignatius of Antioch. On his way from Antioch to martyrdom in Rome, he wrote, as we know, six letters to the people of the Churches in Ephesus, Magnesia, Tralleis, Rome, Philadelphia, and Smyrna, and one letter to Polycarp, the Bishop of Smyrna. Those letters share among other things a common and remarkable characteristic: the striking way in which the word *God* (Θεός) has been used in them. Let me give you a few examples.[2]

1) The term *Θεός* occurs approximately 180 times in the seven letters of Ignatius. In the Bihlmeyer-Schneemelcher edition of the *Apostolic Fathers* the entire text of Ignatius' letters covers 820 lines, which means that the word *God* is to be found once in every 4.5 lines. A comparison will be helpful in determining the significance of this ratio. Three texts taken at random from the same edition of the Apostolic Fathers show the following figures: In the *Didache*, *God* appears once in every 17.5 lines, in *Barnabas* once in every 12.7 lines, and in *1 Clement* once in every 9.2 lines. The difference from the ratio in Ignatius is noticeable and cannot be accidental.

2) Ignatius favors compound words in which one of the components is the word *Θεός*. Thus we come across the words θεοφόρος ("God-bearer"; found in the inscriptions of all of the seven letters and also in *Eph.* 9.2), θεοδρόμος ("God's runner"; *Phld.* 2.2; *Pol.* 7.2), θεομακάριστος ("blessed by God"; *Smyrn.* 1.2; *Pol.* 7.2) or Θεομακαρίτης (*Smyrn.* 1.2 as an alternative reading), θεοπρεπής ("befitting of God"; *Magn.* 1.2; *Smyrn.* inscr.; 11.1; 12.2; *Pol.* 7.2), θεοπρεσβευτής or θεοπρεσβύτης ("ambassador of God" or "old man of God"; *Smyrn.* 11.1), and ἀξιόθεος ("worthy of God"; *Magn.* 2.1; *Trall.* inscr.; 1.1; *Smyrn.* 12.2). Compound

[2]In the cited examples, I am using material from my essay "God Language in Ignatius of Antioch", in *The Future of Early Christianity. Essays in Honor of Helmut Koester*, ed. B. A. Pearson (Minneapolis: Fortress Press, 1991), 423-26.

words with θεός are encountered in the Septuagint, the New Testament, and in some of the early Christian texts. They are also found in several of the authors of the classical or Hellenistic periods. What is remarkable in Ignatius, however, and what sets him apart, is the accumulation of so many such words in a limited body of literature, and, all the more, the fact that some of them, e.g., θεοδρόμος, θεομακάριστος or θεομακαρίτης, and θεοπρεσβευτής or θεοπρεσβύτης are *hapax legomena,* i.e. once said, in the Greek literature.

3) Ignatius uses a number of short phrases in which the word *θεός* appears in the genitive together with an abstract or concrete substantive: ἐν αἵματι θεοῦ ("in the blood of God"; *Eph.* 1.1), πληρώματι θεοῦ ("in the fullness of God"; *Eph.* inscr.), χρῶμα θεοῦ λαβόντες ("having received God's melody"; *Eph.* 4.2), ἐν ὁμονοίᾳ θεοῦ ("in God's concord"; *Magn.* 6.1; 15.1; *Phld.* inscr.), ὁμοήθειαν θεοῦ λαβόντες ("having received God's unity of ethos"; *Magn.* 6.2; *Pol.* 1.3), τὸ πάθος τοῦ θεοῦ ("the passion of God"; *Rom.* 6.3), πόμα θεοῦ ("the drink of God"; *Rom.* 7.3), ἐλάλουν θεοῦ φωνῇ ("I spoke with the voice of God"; *Phld.* 7.1), εἰς ἑνότητα θεοῦ ("to the unity of God"; *Phld.* 8.1), τῇ γνώμῃ τοῦ θεοῦ ("with God's mind"; *Eph.* 3.2 etc.), ἄρτον τοῦ θεοῦ ("the bread of God"; *Eph.* 5.2), ἐν ἡσυχίᾳ θεοῦ ("in the quietness of God"; *Eph.* 19.1), ἐν ἑνότητι θεοῦ ("in the unity of God"; *Eph.* 14.1, etc.), χαρακτῆρα θεοῦ ("the character of God"; *Magn.* 5.2), μιμηταὶ θεοῦ ("imitators of God"; *Trall.* 1.2), ἐγὼ λόγος θεοῦ ("I, word of God"; *Rom.* 2.1), σῖτος θεοῦ ("the wheat of God"; *Rom.* 4.1), ἐν ἀγάπῃ θεοῦ ("in the love of God"; *Phld.* 1.1), τὴν χαρὰν τοῦ θεοῦ ("the joy of God"; *Phld.* 10.1), ἀμεριμνία θεοῦ ("God's freedom from care"; *Pol.* 7.1).

Noteworthy in this instance is the variety of nouns connected with God and the rather bold usage of that word in reference to human conditions or material entities. Ignatius did not say "divine melody" [θεῖον χρῶμα] or "divine voice" [θεία φωνή], but "God's melody" [χρῶμα θεοῦ], "God's voice" [φωνὴ θεοῦ], which means that he shows a preference for the noun *God* (θεός) over the adjective *divine* (θεῖος). Of course, he knows the adjective *divine* (θεῖος), but he uses it only once, in a reference to the prophets (*Magn.* 8.2). This signifies that in the phrases listed above, where the word *God* (θεός) is employed in a qualifying genitive, something more than an adjectival understanding is implied.

4) Ignatius uses a number of expressions in which the word *θεός* (God) in the genitive again, is the object of a verb indicating an intimate and / or strong relationship with believers. Five such expressions are encountered in the letters of Ignatius: γέμειν θεοῦ ("being full of God"; *Magn.* 14.1), μετέχειν θεοῦ ("to participate in God"; *Eph.* 4.2), εἶναι θεοῦ ("to be of God"; *Eph.* 8.1; *Phld.* 3.2), λείπεσθαι θεοῦ ("to lack God"; *Trall.* 5.2), and ἐπιτυγχάνειν θεοῦ ("to attain God"; *Magn.* 14.1; *Trall.* 12.2; *Rom.* 4.1; *Smyrn.* 11.1, etc.).

In this category Ignatius is once more unique among early Christian authors, in whom phrases like these mentioned above are not easily found, much less accumulated. But even outside of early Christian literature, it is difficult to find examples similar to the Ignatian ones. The Ignatian terminology clearly presupposes the possibility of intense and ultimate relationships between believers and God.

5) Ignatius favors the prepositional phrase "in God" [ἐν θεῷ]. This phrase appears within differing contexts and in a variety of references: ἀποδεξάμενος ἐν θεῷ ("having received in God"; *Eph.* 1.1), ἡ ἐν θεῷ εὐταξία ("orderliness in God"; *Eph.* 6.2), εὔχομαι ἐν θεῷ ("I pray in God"; *Magn.* inscr.), ὡς φρόνιμοι ἐν θεῷ ("as wise in God"; *Magn.* 3.1), φρονεῖν ἐν θεῷ ("to think in God"; *Trall.* 4.1), τὸ ἐν θεῷ

πλῆθος ("God's crowd"; *Trall.* 8.2), ὀναίμην ἐν θεῷ ("may I have joy in God"; *Pol.* 1.1), μέρος ἔχειν ἐν θεῷ ("having a lot in God"; *Pol.* 6.1), etc.

It has been appropriately pointed out that this broad and somewhat flexible use of "ἐν θεῷ" constitutes one of the most remarkable features of Ignatius' practice with regard to prepositions. In this case, sentences in which "ἐν θεῷ" occurs may be read as implicit statements of belief in a deep and direct involvement of God in the life of the believers.

There is no doubt that the frequency and the way of usage of the word *God* (θεός) by Ignatius constitutes a striking phenomenon. Various suggestions have been advanced in order to explain it. Heinrich Schlier and Hans Werner Bautsch, for instance, argued for Gnostic influences; H. Riesenfeld suggested rhetorical and linguistic features related to the literary-rhetorical phenomenon of "Arianism"; and E. Norden claimed that it was the extreme pathos of Ignatius which led him to "personal word formations and constructions of unprecedented boldness."

All of these suggestions are valid, but they cannot fully explain the strong and persuasive God language in Ignatius, because such language, beyond style, rhetoric and passion, involves concrete, theological concepts, ideas, experiences, and even life attitudes. At this point we could submit the idea that God language in Ignatius is the result of his fervent belief in the absolute priority of God, the centrality of God, the accessibility of God, the necessity for an intimate relationship with Him. Such a belief is of course based on the Christ event, on the reality of a God who became human being. Ultimately, however, the reference is to God. Ignatius is not talking about religion in general; he is not offering religious ideology. He is talking about God, or rather he is talking God. He would go so far as to say to the Philadelphians: "While I was with you, I cried out [ἐκραύγασα], I spoke with a great voice [ἐλάλουν μεγάλῃ φωνῇ], God's voice." What follows is not a biblical passage, but Ignatius' own admonition to the Philadelphians, fully understandable through his strong relationship with God.

The absolute priority of God, the vital need for a real, existential connection with Him, the urgency of focusing on Him and entering into an advanced, total relationship with Him, seems to be the Ignatian message reaching our present.

Our present time, especially since September 11, involves extensive discussions about the role of religion within the contemporary world, especially the role related to eliminating violence and war and to advancing peace and friendship among people and nations. What happens quite often, however, is that the discussions deal mostly with religion as a system, as ideology, as organized entity, socially and culturally identifiable. There is no extensive and intensive talk about God as the center of religion, as the One, the First and the Last, as the immediate and also the ultimate reality, as the decisive player on the universal and local scenes.

Ignatius' message is focusing on God, making the connection with Him alive and dynamic, and, if I can use a rather paradoxical language, moving from religion to God, from a formless religiosity to a personal relationship, from the distant, neutral position of a spectator to the face to face encounter, even to a confrontation with Him.

Ignatius' theocentric attitude is important not only in contradistinction from a religiocentric one, but also from an anthropocentric one. And for our present, which is strongly anthropocentric, the need to enhance theocentric attitudes and solutions for contemporary problems is vital.

Justin Martyr: Dialog as Sharing the Words

The second voice from the past addressing our present is the voice of Justin Martyr. His message refers to a basic phenomenon, namely, to the phenomenon of dialog in the realm of religion. This is something ongoing which is clearly discernable among theologians, philosophers and historians of religion, churches, and various religious bodies. Recently, and more specifically after September 11, 2001, it became a steady feature encountered in meetings among political, economic and religious leaders. As a characteristic example, we could mention the World Economic Forum held in New York in February 2002, in which in addition to participants coming from the economic, political and technological fields, approximately forty-five religious leaders were invited to participate fully in every aspect of the meeting.

There is no doubt about the necessity and the significance of dialog related to religion. The old and perennial question is "what kind of dialog?" Or, rather, "what quality of dialog?" Or "what principles determine dialog?"

The voice of Justin the Philosopher and Martyr is a voice from the past offering some interesting if not stimulating suggestions, which may perhaps facilitate our efforts to answer the above questions. It is the voice of a thinker of the Early Church. Justin is truly a man of dialog.[3] We see this immediately in his major work. There is nothing accidental in the fact that his *Dialog with Trypho* is the first theological

[3]Elaborate material of this section has been drawn from my essay "Κοινωνῶν ὑμῖν τῶν λόγων" in *The Contentious Triangle, Church, State and University, Festschrift in Honor of Prof. G. H. Williams*, ed. R. L Peterson and C. A. Pater (Kirksville, MO: T. Jefferson University Press, 1999), 71-80.

work in the form of a full dialog between a Christian and a Jew that appears in the field of Early Christian literature. The reasons why Justin selected this literary genre to present his views might be several. One of them probably is the imitation of Plato and the ambition to transfer to the Christian soil a celebrated literary form. Justin, however, seems to be doing more than simply following or imitating a literary genre. When we read carefully the *Dialog with Trypho*, we can easily see that the author is seriously involved in a real discussion with a Jewish thinker who raises several questions about the validity and the veracity of the Gospel and the Christian faith and practice in general. The truly favorable way Justin presents his opponent's person and ideas in his *Dialog with Trypho* is indicative of an alive and responsible adherence to dialog as a substantive and vital exchange of ideas between humans and not as a simple literary technique.

The above observation is corroborated by the fact that in the very beginning of the discussion with Trypho, Justin reiterates a lengthy discussion between him and an old man which caused his conversion to Christianity. He obviously knows by experience the tremendous existential significance of dialog, since it radically changed his life.

The decisive significance that dialog has for Justin is further evidenced in his two other works, namely his *First Apology* and *Second Apology*. These works, of course, do not take the form of a dialog in the strict technical sense. Yet the argumentation, the presentation of the main theses, the dialectical flow of ideas, and the continuous explanations show an author who is in a condition of genuine dialog, discussing step by step all possible viewpoints, reactions, disagreements, or criticisms. In his two *Apologies*, Justin is in constant conversation with the recipients and readers of his texts, anticipating or answering all possible objections or questions.

Justin proves to be a man of dialog not only by using pertinent literary forms, but also by his determination to actively participate in all major religious and/or philosophical debates of his times.

We can begin with Justin's dialog with Judaism. His basic work, *Dialog with Trypho*, is an eloquent example of a Christian theologian who is thoroughly and sincerely engaged in a discussion with Judaism. All greater issues pertaining to the Jewish faith and religious practices are carefully presented and discussed. Even textual problems are the objects of an animated and hot exchange of opinions.

Justin's willingness and eagerness to discuss everything related to the Jewish faith brings him to the field of the history of Ancient Israel, and the theophanies made to Abraham, Jacob, Joshua, and Moses. The dialog here reaches conflictual levels. It remains, nonetheless, decent and sincere, and, more importantly, it remains a true dialog.

Justin diligently reports every possible objection or attack on the part of Trypho. He even advances arguments which seem to be supportive of Trypho's positions, thus creating an atmosphere of a frank debate which boldly and without any restrictions confronts all aspects of the question pertaining to the relationship between Judaism and Christianity.

Beyond Judaism, Justin is in an open dialog with the pagan world and its religion. In his *First Apology* and *Second Apology*, he offers the arguments of a good debater who wants to keep the lines of communication open and alive. As we know, in order to achieve such a goal, he presents among others an interesting suggestion. He argues that in essence the religious ideas and worshipping practices of paganism are distorted forms or perverted imitations of Jewish and Christian ideas and practices deriving mostly from the Scriptures. He then ascribes this phenomenon to the influence of the demonic powers. In this case he creates an inviting perspective, since this is not a perspective of a complete and absolute rejection of the pagan religion, but of an overcoming and a correcting of distortions and of discovering the original truth behind them. Thus, the avenue of dialog is made open.

In addition to Judaism and pagan religion, Justin extends his dialog to the area of his contemporary philosophy. We know that he had spent plenty of time before his conversion to Christianity listening to and discussing with philosophers of various Schools. He mentions, more specifically, philosophers of Stoic, Peripatetic, Pythagorean, and Platonic persuasions. Within this context, he proposes a definition of philosophy as "the deep science and the full knowledge of the being and the truth, a deep knowledge and wisdom which offer happiness as reward" (*Dial.* 3,4). This definition shows Justin's deep respect for philosophy and also accounts for his strong belief that he has to be in substantive dialog with it.

In his effort to keep an open dialog with the philosophers of his time he advances the theory of the "*spermatikos logos*," the seminal divine logos. As he clearly states, "Each one of the philosophers, by sharing in the *spermatikos logos* was able to see the kingship and, therefore, spoke well [i.e. truthfully]" ["Εκαστος γὰρ τις ἀπὸ μέρους τοῦ σπερματικοῦ θείου λόγου τὸ συγγενές ὁρῶν, καλῶς ἐφθέγξατο] (2 *Apol.* 13,3). On the basis of this theory, Justin does not hesitate to enter into an open discussion even with the most stubborn, sophisticated, highly biased or unyielding philosopher, who, however, is in essence not totally unrelated to the divine Logos, Christ.

We do not need to prolong our presentation of Justin's other areas of activities such as his dialogs with the Gnostics and the Roman authorities. We should, however, briefly mention one more significant case: his dialog with the Scripture. He clearly is in dialog with the biblical text in the sense of asking insightful and penetrating questions and listening very attentively in order to have a right understanding of the world of the Bible. His exegesis is an alternation between a careful listening to the scriptural text and a formulation of questions going to the depth of the examined passages. He is an author who loves to listen to the voice of the Scriptures as an alive voice, as a part of an ongoing dialog. It is as if he is fascinated by such a voice and does not want to stop listening, even though, in numerous cases, the biblical text has already covered the desired point of argumentation. At this juncture we should add that in several instances Justin introduces the scriptural passages not with the traditional formula "λέγει ἡ Γραφή" [the Scripture says], or "Ἠσαΐας λέγει" [Isaiah says], but with phrases like "Ἠσαΐας βοᾷ" or "κέκραγεν" [Isaiah shouts or cries loudly]. The usage of the verbs βοᾶν and κράζειν (to shout, to cry out loudly) is indicative of the attitude of someone who is not simply reading a text, but who is listening to a text, who is being in a dialog with a text that loudly answers questions raised in a passionate discussion.

One could justifiably make the suggestion that in the *Dialog with Trypho* we do not have two but three participants in the discussion, namely, Justin, Trypho, and Scripture. To a certain degree, the same could be said also for the *First Apology*, where we might detect again three participants in the debate, Justin, the Roman emperor, and Scripture. In fact, Scripture seems to be the main speaker in the discussions. Such a phenomenon would have been impossible if Justin were not in constant dialog with the biblical texts.

The voice of Justin offers a very strong, loud and passionate advocacy for dialog. It is an advocacy for a dialog towards all directions, and among the most differentiated religions, philosophies and scientific theories. Here is something that is directly related to our present status as human beings living in a particular time of history. What is the specific significance of Justin's contribution to the issue of dialog?

First, there is the high quality of the dialog: the truly precious elements of direct, sincere and respectful conversation, the sense that dialog is not an exchange of words, but a real encounter of human beings.

Second, there is the courage to engage in a full discussion, to touch upon all possible, sometimes thorny, aspects of an issue under consideration.

Third, there is an openness to any imaginable partner in a conversation, to any religion, philosophy, or theory willing to enter into discussion. In fact, there is not the mere willingness or readiness for dialog, but the initiative to create avenues and realities of dialog among even unpredictable partners.

The most important, however, and the most insightful contribution of Justin towards a true enhancement of any dialog is his understanding that dialog is a communion of words. At a certain point of his *Dialog with Trypho*, Justin addresses him by saying that "he is sharing with him the words" (*Dial*. 64.2), i.e. that he is with him in a condition of a "communion of words" [κοινωνῶν ὑμῖν τῶν λόγων]. What we encounter here is not the verb *to discuss* or *to converse* (συζητεῖν or διαλέγεσθαι) but to be in communion (κοινωνεῖν). Such a terminology reveals an understanding of dialog as a person to person communication during which words and language become a deeply connecting link, a bonding of human beings to each other. A true communion of words, a sharing of words as a basic characteristic of any genuine dialog, especially in the field of religion, seems to be a much desirable thing today.

Basil the Great: Language as an Expression of Life, Connectiveness and Humor

Saint Basil the Great, Archbishop of Caesarea in Cappadocia of Asia Minor, was a gigantic theological figure of the fourth century. His voice, heard through his massive works covering thousands of pages, touches upon many issues of our times. In concluding this paper, however, I have limited myself to a selection of few excerpts from his 365 letters, indicative of his understanding of language as an expression of life, connectiveness and humor.

In this case, I offer a selection of a few of these excerpts which are not only insightful, but also truly enjoyable. I am limiting myself to reading a few of these excerpts. First there are some excerpts in which Saint Basil offers the necessity for this connection through language, especially through correspondence by means of letters. They are very short and to the point. He writes to a friend, Olympius:

> You use to write to us little enough, but now you do not write even that little; and if your brevity keeps increasing with the time, it seems likely to become complete speechlessness [voicelessness]. Therefore, return to your old custom, for I shall never again find fault with you for practicing…brevity on my letter. Nay, even your little letters, seeing that they are tokens of magnanimity, I shall value highly. Only write to me. (Letter 12, *To Olympius*)

The last phrase reveals the significance that Basil ascribed to even a short communication. He returns in a shorter letter to the same friend:

> Just as all things that come with the seasons have each its own proper season for recurring—the flowers in spring, the ears of corn in summer, the apple in autumn—so winter's fruit is conversation. (Letter 13, *To Olympius*)

Then, we have something worth noticing, the idea that communication by speech is an evidence of being alive:

> One indication of life is speech. ...Come, put aside your silence, writing to us and making yourself manifest—that you are alive. (Letter 332, Without Address)

To another friend named Phalerius he writes:

> I was very pleasantly delighted with the river fish [a gift of Phalerius to Basil]. But of greater worth than the fish is your letter. Therefore write rather than send [fish]. But if it is more pleasing for you to be silent, at any rate do not cease praying for us. (Letter 329, *To Phalerius*)

To Antipater, the Governor, who suffered from anorexia, Basil writes in a way exhibiting a sharp sense of humor:

> How noble is philosophy in every respect, and especially because she does not allow her children to be healed at great cost! Nay, with her the same thing is both appetizing and useful for health. For as I have learned, you have revived your failing appetite with cabbage pickled in vinegar, a food which I once could hardly endure.... Now, however, I am inclined to change my view, and to laugh at the proverb, as

> I observe that cabbage, which has restored our ruler to health, is so good a fostering mother. And in the future I shall consider that nothing is to be compared with it,—to pass over the lotus of Homer, not even that ambrosia, whatever it was, which fed the Olympians. (Letter 186, *To Antipater, the Governor*)

In these texts we can see how much Saint Basil, expressing himself as a plain human being, appreciates language and communication as a connecting link, and how much he is using this humor and wit to express his ideas. Sometimes, he would go even to the point of making particular observations not only about the content of a letter, but even about the appearance of the writing as contributing to good communication. He writes to a calligrapher:

> Write straight and keep straightly to your lines; and let the hand neither mount upwards nor slide downhill. Do not force the pen to travel slantwise, like the Crab...; but proceed straight ahead, as if travelling along a carpenter's rule, which everywhere preserves the even course and eliminates all irregularity. For that which is slantwise is unbecoming, but that which is straight is a joy to those who see it, not permitting the eyes of those who read to bob up and down like well-sweeps. Something of the sort has happened to me when reading your writing. For since your lines rest ladderwise, when I had to pass from one to another I was obliged to lift my eyes to reach the beginning of the next line. And then when no sequence was evident at that point, I had to run back again and seek the order, retracing my steps and "following the furrow," just as they say Theseus did the thread of Ariadne. Therefore write straight

> and do not confuse our mind by your oblique and slanting writing. (Letter 334, *To a Calligraphist*)

I will read just one more excerpt from a letter, which is a very beautiful and practical piece. It is a letter to his friend Gregory and offers directions on speaking which are relevant to us today.

> And, first of all, one should take heed not to be boorish in conversation, but to ask questions without contentiousness, and answer without self-display; neither interrupting the speaker when he is saying something useful, nor being eager to interject his own words for the sake of ostentation, but observing moderation both in speaking and in listening. One should not be ashamed to learn, nor should he grudge to teach; and if one has learned something from another, one should not conceal the fact.... The middle tone of the voice is to be preferred, neither so soft as to elude the ears, nor so loud and strong as to be vulgar. One should first reflect upon what one is going to say, and then deliver one's speech. One should be affable in conversation and agreeable in social intercourse, not resorting to wit as a means of gaining popularity, but depending upon the charm which comes from gracious politeness. On all occasions abjure asperity, even when it is necessary to administer a rebuke; for if you first abase yourself and show humility, you will easily find your way.... (Letter 2, *To Gregory*)

These are examples randomly selected only from Saint Basil's letters. If we would have gone through the thousands of pages of Saint Basil's works, we could have stayed here for days, listening to a never ending lecture.

But what was presented in a furtive glance is indicative of the way Saint Basil views language and uses it as a vital expression of life, as a means of real connection among people and as a vehicle for humor and simple yet sophisticated laughter.

Our present is a present of often cataclysmic and certainly inflationary usage of language. We have multiplied the means of talking to each other: immediate oral delivery, telephone conversation, Internet, correspondence by letter, e-mail, etc. How much life and appreciation for life is included in the daily circulation of billions of words on our planet? How much of language is an alive connector? How much joy is carried by our words as such? And how much speaking in any form is a real *modus vivendi*? These are questions raised in our present by listening to a voice from the past.

Epilogue

Today, in this renowned Sperry Room, which for many years has heard plenty of voices, coming from all places, all ages, all religions, philosophies, and scientific and artistic fields, we have heard three more voices from the past: Ignatius of Antioch, Justin the Philosopher and Martyr, and Basil the Great of Caesarea. They conveyed to us precious messages:

1. The Theocentric principle in the Ignatian mode which emphasizes the absolute priority of God, the vital importance of the reality of God for both individuals and societies, and the need to balance the uncontrollable anthropocentric attitudes of our times;

2. The Dialogic principle in the Justinian mode which advocates the total openness to a dialog without exclusions and discriminations, to a dialog as an expression of com-

munion between human beings, of sharing the invaluable wealth of ideas through words;

3. And finally, the usage of the language principle in the Basilian mode which opens the horizon to the immense universe of language as life, communication, and joy.

I did not present to you a majestic symphony from the amazing Patristic repertoire. I just offered a select, highly harmonious trio: Ignatius, Justin, Basil. If the splendid melody did not come out the way the composers intended and their texts imposed, there is no one else to blame but the presenter. I am sure that the ears of the listeners will recognize the beautiful voices and will complete what the voice of the presenter left unheard.

Answers from the Past to Questions of Today

The Costantinos D. Paparrigopoulos Lecture
at the Center for
Byzantine and Modern Greek Studies

Queens College

New York, NY
May 30, 2002

Dear Professors, Students, and Friends,

Χριστός 'Ανέστη!

It is a great honor for me to be with you tonight on the occasion of offering this lecture, the 24th Constantine Paparrigopoulos lecture. It is an honor because Constantine Paparrigopoulos was a celebrated historian of modern Greece who offered the monumental *History of the Hellenic Nation*. It is also an honor since tonight we pay special tribute to Professor Harry Psomiades, the founder and sustainer, the heart and mind of this center for Greek and Byzantine studies. Tonight we also celebrate the completion of the studies of twenty people, and the bestowal of awards to a number of students who have distinguished themselves in their academic work. So I feel that this evening presents an opportunity to celebrate and to honor people on the professorial level and on the student level at the center for Greek and Byzantine studies, and also to remember gratefully truly great scholars like Constantine Paparrigopoulos.

I started with the paschal greeting "Χριστός 'Ανέστη" purposely because we are in the post-resurrection period, and this is the traditional Greek Orthodox address at this specific time. But I also started that way because I wanted to duplicate, in a different manner, what happened in the State Department in Washington, D.C. two years ago. It was there that the Secretary of State at that time, Mrs. Albright, offered a dinner in the very prestigious Benjamin Franklin Hall of the State Department to honor the Greek Orthodox community. She opened her welcoming address by saying, totally unexpectedly of course, "Χριστός 'Ανέστη" in Greek. On the basis of that address, at the very end of the dinner, I said, "Madame Secretary, since you greeted us with 'Χριστός 'Ανέστη,' please allow us to close the dinner the same way by singing in lieu of a benediction the hymn '*Χριστός 'Ανέστη*.'" So for the first time in history, the very prestigious Benjamin Franklin Hall of the State Department heard in Greek, chanted by two hundred people, the hymn of the Resurrection. I thought of somehow duplicating this event in a varied manner tonight, because of the very special audience and the very special location. If the State Department, a place for political decisions, can hear the hymn of the Resurrection, a university like Queens College, which is a place for decisions related to knowledge and wisdom, can equally well hear Χριστός 'Ανέστη!

And now, let me proceed with my short paper in which I present some basic thoughts under the title "Answers from the Past to Questions of Today," answers given by our traditions of Orthodoxy and Hellenism. I will briefly concentrate on four questions and their relevant answers.

The Problem of Communication

The first question deals with the problem of communication, namely, the need for real, genuine, and full communication among people. We live in a world where we are oversaturated with possibilities for communication: various media, standard and cellular telephones, Internet, e-mail, television, radio. Here is an amazing plethora of means for communication. Do we communicate? Do we feel that as human beings we are in a unique condition whereby we can create a bond among us via communication? The legacy of Hellenism is multiple with regard to this question of communication, and the answer has many aspects. I have isolated purposely just one aspect of communication, namely, the power, value, and quality of language.

For the classical Greek mind, language is the means of real communication, but not language as words thrown at random. The Greek classical understanding of language as communication involves precision, completeness, and beauty. The classical world is characterized by this precision, this accuracy, this concern to render meaning in the best and most accurate way, to not do any damage to what you mean by what you say. At the same time, there exists in the classical linguistic tradition the concern to keep language free from a captivity to rigid forms and limited modes of expression. This is why in the Greek language there exists a tremendous vocabulary that seems to be inexhaustible. At the same time, there exists a grammar that creates the possibility for completeness and accuracy when appropriate syntactical and grammatical forms of verbs, nouns, adjectives, adverbs, and prepositions are used.

Paramount, however, in the mind of the Greek classical legacy regarding language as communication, is the concept of beauty. Communication is an item of beauty. There cannot exist communication in a linguistically ugly way. Aesthetics is part of viewing language as communication. This is true for Homer, the pre-Socratic philosophers, Plato, Aristotle, the Stoics, the middle Stoics, the middle Platonics, the tragedians, Sophocles, Euripides, Aeschylos, and even such comedians as Aristophanes. Even in the medical essays of Hippocrates and Galenos, language is encountered as communication in a beautiful manner. Those authors did not write for the sake of writing; they wrote always with the consideration that they were communicating. This is why the texts which they produced are beautiful, precise, and complete. They have this quality because they are perfect specimens of communication using the most sophisticated language possible. They are timeless, and they are geographically international.

Today, in the year 2002, at this very moment in several places in the world, theatrical plays by any of the above mentioned classical authors—for instance Sophocles, Euripides, Aeschylos, or Aristophanes—might be on stage. Recently, I attended a performance of Sophocles' *Oedipus Rex*, and after the final curtain, a good American friend, an erudite man, said to me, "Honestly, if you ask someone who came here tonight without knowing the author of this play in advance, and who was not exactly knowledgeable about classical tragic playwrights, he could say that this very well might have been a play by Tennessee Williams, Eugene O'Neil, or Arthur Miller." Indeed, the play might have been written by any significant modern playwright, yet it was actually written 2,500 years ago. Nevertheless, it was a perfect piece of communication between Sophocles and modern Americans because of its substantive and beautiful language. It was a carrier of something that is trans-time, trans-location, and trans-ethnicity, because Sophocles used language as a means for perfect communication.

The Orthodox Christian component in the answer to the question of communication is that in addition to these characteristics, there exists in language the element of sacredness. There is in Christianity an understanding that language is something sacred, that it connects us with the realm of the holy. This happens because we experience language also as the Word of God—God appearing and speaking in human language, communicating in human language. We experience communication in a different manner because by being Orthodox we encounter language as worship, language as revealed truth, and language as proclamation of the Gospel.

I would like to bring to your attention a passage from the Gospel of Matthew, a statement by Christ. It reads in the original, *"Λέγω δὲ ὑμῖν ὅτι πᾶν ῥῆμα ἀργὸν ὃ λαλήσουσιν οἱ ἄνθρωποι ἀποδώσουσιν περὶ αὐτοῦ λόγον ἐν ἡμέρᾳ κρίσεως· ἐκ γὰρ τῶν λόγων σου δικαιωθήσῃ, καὶ ἐκ τῶν λόγων σου καταδικασθήσῃ"* (Matthew 12:36-37). In English translation, *"I tell you, on the day of judgment people will render account for every careless word they utter, for by your words you will be justified, and by your words you will be condemned."* Amazingly, this statement does not contain references to sin, evil, or anything of the sort. It does not contain anything referring to deeds or works. It speaks only about words. The words become the criterion for vindication or condemnation. Here is revealed the tremendous importance for even one single word. And here is revealed the vital soteriological importance of language as communication.

The Problem of a Healthy Social Symbiosis

The second question deals with the problem of symbiosis, of living together in a way that will promote real happiness and progress in our society. What is the proper formula for a healthy social symbiosis on the communal, the national, or the international level? The answer from the past to this question comes from the Hellenic tradition in the form of the political system known as democracy.

We take democracy for granted, but it is not a simple thing. Democracy was born in ancient Greece and was cherished and cultivated under very special and carefully maintained conditions. It is interesting to note that the word *politics*, a word integrally related to democracy, derives in Greek from the word *πόλις* (city). Politics, in essence, is not related to political matters but to the welfare of the city. Politics is the art, wisdom, and management that guarantees the proper life of the city, the healthy symbiosis of all citizens. Ancient Athenians and Greeks used the term *politics* in a way that emphasizes the need for assisting the population of a city in growing happily and successfully together. That was the fundamental Athenian concept and model of democracy.

From that model, democracy evolved into a general political and administrative system that guarantees the proper function of a given society, city or country. But democracy itself cannot create a real bond among the people. To be fellow citizens in a free democratic country is important, but this does not lead necessarily to a substantive human relationship among the citizens of that country. Here, enters the Orthodox contribution by adding the concept of community to the concept of democracy. Both democracy and community are needed. Community, in this instance, means that people are not only fellow citizens but also brothers and sisters, that they constitute a family, that they are together in a manner which, through democracy, guarantees personal rights and freedoms and, through community, fills everyone with the eagerness to serve and to offer services in the spirit of love and care. Democracy safeguards the structure and proper function in terms of freedom and rights, while community guarantees the function in terms of connectedness amongst people, in terms of serving and loving one another.

The Problem of the Future

The third question has to do with our anxiety about the future of the world in which we live today. I thought of that question again this morning as I was visiting the so-called "pit", which is the very central part of Ground Zero, the place of the September 11 terrorist attack. What is the tomorrow of this world of ours? And what should be our attitude in view of what is happening today locally and internationally?

The ancient Greeks spoke about and believed strongly in a basic attitude towards the world and its future. This attitude consisted of four successive existential steps. The first step was a feeling of admiration in looking at the world, a state of admiring (θαυμάζειν) mixed with a joyful surprise. Admiring led to the second step, which was the raising of questions, the wondering (ἀπορεῖν). When you raise questions you are then led to think (στοχάζεσθαι), to analyze, to look for explanations, to research. This third step is followed by the fourth, which consists of creating (δημιουργεῖν) on all levels. Here, then, is the ancient Greek attitude *vis-à-vis* the world in a synthesis of four components: to admire, to wonder, to think, to create. Such an attitude offers a very positive view of the future, no matter what may be the conditions of the present. How close are we to that attitude? How much time do we spend in admiring, questioning and meditating on the gigantic miracle which is the world? Unfortunately, we usually think of the world as a big problem, and our existential attitude is a mixture of complaints, disappointments, and anxiety, rather than admiration and creativity. The classic Hellenic attitude, however, is vitally important for us today, if we intend to think of the future of our world.

Such an attitude, such an idea of the world as a great miracle (θαῦμα μέγα) worthy of admiration and wise care is amplified and enhanced by the Orthodox understanding, which speaks about this world as the world of God, as the creation of God. This adds to the world the attribute of sacredness, of holiness. No matter what the problems and the contemporary conditions are, our world is the creation of God; our universe partakes of the holiness of its Creator. Therefore, we should view it with admiration and awe.

At this point a passage from the Gospel of Matthew is worth citing. In it, Jesus Christ, using a familiar image known to all of us, asks us to look at the lilies and the grass of the field and raises the question: "*Εἰ δὲ τὸν χόρτον τοῦ ἀγροῦ σήμερον ὄντα καὶ αὔριον είς κλίβανον βαλλόμενον ὁ Θεὸς οὕτως ἀμφιέννυσιν, οὐ πολλῷ μᾶλλον ὑμᾶς;*" (Matthew 6:30) [*If God clothes in such a way the grass of the field which today is alive and tomorrow thrown into the oven, how much more will He take care of you*?].

Normally, we pay attention to the final part of the above question of Jesus thinking that it is a good image to remember in view of the problems we face in this world. If God takes care of the flowers and the grass, He certainly will take care of His entire world today, and of course, tomorrow. But the first part of Jesus' statement is equally important because it introduces the idea of the personal touch and care of God for the least flower of the field, for the least inch of grass. This strengthens the idea of the special care of God even for the grass. An attitude combining the classical Hellenic and the Orthodox approaches *vis-à-vis* the world certainly is the best answer to the question about the future of our world.

The Human Being as Priority

I close my address with the fourth and final question: What are we? And how important are we as human beings in our contemporary world? The Greek answer, the classical Greek answer, declares that human beings are the priority, in fact the absolute priority in this world. I am sure that you are familiar with the classical saying, "πάντων χρημάτων μέτρον ἄνθρωπος" [The human being is the measure, the yardstick of all things]. This phrase clearly suggests the enormous importance of the human being. It projects in a subtle way the priority of man as a unique creature on earth. In the Hellenic tradition, the priority of the human being has been beautifully presented and defended in the major philosophical works, in the masterpieces of literature and unsurpassed creations of sculptors like Pheidias or Praxiteles.

This fundamental concept of the priority of the human being has been decisively enhanced by our Orthodox Christian Tradition. Already the basic article of our faith, by declaring that God became human being in order to save each and every and all human beings, establishes on a firm ground the priority of man. But it is worth noticing that even some of the longest debates in the field of dogmatics which were purely theological like the Christological debates of the Ecumenical Councils of Nicea in 325, Ephesus in 431, or Chalcedon in 452, projected in essence the priority of man. For these debates tried to preserve not only the divinity, but the humanity of Christ since the Fathers of the Church saw the danger of losing the human being if they allowed any diminishing of the human element in Christ. Even the strongest, deepest, and most amazing Christological debates were concurrently anthropological debates, tacitly if not explicitly establishing the priority of the human person.

Conclusion

I have endeavored to present to you in a very short period of time four questions of importance: the question of communication, the question of a healthy social symbiosis, the question of the future of our world and the question of the importance of the human beings in today's society.

From the inexhaustible wealth and treasure of our Hellenic tradition and of our Christian Orthodox tradition we received four suggestions as answers to the above questions: 1) Language is the precise, complete, beautiful and sacred tool for real communication; 2) Democracy and community are the indispensable components of a healthy social symbiosis; 3) Admiration, wondering, thinking and creativity as an attitude towards the world are vital elements for coping with the unknown, if not threatening future; and 4) The priority of human being defines the importance of man on earth.

I started with the greeting "Χριστὸς 'Ανέστη." I am closing with the same greeting to which I add a warm, wholehearted "εὐχαριστῶ." Thank you.

36th Biennial Clergy-Laity Congress Keynote Address

Los Angeles, CA
July 1, 2002

Introduction

The Lord said to His disciples, *"Peace be with you. As the Father sent me, even so I send you"* (John 20:21). This was the great and unique apostolic commission given by the risen Christ to His disciples, a commission that has changed the world.

The Lord says to us today, July 1, year 2002, here in Los Angeles, "Peace be with you. As the Father sent me, even so I send you."

This is our great and holy commission. And this is the essential meaning of the phrase "Offering our Orthodox Faith to Contemporary America," the phrase which constitutes the theme of our 36th Biennial Clergy-Laity Congress. "Offering our Orthodox Faith to Contemporary America" means to respond dynamically, creatively and consistently to the holy call that Christ addresses to us: "As the Father sent me, even so I send you."

God the Father sent to us Christ, the Son. He offered Him to us, to all humanity, to the whole world, so that we may have abundant life, enduring peace and eternal salvation.

But then, Christ our God sends us to the world, to our fellow human beings, specifically, to the people of contemporary America. He sends us to do what He did, to bring the joyful and saving message of the Gospel, to offer the unfailing love of Christ, the fullness of His life and His unwavering truth. We are entrusted by Jesus Christ with the awesome mission and the sacred task to do what He did, to offer wholeheartedly what He offered, without hesitation and without reservations or conditions. We are entrusted by Him to continue His work which He sealed with His sacrificial death on the Cross and His glorious Resurrection. We are called by Him to be in any place and at any time; but particularly, we are called to be here in America, today, His visible, touchable life-giving presence.

Beloved and respected Hierarchs, priests and deacons, lay brothers and sisters, I greet you this morning warmly, and I embrace you with reverence as this visible and touchable presence of Christ, as ambassadors of God, commissioned by Him and gathered here to this holy and sacred meeting of our Archdiocese, our 36th Biennial Clergy-Laity Congress. Welcome to the city of Angels as angels, as messengers of Christ the Lord.

Growth and Progress Since the 2000 Congress

Two years have passed since our last meeting in Philadelphia. Two years filled with activities, events and growth, difficulties and progress, joys and sorrows; years filled with explosive death on September 11, 2001, but also with explosive life. God gave us much more than all that we ask or think (Ephesians 3:20). He gave us the grace to be able to say with Saint Paul, "*In all things we are more than conquerors through Him* [Christ] *who loved us*" (Romans 8:37).

During the past two years, God offered us a multitude of gifts, a plethora of blessings. It would take long hours even to enumerate them briefly. But allow me to bring back from memory just a few of these blessings as indications of the intense love and graciousness of God and as items for a warm thanksgiving prayer.

1) Six churches were consecrated and two had Thyranixia or opening ceremonies in various parts of the country: New Orleans, Louisiana; Cardiff-by-the-Sea, California; Elkins Park, Pennsylvania; Annapolis, Maryland; Bayard, Nebraska; Dallas, Texas; Port Jefferson, New York; and Naples, Florida. In almost all of the cases the consecrated churches belong to elaborate building complexes, including community centers, classrooms, gymnasiums and office space. This shows a tremendous activity by our communities. In addition to the consecration of churches we had inaugurations of community halls, cultural centers, school classrooms or groundbreaking ceremonies for similar projects in places like Houston, Texas; Staten Island, New York; Waterbury, Connecticut; Little Rock, Arkansas; and Denver, Colorado. At this moment significant activity is taking place all over the United States related to building new churches or expanding old ones and constructing buildings and facilities in order to accommodate the ever-increasing needs of the communities. Just in our immediate vicinity here in Los Angeles, in the suburb of Downey, we visited last Friday evening a new, magnificent church under construction. We offer thanks to God for this building and for the expanding activity of our Greek Orthodox Archdiocese.

2) Three new Bishops have been ordained and have been given to the Church. They are the Chief Secretary of our Holy Synod, Bishop Gerasimos of Krateia, the Chancellor of our Holy Archdiocese, Bishop Savas of Troas, and the Director of the philanthropic work of our Holy Archdiocese, Bishop Andonios of Phasiane. They are gifted and dedicated Hierarchs, who will direct important areas of our

Church ministries and serve as Auxiliary Bishops, thus covering vital pastoral and spiritual needs of our communities.

In addition to the bishops, we have had during the same period of the last two years an impressive number of ordinations to the priesthood and to the diaconate. Graduates of our Holy Cross School of Theology of previous years are expressing the willingness to be ordained and serve. At the same time, the percentage of current students ready to commit themselves to the priesthood is rapidly rising. In the two-year period between Philadelphia and Los Angeles we have had 24 ordinations to the diaconate, and 18 ordinations to the priesthood. We give thanks to God for our new bishops, priests, and deacons.

3) In the 35th Clergy-Laity Congress in Philadelphia we reported a sizeable debt from the past, which weighed heavily on our Archdiocese, drastically hampering our work and ministries. A quiet effort was made which started with the members of the previous Archdiocesan Council and continued with the members of the present one. The eagerness of the truly distinguished members of our Church to assist with the task of eliminating this debt was amazing. Here, a remarkable phenomenon emerged, and something unexpected happened. Who would really think that people would give large amounts of money for the dissolution of past loans, deficits and debts? However, the unexpected happened! Between Philadelphia of 2000 and Los Angeles of 2002, within less than two years, some astonishingly generous brothers offered more than five million dollars in donations, thus radically reducing our debt—quite a blessing. Just last April one such truly noble brother came up to me after a meeting and said: "I know that we still have a remaining debt of 1.5 million dollars to a bank. I think our dignity, our identity, as the Greek Orthodox Archdiocese of America obliges us to eliminate it as soon as possible." "For this reason," he added, "please

accept a half a million dollar donation from me, but anonymously, toward this goal." We give thanks to God for the very noble souls, the truly champion contributors of more than five million dollars towards the elimination of the heavy debt which tormented our Archdiocese.

4) September 11, 2001 was a day of death, darkness and unbelievable pain. As a Greek Orthodox community we lost approximately twenty-five members. The number of persons who were lost might have been more, but unfortunately there is no secure data available. May the memory of our brothers and sisters slaughtered on September 11 be eternal. At the same, exceedingly painful time, however, God granted to our Church the opportunity to offer in the midst of death, destruction and unbearable pain, love and comfort and assistance.

September 11 gave to our Church the sacred occasion to rise up to an admirable level of sensitivity, care and offering in may ways: continuous prayer services, blood donations, support and counseling availability, and fundraising for the families of the victims, especially the orphans of the tragedy. I personally witnessed the tremendous outpouring of love demonstrated by our parishes and individually by members of our Church, both clergy and laity. It will take not hours but days and months to speak adequately and to report accurately the many touching stories and incidents in which our Greek Orthodox people showed unusually high human qualities of love, generosity and valiance. Let me temporarily close this subject by also giving you two specific numbers. The one is the amount collected in the September 11 Relief Fund: $2,050,000. The other is the Saint Nicholas Fund which has been assisted by unexpected sources: $1,300,000. We give thanks to God for deeming us worthy as the Greek Orthodox Archdiocese of America to offer a strong witness of love and faith in the midst of a catastrophic event of huge proportions such as the September 11 terrorist attack.

5) Another special blessing during this two-year period has been the progress at our Hellenic College and Holy Cross School of Theology. A concerted effort by our bishops, priests, and communities and various individuals, together with the substantial assistance of a generous offering of scholarships by Leadership 100 resulted in a doubling of the number of first year students, especially in the School of Theology, for the academic year 2001-2002. We have the same phenomenon for the academic year 2002-2003. This practically means that we reasonably expect a dramatic increase of people who are preparing for the priesthood, and thus, will address a vital need of our Church in America. We give thanks to God for the progress of our sacred institution of Hellenic College and Holy Cross Greek Orthodox School of Theology.

6) Among the special blessings of these past two years, we should also include the activities of our Archdiocese related to SCOBA. IOCC (International Orthodox Christian Charities), which this year completed ten years of existence, continues to develop and increase its activities to a considerable degree, spending millions of dollars in assistance to areas of disaster and urgent needs around the world. The same holds true for OCMC (the Orthodox Christian Mission Center), which at this point in time has fifty-four of our people fully working in the missionary field outside of the United States and supports financially many Orthodox Churches in Africa, the Far East, and Albania. OCMC has a budget of approximately two million dollars per year, which is increasing, a fact indicative of its activities and bright prospects. We give thanks to God for the work of IOCC and OCMC.

Offering Our Orthodox Faith to Contemporary America

As the Greek Orthodox Church we have been the blessed recipients of the precious and unique gifts of God for the past two thousand years all over the world, and for the past one hundred plus years here in America, starting with our heroic pioneers. Today, in view of such an amazing past loaded with gifts and blessings, in view of the progress and astonishing achievements of our community, and in view of the immediate and the distant future, we hear again and again the commission of our Lord: *"Peace be with you. As the Father sent me, even so I send you"* (John 20:21). This is the commission to continue with more intensity, creativity and effectiveness the offering of our Orthodox Faith to contemporary America.

What are the prospects before us? How do we see such an offering on our part? What is the true vision of transforming a divine mandate into powerful action?

1) Offering our Orthodox Faith to contemporary America begins with each one of us individually. The Lord Jesus Christ sends personally every member of our Church to offer the treasures of the Orthodox Faith to the people we meet, to the people who constitute contemporary America. He gives us the privilege to share with others the treasures of the absolute and liberating truth of God and the infinite, life-giving love of Christ. Are we ready and well prepared as individuals to respond to such an awesome call? Are we growing in the knowledge of Christ and in a sustained, personal close relationship with Him? Is our knowledge of the truth of God adequately advanced? Are we well aware of our Hellenic Orthodox tradition? Is our individual life of worship and prayer sufficiently rich? Are we in a state of continuous growth in our love and care for others who are assuredly contemporary Americans? If our Orthodox

Faith is not organically and inseparably related to our personal life, there is no real way to offer it to anyone. In the final analysis, we cannot offer our faith to contemporary America; we cannot be ambassadors of Christ; we cannot be the true, whole image of Christ if we are not personally and fully committed to Him. Such a commitment must be characteristic of each and every member of our Church if we are serious about offering our Orthodox Faith to contemporary America.

2) The commission, however, to share what we have and to give what we have generously received from God, the commission to offer our Orthodox Faith to contemporary America, goes beyond individuals and addresses the Church as such. The center of the Church as a witness of faith is the parish, the community of believers gathered around the Eucharistic holy table. It is the parish, it is the local community which has been, is, and will forever be the central, indispensable agent for offering our Orthodox Faith to contemporary America.

This 36th Clergy-Laity Congress should be the Congress which will cultivate the awareness of the tremendous importance of the parish, of the need to support the parish with all possible means, to help develop its life and activities, to make the parish a powerful witness and passionate promoter of Orthodox Faith and Tradition. In this Congress we should designate the two years between now and the next Biennial Congress as years of an intense care for the parish in order to facilitate its unrestricted growth.

The Archdiocese as a whole and the Dioceses as parts of it must focus on the parishes, constantly assist them, consistently serve them, providing them with all means available so that they can be true witnesses of the Gospel, genuine transmitters of the life of Jesus and His salvation offered to all people and to contemporary America.

As the Archdiocese we will intensify and enlarge our efforts to be focused on our parishes; we will steadily persist in our task to be of substantive and effective assistance to our communities. With the help of God we intend to establish a relationship in which the primary concern of the Archdiocese is to serve the parish, to promote and enhance the life and activities of local communities all over the country. Only strong, healthy and constantly developing church communities can offer our Orthodox Faith to contemporary America in a realistic way. But how are we going to strengthen and develop our parishes? What are the specific steps we intend to take in order to make them units of vitality and powerful witnesses of faith?

3) In order to advance the real serving attitude of the Archdiocese toward our parishes, we have already started or are about to start a number of specific major projects. Allow me to report briefly on them.

(a) The existing department of Family and Marriage at the Archdiocese, dealing mostly with cases of the so-called mixed or interfaith marriages, is rapidly developing and becoming the Center for Family Care. It will be located and will operate at Saint Basil Academy in Garrison, N.Y. The Center for Family Care will develop programs and resources that will address questions and issues related to preparation for marriage, marital difficulties, interfaith marriages, clergy families, and families of divorce. It will also produce video, audio and printed material relevant to the abovementioned areas, and it will make these resources available to parishes and families. It will organize seminars and educational opportunities that will address areas of family life and development and will make available counseling possibilities via telephone or the Internet. All of these resources will be available and easily deliverable to our parishes so that the families within each community will become the object of constant and methodical attention, care and assistance. Our vision and our objective in this instance is to create with the help of God a Center for Family Care that will be a model institution for the advancement of healthy, happy, and dynamic Orthodox families, and for the full incorporation of interfaith marriages into the life of each and every parish. Our vision is to create a model institution, which will be a leader in the field of family care among the Christians denominations of contemporary America.

(b) The Youth Department is also being restructured and expanded so that it will be able to offer to our parishes the necessary help in organizing ministry related to youth. In cooperation with the Department of Religious Education and the Greek Education Department, which provide hundreds of educational resources, the Youth Department will assist the communities in their tasks related to JOY, GOYA and YAL. Particular attention has been given to YAL, the vital young adult group of our Church, which probably has not been provided with the proper means for a healthy growth in recent years. Particular attention is also being given to the revitalization of the Orthodox Campus Fellowship, a ministry under SCOBA, which is directed towards the thousands of Orthodox students in our colleges and universities. Our vision and our objective is to overcome the sad phenomenon observed in almost all religious entities in America, according to which adolescents and young adults in the age bracket of 16 to 30 drop out of their respective religious communities. A mighty way to offer our Orthodox Faith to contemporary America is to demonstrate as a fact that Orthodoxy can create a vigorous and productive youth that remain faithfully within the Church and constitute her most exciting and effective age group. The steady orientation of the Youth Department will be to the youth of the parish, and it is to the parish that the pertinent activities will be incessantly channeled.

(c) There is a third major development in organizing important Archdiocesan services for the parishes, thus rendering our offering of our Faith to contemporary America more effective. This is the creation of the Philanthropy Department. The charitable work of the Church is a huge area of action. Our Ladies Philoptochos Society has been doing a truly remarkable work over the years, for which we all are very proud. The area of philanthropy, however, presents us with the potential for further, unlimited growth, encompassing vital needs of contemporary America. The case for our aging people, for instance, is such an immediate need. Several of our communities have already established various types of homes for the aged. We have, for instance, a central place of this type in Yonkers, N.Y., Saint Michael's Home. But the needs are overwhelming. The Philanthropy Department will aim to support all pertinent efforts, providing the appropriate resources and guidance.

The same Department will further assist all philanthropic tasks undertaken by the communities, developing at the same time a complete file of all philanthropic activities of the parishes. This way pertinent information and experience emanating from local efforts could be communicated nationally to all parishes for possible developments of similar tasks.

There are cries for help coming from various places. People with special needs, people who are hungry and poor, people who are sick and abandoned are reaching out, begging for support. The new department will gradually and systematically enlarge its realm of activity and do anything possible to assist our parishes in their sacred efforts to offer our Orthodox Faith to contemporary America in the form of philanthropic witness, in the form of a limitless love in the name of Christ and in continuity with His unique ministry of love, compassion, and care. Our vision and objective here is to project through our parishes, Dioceses and Archdiocese a witness of our Orthodox Faith to contemporary America by means of offering love the way that Christ offered it to the world.

(d) The fourth major project, a project of truly impressive proportions concerns the demanding task of Communications. Here we have the whole area of web sites and the Internet in general, video and audio productions, the preparation and distribution of printed material, and our relations with the media.

Already, our progress in these truly critical areas is well-advanced, as we are providing significant services to our parishes. We are in the joyful position to announce that the new and upgraded web site of the Archdiocese was released last week. Our goal, however, is to increase this offering and provide our parishes on a regular basis with substantive material which will be of immediate use for them. For instance, we plan to issue formatted material to be used for the weekly bulletin of the community, to make available homiletical, educational, and catechetical material and other resources, and to help parishes with information related to pastoral, philanthropic and evangelistic ministry. The communications opportunities, immediately accessible to our communities, will be one of the most dynamic services of the Archdiocese, and certainly it will be a central task in the present and in the years to come.

We strongly believe that with the multifarious assistance provided by the Communications Department to our parishes, they will be in a better position to offer our Orthodox Faith to contemporary America. Our vision and objective in this case is to develop and to use a communications system that will be a powerful vehicle for the transmission of the Gospel message to the hearts of our fellow Americans, for the transmission of the very voice of Christ to the ears and the hearts of the people of the world.

(e) The last major development related to our mission of offering the witness of our Orthodox Faith to today's American society, is the intensification and growth of the educational activities of our Church. There is an urgent need to advance the knowledge of our Orthodox Tradition and our truly universal Hellenic heritage. This is a splendid heritage that is integrally connected with our Orthodox Faith, encompassing vast areas of culture, civilization and language. Our heritage is not narrowly ethnic but belongs to the whole civilized world. There is an urgent need for creating a body of faithful who will be truly illumined, truly educated, truly and fully informed about our Greek Orthodox identity.

Through our unique institution of Hellenic College and Holy Cross School of Theology, through our Departments of Religious Education and Greek Education, through our schools, and through all other means available we plan to promote education, *paideia* as a central, vital issue in the life of our Church here. This is an issue that has to be nurtured and cultivated in our parishes, thus enabling them to promote effectively our Faith and offer it to contemporary America, the place of astonishing progress in matters of science and learning.

Conclusion

We have presented five major developments of great importance for offering our Orthodox Faith to contemporary America:

1) The Center for Family Care;
2) The restructuring and intensification of the work of Youth Ministry;
3) The creation of the Philanthropy Department;

4) The reorganizing of the Communications Department for maximum, state of the art performance; and
5) The enhancement and promotion of our educational activities.

The importance of the abovementioned developments is also seen in that these are developments that are fully directed toward our parishes and for their benefit.

There is, however, another aspect of importance related to these developments which I am in the exceedingly blessed position to share with you today. There are distinguished members of our Church here in America who are deeply appreciative of such developments and such progress, which shows the potential for the unprecedented growth of our parishes and our Archdiocese. These remarkable brothers, these true pillars of the work of the Church, have declared their willingness and their commitment to support these projects and programs financially. And the commitment is millions of dollars—a truly tremendous contribution that is readily available.

But this is not a matter for a very few major donors. This is a matter for all of our faithful. The projects we are talking about must be warmly embraced by all, strongly supported by all, and passionately promoted by all. They are projects aimed at offering our Orthodox Faith to contemporary America in a well-focused, carefully balanced, and all-encompassing manner.

The results might far exceed our thoughts, expectations and visions. The results might not be many, but one: the creation of a new era in the history of Orthodoxy, the creation of a new model in ecumenical Orthodoxy, the model of Greek-American Orthodoxy of the twenty-first century and beyond. Who knows if God has not sent us in this blessed country at this time, at this hour, precisely in order to offer this model of universal Orthodoxy, a model destined to carry the authentic, whole, life-giving and holy voice of Christ to every person in every place, but primarily here in contemporary America.

We are invited in the name of Christ our Lord and God and with His invincible power to have the vision to work and to pray for an America which will become the place of a shining, pioneer, model and leading Orthodox Faith. This invitation might have been issued some time ago. Today, however, in this 36th Clergy-Laity Congress of our Archdiocese, it is heard clearly and loudly. We have to respond to God. We have to work with Him. We have to create with Him a shining Orthodoxy for America.

The Impact of September 11, 2001 On the Religious and Social Life of People

Bucharest, Romania*
August 29, 2002

Introduction

I express my sincere thanks for the honor given to me to address this important conference organized jointly by distinguished members of the European Parliament and the Ecumenical Patriarchate.

I have had the great honor of participating and speaking at the first conference of this kind in Constantinople at the Ecumenical Patriarchate in 1996. Today, however, we meet here in Bucharest under different conditions. We meet under the heavy shadow of the post September 11, 2001 events.

What I am about to offer, because of the limitations of time, are some thoughts and ideas related to the basic consequences and the way life changed for the people in America in the aftermath of the horrendous terrorist attack of September 11, 2001. In summary, I will present my comments in two groups, a) The tragic and negative impacts on life following the attacks of September 11, and b) the possible positive effects on life as consequences of the events of

*This address was presented at The Sixth Dialogue between the Group of the European People's Party (Christian Democrats) and European Democrats and the Ecumenical Patriarchate. The text was published in a book of conference papers under the conference title.

September 11. Of course, I will present primarily personal experiences drawn from direct contact with the events of September 11, since I have had the distinct, yet painful privilege to reside in the place where these unprecedented and barbaric attacks took place.

Tragic and Negative Impacts of September 11, 2001

The negative and sad consequences of September 11 on the life of the people living in America are many and sharply differentiated. From the vast number of these consequences I would like to present three that seem to be major consequences inclusive of some variations on the same theme.

1. The Emotional Trauma

The first clearly visible impact of September 11 is the enormous pain inflicted upon thousands of people. The people who immediately received this unexpected blow of immeasurable and tremendous emotional trauma were the families of the victims. Thousands and thousands of wives, children, parents, brothers and sisters, relatives and friends were involved in an emotionally heavy time filled with anxiety immediately after the first of the Twin Towers was hit by the terrorists, since trapped inside the tower were their loved ones. After the collapse of the second tower, their emotions reflected a grim reality of devastation and death. And as the hours passed and the magnitude of the loss was gradually made known to millions of people in the greater New York area, it seemed that a gigantic wave of the most unbearable pain covered the entire megalopolis of New York and the whole of America.

I cannot forget the piercing and indescribable intensity of sorrow and pain that I felt going from funeral to funeral of the victims of the terrorist attack. You are in a church packed with thousands of people and you have in the front row a young widow with her three now-orphaned children praying at the funeral being conducted for their husband and father without the presence of a body. In fact, many bodies of the victims who lost their lives on September 11 were never recovered. And then you go to a funeral being held at another church, with a similar scene, only this time the father and the mother, two brothers and two sisters mourn the loss of their son and brother, a victim of this attack who simply disappeared from life in one of the Twin Towers. Who could adequately and precisely describe and leave for posterity the truly indescribable funeral scenes like the ones I just shared with you, scenes that were generated by other indescribable scenes of death of thousands of innocent people in the Twin Towers at Ground Zero, at the Pentagon in Washington, and in Pennsylvania?

If one wants to have a most impressive image of excruciating pain and immense sadness one could simply call to mind the image of the people of America in the hours, days, and months following the morning of September 11, 2001.

2. *The Existential Trauma*

The pain and sadness we are talking about do not belong to ordinary, expected, understandable, or easy to deal with experiences. The tragic events of September 11 wounded humanity in such a way that immediately human beings sought answers to very difficult existential questions: What is human life? Why should innocent people of all ethnicities, religions, races, who have nothing to do with anything that could justify their massacre, be killed in such a cruel way? Why must human life, given just once to each person, be taken abruptly in the most inhuman way? Why do human beings, who posses the gift of freedom, a freedom granted to any and every person on earth, use this freedom not only to deprive others from their freedom, but from their elementary, unique, and once and for all right to live a full and peaceful life on earth? Indeed, the question arose, "Does human existence have any meaning?" These are questions that tormented people continuously.

On one of my earliest visits to Ground Zero, the very place where thousands of people were buried under the piles of debris, I remember as I was exiting the immediate zone of catastrophe and making my way through the people of the media, I was asked by one of them the following question, "Don't you feel your faith strongly shaken, if not fatally wounded, by what you just saw?"

It is precisely the abovementioned questions which I classify as an existential trauma knowing the results of the horrendous events of September 11. It is obvious that this existential trauma in conjunction with the emotional trauma of unbearable pain has had a strong impact on the religious life of people, producing situations and questions that we as pastors never before encountered.

3. The Financial Trauma

Even for someone who is not familiar, and not a specialist in the field of financial and economic issues, it is not difficult to observe the catastrophic impact of September 11 on the economy. New York, especially, as a central place for economic development in the United States, suffered terribly seeing within hours the collapse of her symbols of economic prosperity. The upheaval in the financial market, the negative chain reactions in main financial enterprises like transportation, hotels, and communications, all attest to this economic catastrophe. Thousands of people were instantaneously unemployed, and their families found themselves without the elementary means for survival. We do not need to emphasize at this point the radical changes experienced by millions of people because of the new unexpected financial conditions. September 11, through the resulting terrible financial conditions, caused a dramatic change on the purely social level of contemporary people living in America and by extension all over the world. But thanks to the resilience of the American people and the careful networking of resources, the negative financial repercussions that resulted from the events of September 11 gradually started to diminish. It will take, however, quite a significant amount of time and resources and an enormous coordination process on the part of the government and various corporations and agencies involved in economic development, and on the part of individual citizens of the United States, in order to fully recuperate and advance beyond the financial conditions existing before September 11.

The Possible Positive Consequences of September 11

As I said at the opening of my remarks, September 11 became a catalyst that brought to the surface unknown positive forces and possibilities that constitute a tremendous asset for the life of people. Allow me to present briefly three of them that could be considered the most important, but not the only, significant positive changes.

1. The Explosion of Love

In the aftermath of September 11 we experienced an explosion of something quite different than the horrendous explosions of the hijacked aircrafts. We are referring to the explosion of love, care, and concern, that all of a sudden became the very characteristic of people's lives following September 11. This solidarity between the people of America characterized every person and transcended the boundaries of race, color, and creed. Indeed, the level of solidarity between people who were dissimilar on many different levels reached unbelievable proportions. People unknown to each other came together, worked day and night together, offered their talents together, ran to help together, all in a tireless never-ending amazing explosion of love, service, and assistance.

How can I forget, and please allow me again to be personal, the scene in which people were assisting the wounded and bereaved families while others at the same time brought food and all sorts of supplies to the trauma centers. Others traveled long distances to offer comfort through music and other means to the hard working volunteers, who clearly out of love pushed themselves to work far beyond the human limits of tiredness and long, sleepless nights.

You have, for instance, the scene at Saint Vincent's Hospital in Manhattan, N.Y.—the receiving hospital for the wounded survivors of September 11—surrounded by huge groups of volunteers bringing food to the relatives of the victims, while just across the street a large group of young adults, who arrived that morning from Alabama after a two-day long and difficult journey, sings and offers the relief of religious music to this whole huge mass of people. Here is pain, and undeniably existential trauma, but here also is the triumph of love and charity and the beauty of people realizing and actualizing a splendid expression of unity and solidarity. This is not a personal observation; this is a common experience.

Let me close this part of my remarks by another image that has been indelibly engraved in my heart. This is the image of a long line of people waiting outside of the house of the family of one of the victims. The line of people extends out the front gate of the home to the corner of the street. People are standing there in the winter cold, awaiting their turn to enter the home and express their support to the members of the family. The hour is past midnight, and they have been standing for hours simply to embrace, to hug, and to let the family know that they are there for them and that they will be back again the next day, and the next day, and the next. Their burning love for their neighbor gives them the courage to stand in the home of a friend that is filled with the cold presence of death.

2. *From Coexistence to Living Together*

After September 11 everybody almost without exception realized that we live in a world where there are religious, cultural, and financial differences, and that we cannot live in isolation any longer. People realized that the socioeconomic and geopolitical conditions imposed, under the circumstances, the necessity to understand and to learn to live with full awareness of creeds and traditions that were different from their own. We used to talk about the need for developing the so-called "tolerance of coexistence." After September 11, the prevailing feeling and thinking is that we have to move beyond a simple tolerance of coexistence to a conscious decision to live together and not simply to coexist.

This is a very positive impact because it creates a promising series of actions, efforts, and a variety of endeavors to advance cooperation among different entities, to overcome enmities that may be due to ignorance, and to cultivate a rapprochement and authentic friendship. Indeed, fertile ground is therefore open, inviting truly creative thinking, benevolent planning, and dramatic improvement of relationships between formerly opposing forces. This perspective is truly heartwarming both for the immediate and the distant future.

3. Towards a Better Understanding and Cooperation Among Religions

The third major positive and beneficial result of September 11 is a new development related to the mutual understanding and further cooperation among different religious bodies. Just three days after the attack, on the afternoon of September 14, a number of religious leaders representing various religious communities of New York were invited to Ground Zero in order to offer prayers for the victims. We stood by the side of the President of the United States, the Mayor of New York, and the Governor of New York, and prayed together under the shadow of the remaining skeleton of one of the towers and in front of the truly sacred ground under which were buried thousands of innocent people. Since then, there were numerous occasions where religious leaders met and discussed means of implementing common efforts to alleviate the excruciating pain, to assist in the rebuilding of what was senselessly destroyed, and to offer support to the families which suffered loss of persons, properties, and all kinds of resources. Among those meetings which took place within a month of the attacks was one of prominent significance, and this was the long meeting of twenty-six religious leaders from all over the country with President Bush in the White House.

In this instance, the occasion was given for significant discussions about coping in the most effective way with the tragic consequences of the terrorist attacks of September 11. It is important to note that precisely because of the same tragic event a series of meetings of representatives of major faiths, which otherwise may not have occurred, started taking place not only inside America, but also outside in various parts of the world, for instance, in Brussels, Assisi, Cairo, and of course here in Bucharest. Under the circumstances we can see a spirit developing and a willingness that is growing for the increasing of mutual knowledge and of cooperation for advancing the cause of peace among the significant religious entities to which billions of the inhabitants of earth belong today.

Conclusion

I have tried to present in a telegraphic manner three major negative and three major positive results of September 11.

The negatives: The Emotional Trauma, the Existential Trauma, and the Financial Trauma.

The positives: the Explosion of Love, From Coexistence to Living Together, and Towards a Better Understanding and Cooperation Among Religions.

This has been only a less-than-elementary glimpse of a gigantic panorama that would need not simply hours or days, but a long time to look at and understand, analyze, and proceed with the effort of transforming a tragedy into a triumph of good. But this was done to provide an opportunity for a contact with this panoramic view and to proclaim once more the eternal truth that human beings can reverse the irreversible, overcome the evil and the ugly, and create a world of promise, hope, and vision out of the most disheartening ruins and encounters with death.

Ο Αληθης Σκοπος της Εκκλησιας και της Χριστιανικης Ζωης και η Πρακτικη Συνεπεια Τουτων δια την Ζωην του Συγχρονου Χριστιανου

Synaxis of the Reverend Hierarchs of the Most Sacred Ecumenical Throne

Ecumenical Patriarchate, Constantinople
September 1, 2002

Παναγιώτατε,

Ὑποβάλλω εὐλαβῶς πρός Ὑμᾶς καί τήν περί Ὑμᾶς Ἁγίαν καί Ἱεράν Σύνοδον τοῦ Οἰκουμενικοῦ ἡμῶν Πατριαρχείου τάς θερμοτάτας εὐχαριστίας μου διά τήν ἐξαιρετικήν τιμήν τήν προσγενομένην εἰς τήν ταπεινότητά μου νά κληθῶ ἵνα παρουσιάσω τήν παροῦσαν εἰσήγησιν εἰς τήν Ἱεράν ταύτην Σύναξιν τῶν Ἁγίων Ἱεραρχῶν τοῦ πανσέπτου Οἰκουμενικοῦ Θρόνου.

Τό θέμα ὡς διετυπώθη εἶναι εὐρύτατον καί καλύπτει πλευράς αἵτινες θά ἀπήτουν μακρόν χρόνον πρός ἐπαρκῆ παρουσίασιν:

Ὁ ἀληθής σκοπός τῆς Ἐκκλησίας καί τῆς χριστιανικῆς ζωῆς καί ἡ πρακτική συνέπεια τούτων διά τήν ζωήν τοῦ συγχρόνου χριστιανοῦ.

Κατ' ἀνάγκην, ἡ εἰσήγησίς μου θά εἶναι διαγραμματική μᾶλλον παρά ἀναλυτική καί ἐμπεριστατωμένη. Ἁπλῶς θά θίξω ὡρισμένας πλευράς πρός περαιτέρω μελέτην καί συζήτησιν, προϋποθέτων ἐπίσης τάς ἐπί μέρους εἰσηγήσεις τῶν πρός τοῦτο ὡρισθέντων τριῶν ἁγίων ἀδελφῶν, εἰσηγήσεις αἱ ὁποῖαι κατ᾽ οὐσίαν ἀναλύουν τάς βασικάς πλευράς καί τό συγκεκριμένον περιεχόμενον τοῦ κυρίου θέματος. Ἐπίσης προϋποθέτω τά βασικά θέματα τῶν προηγηθεισῶν συνάξεων κατά τά ἔτη 1994, 1996 καί 1998.

Ἡ εἰσήγησίς μου διαιρεῖται εἰς πέντε μέρη τά ὁποῖα ἐν συνόψει ἀναφέρονται:

1. Εἰς τό συγκεκριμένον ἀνθρώπινον περιβάλλον τοῦ συγχρόνου κόσμου ἐντός τοῦ ὁποίου ζεῖ καί δρᾶ ἡ Ἐκκλησία μας σήμερον,
2. Εἰς τό συγκεκριμένον ἀνθρώπινον στοιχεῖον τό συγκροτοῦν τήν Ἐκκλησίαν μας σήμερον,
3. Εἰς τόν σκοπόν τῆς Ἐκκλησίας μας σήμερον ἐν ὄψει τῆς ἰδιότητός της ὡς σώματος Χριστοῦ καί τῆς θεοσδότου κλήσεώς της νά συνεχίσῃ εἰς αἰῶνα αἰῶνος τό ἔργον Του ἐπί τῆς γῆς,
4. Εἰς πρακτικάς συνεπείας ἀπορρεούσας ἐκ τῆς ὡς ἄνω ἰδιότητος καί κλήσεως τῆς Ἐκκλησίας, καί
5. Εἰς συμπερασματικάς τινας παρατηρήσεις.

Τό σύγχρονον ἀνθρώπινον περιβάλλον καί τά συνοδεύοντα βασικά προβλήματα

Δέν εἶναι δυνατόν νά προσδιορισθῇ μέ ἀκρίβειαν καί ρεαλιστικότητα ὁ σκοπός τῆς Ἐκκλησίας καί τῆς χριστιανικῆς ζωῆς ἐντός τοῦ συγχρόνου κόσμου ἐάν δέν κατανοηθῇ ποῖος εἶναι αὐτός ὁ κόσμος ἀπό πλευρᾶς συγκεκριμένης καταστάσεως, προβλημάτων, προοπτικῶν καί τοποθετήσεων. Ἐπισημαίνω ἐπιτροχάδην μερικά ἐξ αὐτῶν.

1) Ὁ κόσμος μας εἶναι κόσμος μαζικῶν πληθυσμιακῶν μετακινήσεων. Ἡ Εὐρώπη, ἡ Ἀμερική, ἡ Ἀσία, ἡ Ἀφρική ζοῦν μίαν συνεχῆ ποικιλότροπον μετακίνησιν ἀνθρωπίνων μαζῶν. Τοῦτο σημαίνει ὅτι αἱ Ἐκκλησίαι μας καί οἱ πιστοί μας ζοῦν καταστάσεις συνυπάρξεως μέ ριζικῶς διαφοροποιημένα πολιτιστικῶς καί θρησκειολογικῶς στοιχεῖα, χαρακτηριζόμενα εἰς πολλάς περιπτώσεις ἀπό ἔντονον θρησκευτικοπολιτιστικόν φανατισμόν. Τό ἐπί πλέον ἰδιάζον χαρακτηριστικόν τοῦ φαινομένου εἶναι ὅτι αἱ ὡς ἄνω εὐρύταται μετακινήσεις πληθυσμῶν εἶναι ἐν πολλοῖς ἀσταθεῖς καί ὡς ἐκ τούτου αἱ δυνατότητες ταχείας προσαρμογῆς καί ἁρμονικῆς συνυπάρξεως μειωμέναι. Σχετικά παραδείγματα ἔχομεν ἀπό τήν Ἀμερικήν, τά Βαλκάνια, τήν Ἐγγύς Ἀνατολήν κ.λ.π. (Παράδειγμα σχολείων τοῦ Brooklyn, New York, Ἐνορία Ζωοδόχου Πηγῆς, Manhattan, New York, Ἐνορία Ἁγίου Σπυρίδωνος).

2) Ὁ σύγχρονος κόσμος, δεύτερον, εἶναι κόσμος παγκοσμιοποιήσεως τῆς ἐπικοινωνίας καί τῆς πληροφορίας. Ὅλοι οἱ ἄνθρωποι, τοὐλάχιστον ἐν δυνάμει, ἔχουν πρόσβασιν εἰς τάς αὐτάς εἰδήσεις, τάς αὐτάς πληροφορίας καί τά αὐτά προγράμματα πολυεπιπεδικῆς ἐνημερώσεως. Οὕτω καλλιεργεῖται μιά ἐπικρατοῦσα αἴσθησις κοινοκτημοσύνης τῆς γνώσεως καί τῆς ἐνημερώσεως περί τοῦ τί συμβαίνει ἀνά πᾶν λεπτόν εἰς τόν πλανήτην μας. Τοῦτο εἰς πλείστους ἀνθρώπους δημιουργεῖ μίαν βεβαιότητα γνώσεως τῆς ἀληθείας περί τοῦ ἐν τῷ κόσμῳ εἶναι καί γίγνεσθαι, πρᾶγμα τό ὁποῖον ἔχει δραματικάς ἐπιπτώσεις ἐπί τοῦ θέματος τῆς Ἐκκλησίας ὡς μοναδικοῦ φορέως καί ἐκφραστοῦ τῆς ὑπερτάτης καί ἀπολύτου ἀληθείας περί τοῦ ἐν τῷ κόσμῳ εἶναι καί γίγνεσθαι. Διά τόν ρεαλιστήν ἄνθρωπον τῶν καιρῶν μας ἡ ἀλήθεια σχετικοποιεῖται

καί ἐκφράζεται διά τῆς συνεχοῦς πληροφορήσεως εἰς τήν ὁποίαν ἔχουν ἄμεσον πρόσβασιν οἱ πάντες.

3) Τρίτον, ὁ κόσμος μας εἶναι κόσμος πρωτοφανοῦς εὐθραυστότητος ἀβεβαιότητος καί ἀνασφαλείας. Εἶναι κόσμος ἐντός τοῦ ὁποίου τό μόνον οὐσιαστικῶς προβλέψιμον εἶναι τό ἀπρόβλεπτον καί ἀπροσδόκητον. Ἰδίως μετά τήν 11ην Σεπτεμβρίου 2001, οἱ ἄνθρωποι ζοῦν μέ τήν αἴσθησιν ὅτι εἶναι εὐάλωτοι, ὅτι ἡ ζωή των ἐξαρτᾶται ἀπό παράγοντας κατ' οὐσίαν ἀνεξελέγκτους. (Παράδειγμα ἀπό τό World Economic Forum: Thinking the Unthinkable). Ἐν ὄψει αὐτῆς ἀκριβῶς τῆς αἰσθήσεως τό αὔριον τῶν ἀνθρώπων εἶναι χρόνος ὑπό αἵρεσιν, ὑπό σκιάν ἰσχυρῶν ἀμφιβολιῶν. Τό θέμα ἔχει προφανεῖς ἐπιπτώσεις ἐπί τοῦ ἔργου καί τῆς προοπτικῆς τῆς ἐκκλησιαστικῆς διακονίας, δηλ. ἐπί τοῦ συγκεκριμένου σκοποῦ τῆς Ἐκκλησίας σήμερον.

4) Τέταρτον, ὁ σύγχρονος κόσμος εἶναι κόσμος ηὐξημένου πόνου καί θλίψεως ἐπί παγκοσμίου ἐπιπέδου. Πεῖνα, ἀσθένειαι, πόλεμοι, θάνατοι ἀδόκητοι ἤ βίαιοι ἑκατομμυρίων ἀνθρώπων, ἀποτελοῦν συμπτώματα μόνιμα καί θλιβερά τῆς συγχρόνου ἀνθρωπότητος. Παραλλήλως ὁ πόνος, ὡς πολύ καλῶς γνωρίζομεν, μεταλλάσσεται εἰς ἀγανάκτησιν καί εἰς ἐκρηκτικήν ἐπαναστατικότητα λόγῳ τῆς προκλητικῆς ἀδικίας καί ἀνισότητος, λόγῳ τῆς ἀγρίας ἐκμεταλλεύσεως τῶν ἀδυνάτων ἀπό τούς ἰσχυρούς καί τῆς ἐντεινομένης διαφορᾶς μεταξύ ἐχόντων καί μή ἐχόντων. Καί ἐνταῦθα ἡ Ἐκκλησία δέν δύναται νά ἀγνοήσῃ τά τεράστια προβλήματα.

5) Τέλος, πέμπτον, διά νά περιορισθῶμεν εἰς στοιχειώδη δειγματοληπτικήν ἀναφοράν, ὁ κόσμος μας εἶναι κόσμος μερικῆς ἤ ὁλικῆς ἐκλείψεως τῆς χαρᾶς καί ἀντικαταστάσεώς της διά τῆς ἡδονῆς καί τῆς ἀπολαύσεως. Ἡ ἡδονοθηρία καί ἡ ἀχαλίνωτος τάσις πρός

παντός εἴδους ἀπολαύσεις ἔχουν δημιουργήσει παγκοσμίως τάς γνωστάς καταστάσεις ἑνός σεξολογικοῦ πληθωρισμοῦ καί μιᾶς θλιβερᾶς κυριαρχίας τῶν ναρκωτικῶν καί τῶν ἐθιστικῶν ἐν γένει οὐσιῶν συνδεομένων μέ παντοειδεῖς ἀπολαύσεις. Τό ἐπί πλέον ἰδιάζον χαρακτηριστικόν τῶν καταστάσεων αὐτῶν εἶναι ὁ φρενήρης ρυθμός ἀναπτύξεως καί ἡ ἀμεσότης τῆς ἐπιζητουμένης ἀπολαύσεως. Νέοι πρίν ἤ κλείσουν τόν κύκλον τῆς ἐφηβείας των ἔχουν δοκιμάσει τά πάντα, ὅπως οἱ ἴδιοι δηλώνουν, μέ συνεπείας ἤ νά ἔχουν αἰχμαλωτισθῆ εἰς ἕνα ψυχοφθόρον, σαρκοβόρον, καί τελικῶς θανατηφόρον τρόπον ζωῆς ἤ νά ἔχουν βυθισθῆ εἰς καταστάσεις καταθλίψεως λόγῳ ἀνίας καί πλήρους ἀδιαφορίας διά τήν ζωήν ἡ ὁποία δέν ἔχει πλέον νά τούς προσφέρῃ ἐνδιαφέροντα καί ἀξιόλογα πράγματα. Εἰς ἀντιμετώπισιν τῶν ὡς ἄνω θλιβερῶν καταστάσεων, ὁ σκοπός τῆς Ἐκκλησίας καί τῆς χριστιανικῆς ζωῆς προφανῶς κέκτηται ἀποφασιστικόν ρόλον.

Τό συγκεκριμένον ἀνθρώπινον στοιχεῖον τό συγκροτοῦν τήν Ἐκκλησίαν μας σήμερον

Ἕνα δεύτερον μεῖζον θέμα διά τό ὁποῖον πρέπει νά εἴμεθα ἐνήμεροι ὅταν ὁμιλῶμεν περί τοῦ σκοποῦ τῆς Ἐκκλησίας, εἶναι τό θέμα τοῦ ποῖοι ἀκριβῶς ἀποτελοῦν τήν Ἐκκλησίαν μας σήμερον. Ποῖον εἶναι τό ἀνθρώπινον στοιχεῖον τό ὁποῖον ἀποτελεῖ τό σύνολον τῶν πιστῶν τῶν θεοσώστων Ἐπαρχιῶν μας; Γενικεύοντας καί ἁπλουστεύοντας διά λόγους εὐχερεστέρας παρακολουθήσεως, θά ἠδυνάμεθα νά διακρίνωμεν δύο θεμελιώδεις κατηγορίας πιστῶν συγκροτούντων τό ἐκκλησιαστικόν πλήρωμα:

1) Ἡ πρώτη ἀποτελεῖται ἀπό ὅλους τούς βαπτισθέντας οἱ ὁποῖοι μετέχουν συνειδητῶς καί συστηματικῶς εἰς τήν ζωήν τῆς Ἐκκλησίας ὡς στρατευμένα μέλη της. Τοῦτο σημαίνει κατά τό μᾶλλον καί ἧττον συνεπῆ λατρευτικήν ζωήν μέ συμμετοχήν εἰς τά ἱερά Μυστήρια, προσφοράν εἰς τάς διαφόρους δραστηριότητας ἐπί ἐνοριακοῦ ἐπιπέδου και συμβολήν εἰς τά γενικώτερα ἔργα εὐρυτέρων ἐκκλησιαστικῶν συνόλων (Μητροπόλεων, Ἀρχιεπισκοπῶν κλπ.). Σημαίνει ἐπίσης συνειδητήν προσπάθειαν βιώσεως τῆς χριστιανικῆς ζωῆς καί ἐνσαρκώσεως τοῦ γνησίου Ὀρθοδόξου ἤθους καί τῆς ὑγιοῦς εὐσεβείας.

2) Ἡ δευτέρα κατηγορία πιστῶν ἀποτελεῖται ἀπό βαπτισθέντας μέν ἀλλ' ἔχοντας μᾶλλον χαλαράν ἕως καί ἀνενεργόν σχέσιν πρός τήν τρέχουσαν καί ἄμεσον ζωήν τῆς Ἐκκλησίας. Ὁ λατρευτικός των βίος εἶναι ἀπό ἀναιμικός ἕως καί ἀνύπαρκτος, καί ἡ συμμετοχή των εἰς ἐκκλησιαστικάς δραστηριότητας ἐμφανῶς ἐλλιπής.

3) Ὑπάρχει καί μία τρίτη κατηγορία ἡ ὁποία κατ' οὐσίαν δέν εἶναι κατηγορία πιστῶν διότι οἱ συγκροτοῦντες αὐτήν δέν εἶναι βαπτισθέντες ὀρθόδοξοι. Τήν ἀναφέρομεν ἐν τούτοις διότι πρόκειται περί ἀνθρώπων οἱ ὁποῖοι προέρχονται ἐκ μεικτῶν γάμων πρώτης ἤ δευτέρας γενεᾶς καί συνεπῶς ἔχουν ἐξ ἀμέσου κληρονομικότητος στοιχεῖα ὀρθοδόξου καταγωγῆς, καί, κατά τεκμήριον, στοιχεῖα εὐμενοῦς διαθέσεως καί ἀποκλίσεως πρός τήν Ὀρθόδοξον πίστιν.

Ὡς εἶναι φυσικόν, αἱ ὡς ἄνω κατηγορίαι ἀποτελοῦν γενικεύσεις, αἱ ὁποῖαι καλύπτουν ἀπειρίαν ἀποχρώσεων καί διαφοροποιήσεων καί ὑπαγορεύουν ἀναλόγους προσαρμογάς εἰς τόν τρόπον ἀντιμετωπίσεώς των ὑπό τῆς Ἐκκλησίας καί ἐντάξεώς των εἰς τά ποιμαντικά καί παιδαγωγικά προγράμματά της, πρᾶγμα τό ὁποῖον δέν εἶναι εὔκολον.

Μία ἐπί πλέον διευκρίνησις ἐπί τοῦ θέματος αὐτοῦ εἶναι ἀπαραίτητος: Ἡ ἀνωτέρω ἀναφερθεῖσα πρώτη κατηγορία τῶν βαπτισθέντων καί συνειδητῶν, μετεχόντων εἰς τήν ζωήν καί τό ἔργον τῆς Ἐκκλησίας δέν εἶναι ὁμοιογενής κατηγορία πιστῶν. Ἐνταῦθα συμπεριλαμβάνονται ἄνθρωποι μέ ὑπερσυντηρητικάς, συντηρητικάς, μετριοπαθεῖς, καί τέλος φιλελευθέρους τοποθετήσεις, μέ σαφῶς διαφοροποιημένας ἐμφάσεις ἤ πνευματικούς προσανατολισμούς εἰς τήν χριστιανικήν των ζωήν. Εἴς τινας περιπτώσεις οἱ ἐν λόγῳ προσανατολισμοί ἐνδέχεται νά προσλαμβάνουν μορφήν μονομεροῦς προσκολλήσεως εἰς ὡρισμένον κύκλον ἰδεῶν, δογματικῶν προτιμήσεων καί ἐμμονῆς εἰς αὐστηρῶς προσδιορισμένους τρόπους δράσεως τῆς Ἐκκλησίας. Ἀπότοκος τῆς τοιαύτης ἐμμονῆς ἐνδέχεται νά εἶναι μία τάσις ἀπομονωτισμοῦ ἔναντι ἑτεροδόξων, ἑτεροπολιτισμικῶν ἤ ἑτεροεθνικῶν ἀνθρωπίνων συνόλων.

Διά τάς ἐνορίας, αἱ ὁποῖαι ἐσχηματίσθησαν ἐκ μεταναστῶν δέον νά προστεθοῦν δύο ἐπί πλέον διαφοροποιήσεις:

(1) Ἡ πρώτη συνδέεται μέ τό φαινόμενον τῶν μεικτῶν γάμων. Αἱ ἐκ τῶν γάμων αὐτῶν προκύπτουσαι οἰκογένειαι διαφέρουν εἰς σημαντικόν βαθμόν τῶν κλασσικῶν οἰκογενειῶν ὁμοδόξων-ὁμοεθνῶν καί ἀπαιτοῦν εἰδικήν ποιμαντικήν μέριμναν.

(2) Ἡ δευτέρα διαφοροποίησις ὀφείλεται εἰς τήν διαφοράν χρόνου καί σταδίου μεταναστεύσεως. Δέν εἶναι ὁμοία ἡ νοοτροπία καί ἡ αὐτοσυνειδησία τοῦ πρωτογενοῦς μετανάστου τοῦ προερχομένου ἐξ ἀγροτικοῦ χωρίου τοῦ τόπου καταγωγῆς του καί τοῦ τρίτης ἤ τετάρτης γενεᾶς ἑλληνοαμερικανοῦ νέου γεννηθέντος καί διαβιοῦντος εἰς πολυάνθρωπον ἀστικόν κέντρον τῶν

Ἡνωμένων Πολιτειῶν. Ἡ ἀπόστασις νοοτροπίας καί ἤθους μεταξύ τῶν ἀνωτέρω εἶναι ἐνίοτε ἀγεφύρωτοι, μέ δυσμενεῖς ἐπιπτώσεις ἐπί τοῦ σκοποῦ καί τοῦ ἔργου τῆς Ἐκκλησίας.

Ὁ ἀληθής σκοπός τῆς Ἐκκλησίας σήμερον ἐν ὄψει τῆς ἰδιότητός της ὡς σώματος τοῦ Χριστοῦ

Ὡς εἶναι ἀναμενόμενον, δέν πρόκειται ἐνταῦθα νά ἐπινοήσωμεν κάποιον σκοπόν ἤ νά προσδιορίσωμεν κάποιον σκοπόν ἐνσωματοῦντες εἰς αὐτόν ὅραμα καί καινοφανεῖς προοπτικάς. Ὁ σκοπός τῆς Ἐκκλησίας ἁπλούστατα εἶναι δεδομένος. Ἔχει δοκιμασθῆ ἐπί εἴκοσι αἰῶνας καί παραμένει ὁρατός καί ψηλαφητός ὡς μακρά ἱστορία καί πολυτιμωτάτη ἐμπειρία ἐν τῷ Οἰκουμενικῷ ἡμῶν Πατριαρχείῳ. Ἔχει δοκιμασθῆ κατά τήν διαδρομήν μακρᾶς καί πολυκυμάντου πορείας ἐν τῇ ἱστορίᾳ, ἔχει ποτισθῆ μέ τό αἷμα ἑκατομμυρίων μαρτύρων, ἔχει ἐπιβεβαιωθῆ μέ ἑκατοντάδας χιλιάδων σελίδων κειμένων ἀποσταγμάτων τῆς εὐλαβείας καί μεγαλοφυΐας τῶν Πατέρων τῆς Ἐκκλησίας, καί ἔχει σφραγισθῆ μέ τήν μαρτυρίαν τῆς ἁγιότητος τῶν εὐγενεστέρων πνευμάτων τῆς ἀνθρωπότητος, δηλαδή τῶν ἁγίων. Ὁ σκοπός τῆς Ἐκκλησίας εἶναι νά συνεχίσῃ ἐν τελείᾳ πληρότητι, ἀπολύτῳ γνησιότητι καί ἀπαραλλάκτῳ ἀκριβείᾳ τό ἔργον καί τήν ἀποστολήν τοῦ θείου ἱδρυτοῦ καί θεμελιωτοῦ της, τοῦ Κυρίου ἡμῶν Χριστοῦ. Κατά μίαν γνωστήν ἔκφρασιν ἡ Ἐκκλησία εἶναι ὁ Κύριος Ἰησοῦς Χριστός παρατεινόμενος εἰς τούς αἰῶνας. Ἑπομένως ἀληθής σκοπός τῆς Ἐκκλησίας ὡς σώματος τοῦ Χριστοῦ μέ κεφαλήν αὐτόν τοῦτον τόν Κύριον εἶναι

Νά σκέπτεται ἐν Χριστῷ
Νά φρονῇ ἐν Χριστῷ
Νά ζῇ ἐν Χριστῷ
Νά ὁμιλῇ ἐν Χριστῷ
Νά δρᾷ ἐν Χριστῷ, καί
Νά διακονῇ τόν ἄνθρωπον καί τόν κόσμον ὡς αὐτός οὗτος ὁ Χριστός.

Ἡ Ἐκκλησία ἐβίωσε τόν σκοπόν αὐτόν ἐν μέσῳ ἑνός κόσμου θλίψεως, ἁμαρτίας, ἀλλά καί ἀναζητήσεως τοῦ Θεοῦ, ἐν τῇ πίστει ὅτι ὁ Κύριος Ἰησοῦς εἶναι μονίμως παρών συμφώνως πρός τήν ρητήν ὑπόσχεσιν Του "*ἰδού ἐγώ μεθ' ὑμῶν εἰμί πάσας τάς ἡμέρας ἕως τῆς συντελείας τοῦ αἰῶνος*" (Ματθ. 28, 20). Καί τόν ἐβίωσε ἔχουσα ἐπίσης τήν διηνεκῆ ἐνοίκησιν καί καθοδήγησιν τοῦ Ἁγίου Πνεύματος ὥστε νά παραμείνῃ ἀνά τούς αἰῶνας σῶμα καί στόμα καί ζῶσα εἰκών καί παρουσία Ἰησοῦ Χριστοῦ εἰς τόν κόσμον. Ἡ Ἐκκλησία, ὡς σύνολον καί ὡς ἐπί μέρους μέλη, ὡς χριστόμορφος ὀντότης, πραγματοποιεῖ τόν ὡς ἄνω σκοπόν ἀκολουθοῦσα ἀπαρεγκλίτως τά βήματα τοῦ ἐνανθρωπίσαντος Θεοῦ καί συνεχίζουσα τό ἔργον Του.

Ἡ Καινή Διαθήκη μᾶς προσφέρει τέσσαρας μείζονας ἀπόψεις, αἱ ὁποῖαι περιγράφουν τό ἔργον αὐτό τοῦ Κυρίου. Ἡ Ἐκκλησία, ὡς συνεχίζουσα ἐν πιστότητι καί γνησιότητι τό ἔργον αὐτό, τό ὁποῖον ἀποτελεῖ καί τόν σκοπόν, προορισμόν καί ἀποστολήν της ἐν τῷ κόσμῳ, διατηρεῖ ἀναλλοίωτον τήν συνείδησιν τῶν τεσσάρων Καινοδιαθηκικῶν ἀπόψεων περί τοῦ ἔργου τοῦ Κυρίου. Ἀξίζει νά παραθέσωμεν τάς Χριστολογικάς αὐτάς ἀπόψεις ἐν ἄκρᾳ συντομίᾳ.

1) Ἡ πρώτη ἄποψις ἀναφέρεται εἰς τό ἔργον τοῦ Κυρίου ὡς ἀποκαλύπτοντος καί διδάσκοντος τήν ἀπόλυτον ἀλήθειαν. Οἱ θεόπνευστοι Εὐαγγελισταί Ματθαῖος

καί Ἰωάννης μᾶς ἔδωκαν ἀνάγλυφον τήν εἰκόνα αὐτήν. Τά μακρά διδακτικά κείμενα τοῦ Ματθαίου ὅπως ἡ ἔξοχος "Ἐπί τοῦ ὄρους Ὁμιλία", προβάλλουν τήν μοναδικότητα τοῦ Ἰησοῦ ὡς διδασκάλου αὐθεντικῶς ἀποκαλύπτοντος τήν ἀλήθειαν. Ὁ δέ Εὐαγγελιστής Ἰωάννης διέσωσε διά τήν Ἐκκλησίαν μίαν μακράν καί μοναδικήν εἰς τά Εὐαγγέλια σειράν λόγων τοῦ Κυρίου, εἰς τούς ὁποίους κυριαρχεῖ ἀκριβῶς ἡ ἔννοια τῆς ἀληθείας ὅπως λ.χ. "*Ἐγώ εἰς τοῦτο γεγέννημαι καί εἰς τοῦτο ἐλήλυθα εἰς τόν κόσμον ἵνα μαρτυρήσω τῇ ἀληθείᾳ*" (Ἰωαν. 18, 37), "*Ἐγώ εἰμί ἡ ὁδός καί ἡ ἀλήθεια καί ἡ ζωή*" (Ἰωαν. 14, 16), "*Ἐγώ τήν ἀλήθειαν λέγω*" (Ἰωάν. 8, 45), καί "*γνώσεσθε τήν ἀλήθειαν καί ἡ ἀλήθεια ἐλευθερώσει ὑμᾶς*" (Ἰωάν. 8, 32).

Ἡ Ἐκκλησία, ὡς συνεχίζουσα τό ἔργον τοῦ Χριστοῦ καί οὖσα τό στόμα αὐτοῦ δέν δύναται νά μή ἔχῃ ὡς πρωταρχικόν σκοπόν τήν ἀδιάκοπον προσφοράν τῆς καθαρᾶς ἀληθείας τῆς ἐν Χριστῷ ἀποκαλυφθείσης.

2) Ἡ δευτέρα μείζων Χριστολογική ἄποψις ἀναφέρεται εἰς τό ἔργον τοῦ Κυρίου ὡς φιλανθρώπου ἰατροῦ, ὡς θεραπευτοῦ τῶν ποικίλων πληγῶν καί τῶν τραυμάτων τῶν ἀνθρώπων. Ὁ ἱερός Εὐαγγελιστής Λουκᾶς, διεζωγράφησε μέ ἀπαράμιλλον τρόπον τήν χριστολογικήν αὐτήν ἄποψιν τοῦ ἔργου τοῦ Κυρίου καί μεταξύ ἄλλων παρέδωκε διά τοῦ Εὐαγγελίου του εἰς τήν Ἐκκλησίαν τόν ὑπέροχον θησαυρόν τῶν παραβολῶν τοῦ καλοῦ Σαμαρείτου καί τοῦ Ἀσώτου (Λουκ. 10, 30-37 καί 15, 11-32). Ἐνταῦθα προβάλλεται μέ ἀνάγλυφον τρόπον ἡ ἀπύθμενος θεραπευτική στοργή τοῦ Ἰησοῦ, τοῦ μονίμως καί ἀενάως ἐπιχέοντος ἔλαιον καί οἶνον (Λουκ. 10, 34) ἐπί τάς πληγάς τῶν ἀνθρώπων, τοῦ "*θεραπεύσαντος πάντας τούς κακῶς ἔχοντας*" (Ματθ. 8, 16) "*ἐπί ἑκάστῳ αὐτῶν τάς χεῖρας ἐπιτιθείς*" (Λουκ. 4, 40). Ἐκφραστικώτατα ὁ Ἀπόστολος Πέτρος εἰς τήν

συγκινητικήν περίπτωσιν τοῦ ἑκατοντάρχου Κορνηλίου, τήν ὁποίαν ὁ εὐαγγελιστής Λουκᾶς περιγράφει εἰς τάς Πράξεις τῶν Ἀποστόλων (Πραξ. 10, 1-48), διεκήρυξεν ὅτι ὁ "*Ἰησοῦς ὁ ἀπό Ναζαρέτ...διῆλθεν εὐεργετῶν καί ἰώμενος πάντας...*" (Πραξ. 10, 38). Ἐντεῦθεν ἐξηγεῖται διατί ὁ Κύριος κατά τήν χαρακτηριστικήν διατύπωσιν τοῦ ἱεροῦ Εὐαγγελιστοῦ Λουκᾶ ἀπέστειλε τούς ἀποστόλους "*κηρύσσειν τήν βασιλείαν τοῦ Θεοῦ καί ἰᾶσθαι τούς ἀσθενοῦντας*" (Λουκ. 9, 2) καί ἔδωκε τήν σαφεστάτην ἐντολήν "*εἰς ἥν δι᾽ ἄν πόλιν εἰσέρχησθε... θεραπεύετε τούς ἐν αὐτῇ ἀσθενεῖς καί λέγετε αὐτοῖς, ἤγγικεν ἐφ᾽ ὑμᾶς ἡ βασιλεία τοῦ Θεοῦ*" (Λουκ. 10, 8-9).

Σκοπός τῆς Ἐκκλησίας ὡς σώματος Χριστοῦ εἶναι ἡ συνέχισις εἰς ὅλα τά πιθανά καί δυνατά ἐπίπεδα τοῦ θεραπευτικοῦ ἔργου τοῦ Κυρίου. Ἡ Ἐκκλησία καί οἱ ἄνθρωποί της ὀφείλουν νά διέρχωνται ὡς Ἐκεῖνος, "*εὐεργετοῦντες καί ἰώμενοι πάντας*" (Πραξ. 10, 38).

3) Ἡ τρίτη μείζων Καινοδιαθηκική Χριστολογική ἄποψις μέ ἀποφασιστικάς συνεπείας διά τόν προσδιορισμόν τοῦ σκοποῦ τῆς Ἐκκλησίας ἀναφέρεται εἰς τό λυτρωτικόν ἔργον τοῦ Κυρίου ὡς σταυρωθέντος καί ἀναστάντος διά τήν σωτηρίαν τῶν ἀνθρώπων. Ὁ ἱερός Εὐαγγελιστής Μᾶρκος καί ὁ Ἀπόστολος Παῦλος ἐστιάζουν ἰδιαιτέρως τήν προσοχήν μας εἰς τό κεντρικόν αὐτό θέμα, τό ὁποῖον καί συνιστᾶ τήν οὐσίαν τοῦ Εὐαγγελίου. Τό μέγιστον τοῦ πόνου καί τοῦ πάθους ἐν ὄψει τῆς ἁμαρτίας καί τοῦ θανάτου ἐν ἀδιακόπῳ συνυπάρξει μέ τό μέγιστον τῆς χαρᾶς καί τῆς δυνάμεως ἐν ὄψει τῆς σωτηρίας καί τῆς ἀναστάσεως, ἀποτελοῦν ὡς γνωστόν σταθερά θέματα τοῦ κατά Μάρκου εὐαγγελίου καί τῶν ἐπιστολῶν τοῦ Παύλου.

Εἶναι χαρακτηριστική, καί βεβαίως ὄχι τυχαία, ἡ προαναγγελία τοῦ πάθους τοῦ σταυροῦ καί τῆς ἀναστάσεώς Του ὑπό τοῦ ἰδίου τοῦ Κυρίου εἰς τρία συνεχόμενα κεφάλαια τοῦ Εὐαγγελίου τοῦ Μάρκου (8, 31, 9, 31 καί 10, 33) μέ κατάληξιν τήν διακήρυξιν ὅτι "*ὁ υἱός τοῦ ἀνθρώπου οὐκ ἦλθε διακονηθῆναι, ἀλλά διακονῆσαι καί δοῦναι τήν ψυχήν αὐτοῦ λύτρον ἀντί πολλῶν*" (Μαρκ. 10, 45). Ὁ δέ Ἀπόστολος Παῦλος προσέφερεν εἰς τήν ἀνά τούς αἰῶνας καί μέχρι συντελείας τοῦ κόσμου ζῶσαν Ἐκκλησίαν ἀναριθμήτους διακηρύξεις τῆς θεμελιώδους αὐτῆς σωτηριολογικῆς πραγματικότητος. Τάς προσέφερεν ὑπό τήν μορφήν παραλλαγῶν τῆς μεγαλειώδους ὑμνολογικῆς ἐκφράσεως τοῦ δευτέρου κεφαλαίου τῆς πρός Φιλιππησίους ἐπιστολῆς (Φιλιπ. 2, 5-11),

> *Τοῦτο γάρ φρονείσθω ἐν ὑμῖν ὅ καί ἐν Χριστῷ Ἰησοῦ, ὅς ἐν μορφῇ Θεοῦ ὑπάρχων οὐχ ἁρπαγμόν ἡγήσατο τό εἶναι ἴσα Θεῷ, ἀλλ' ἑαυτόν ἐκένωσε μορφήν δούλου λαβών, ἐν ὁμοιώματι ἀνθρώπων γενόμενος, καί σχήματι εὑρεθείς ὡς ἄνθρωπος ἐταπείνωσεν ἑαυτόν γενόμενος ὑπήκοος μέχρι θανάτου, θανάτου δέ σταυροῦ. διό καί ὁ Θεός αὐτόν ὑπερύψωσε καί ἐχαρίσατο αὐτῷ ὄνομα τό ὑπέρ πᾶν ὄνομα, ἵνα ἐν τῷ ὀνόματι Ἰησοῦ πᾶν γόνυ κάμψῃ ἐπουρανίων καί ἐπιγείων καί καταχθονίων, καί πᾶσα γλῶσσα ἐξομολογήσηται ὅτι Κύριος Ἰησοῦς Χριστός εἰς δόξαν Θεοῦ πατρός.*

Τάς προσέφερεν ἐπίσης εἰς πολλάς περιπτώσεις ὑπό τήν μορφήν τῆς προσωπικῆς ἐξομολογήσεως τοῦ τρίτου κεφαλαίου τῆς ἰδίας ἐπιστολῆς (Φιλιπ. 3, 10) ὅταν ἀποκαλύπτει τόν βαθύτατον πόθον του "*τόν γνῶναι αὐτόν (δηλ. τόν Χριστόν) καί τήν δύναμιν τῆς ἀναστάσεως αὐτοῦ καί τήν κοινωνίαν τῶν παθημάτων αὐτοῦ.*"

Αὐτή *ἀκριβῶς ἡ γνῶσις καί ἡ κοινωνία καί ἡ* παντί τρόπῳ *καί* σθένει μετάδοσις τῆς ἐμπειρίας τῆς διά τοῦ Σταυροῦ *καί* τῆς Ἀναστάσεως τοῦ Κυρίου σωτηρίας, συνιστᾶ τήν οὐσίαν τοῦ ἔργου τῆς Ἐκκλησίας ἀπ' ἀρχῆς καί μέχρι σήμερον. Καί ἑπομένως προσδιορίζει τόν σκοπόν της καί τόν σκοπόν ζωῆς καί ὑπάρξεως τῶν ἐπί μέρους μελῶν της.

4) Ἡ τετάρτη μείζων Χριστολογική ἄποψις τῆς Καινῆς Διαθήκης ἀναφέρεται εἰς τό ἔργον τοῦ Κυρίου ὡς τοῦ μοναδικοῦ Μεγάλου Ἀρχιερέως. Θαυμάσιος πρός τοῦτο ὁδηγός ὑπῆρξεν ἀνά τούς αἰῶνας ἡ πρός Ἑβραίους Ἐπιστολή, ἡ ὁποία κυρίως εἰς μίαν σειράν ἑπτά κεφαλαίων (Ἑβρ. 4, 14-10, 31) ἀναλύει τό ἔργον τοῦ Χριστοῦ ὡς τοῦ μεγάλου Ἀρχιερέως καί ἡγουμένου τῆς λειτουργικῆς πράξεως καί τῆς ἀδιαλείπτου προσευχῆς. Τῆς λειτουργικῆς πράξεως, ἡ ὁποία οἰκοδομεῖται ἐπί τῆς θεμελειώδους προτάσεως τῆς πρός Ἑβραίους ἐπιστολῆς ὅτι "*οἱ μέν πλείονές εἰσι γεγονότες ἱερεῖς διά τῷ θανάτῳ κωλύεσθαι παραμένειν· ὁ δέ (Ἰησοῦς) διά τό μένειν αὐτόν εἰς τόν αἰῶνα ἀπαράβατον ἔχει τήν ἱερωσύνην· ὅθεν καί σῴζειν εἰς τό παντελές δύναται τούς προσερχομένους δι' αὐτοῦ τῷ Θεῷ, πάντοτε ζῶν εἰς τό ἐντυγχάνειν ὑπέρ αὐτῶν*" (Ἑβρ. 7, 23-25). Ὁ Κύριος Ἰησοῦς ὁ ἐπί τοῦ σταυροῦ προσενέγκας ἑαυτόν ζεῖ εἰς τό ἐντυγχάνειν ὑπέρ ἡμῶν. Ἡ Ἐκκλησία δέν δύναται νά μήν ἔχῃ ὡς σκοπόν τό νά ἀντανακλᾷ γνησίως ἐπί γῆς διά τῆς λατρευτικῆς ζωῆς της, τήν λατρευτικήν πραγματικότητα τῆς ἐν οὐρανοῖς ἀσιγήτου, λυτρωτικῆς μεσιτείας τοῦ ἀμνοῦ καί Λόγου τοῦ Θεοῦ.

Σταχυολόγησις πρακτικῶν συνεπειῶν διά τήν Ἐκκλησίαν ἐκ τῶν ἀνωτέρω Χριστολογικῶν ἀπόψεων

Ἐάν σκοπός τῆς Ἐκκλησίας εἶναι ἡ πλήρης, ἀναλλοίωτος καί γνησία συνέχεια τοῦ ἔργου τοῦ Χριστοῦ ὡς διεγράφη ἀνωτέρω, ἐάν ἡ Ἐκκλησία εἶναι ὁ Ἰησοῦς

Χριστός παρατεινόμενος εἰς τό διηνεκές, "*ὁ χθές καί σήμερον ὁ αὐτός καί εἰς τούς αἰῶνας*" (Ἑβρ. 13, 8), τότε προκύπτουν ἐξ αὐτοῦ σαφεῖς συνέπειαι αἵτινες ὑπαγορεύουν τήν ἀκολουθητέαν πορείαν καί προσδιορίζουν προγραμματισμούς ποικίλης δράσεως. Σημειώνομεν σταχυολογικῶς καί διαγραμματικῶς τέσσαρα σχετικά στοιχεῖα.

1) Τό πρῶτον εἶναι ἡ ἀνάγκη πραγματοποιήσεως τοῦ σκοποῦ τῆς Ἐκκλησίας νά εἶναι τό στόμα τοῦ Χριστοῦ ὡς στόμα διακηρύξεως καί μεταδόσεως τῆς ἐκ Θεοῦ ἀποκαλυφθείσης ἀπολύτου καί ἀναλλοιώτου ἀληθείας. Ἐπιτρέψατέ μοι εἰς τό σημεῖον αὐτό νά τολμήσω μίαν μεταφοράν εἰς τήν ὅλην Ἐκκλησίαν σταχυολογημένων φράσεων ἐκ τῶν Στιχηρῶν τῶν Αἴνων τῆς Κυριακῆς τῶν Ἁγίων Πατέρων τῆς Α' ἐν Νικαίᾳ Οἰκουμενικῆς Συνόδου. Ἡ ἐπικαιρότης τῆς μεταφορᾶς εἶναι προφανής: "Ὅλην συγκροτήσασα τήν τῆς ψυχῆς ἐπιστήμην καί τῷ θείῳ Πνεύματι συνδιασκεψαμένη," καί "ὅλην εἰσδεξαμένη τήν νοητήν λαμπηδόνα τοῦ Ἁγίου Πνεύματος," ἔτι δέ "ταῖς τῶν Ἀποστόλων ἑπομένη προδήλως διδαχαῖς" ἡ Ἐκκλησία "ὡς Χριστοκῆρυξ" καί ὡς "πάγχρυσον στόμα τοῦ Λόγου," "Εὐαγγελικῶν προϊσταμένη δογμάτων ἡ μακαρία, καί τῶν εὐσεβῶν παραδόσεων ἄνωθεν λαβοῦσα τήν τούτων ἀποκάλυψιν σαφῶς, καί φωτισθεῖσα, θεοπνεύστως ἀπεφθέγξατο" καί "ἐξέθετο ὅρους θεοδιδάκτους."

Ἡ Ἐκκλησία ἔχει ὡς σκοπόν νά ὁμιλῇ θεοπνεύστως καταθέτουσα εἰς τόν κόσμον τήν θεοδίδακτον ἀλήθειαν τήν ὁποίαν ἔλαβεν ἄνωθεν, ἑπομένη ταῖς διδαχαῖς τῶν ἀποστόλων καί προϊσταμένη τῶν εὐσεβῶν παραδόσεων. Καί πρέπει νά πραγματοποιῇ τό ἔργον αὐτό ἀφ' ἑνός μέν "ὅλην συγκροτήσασα τήν τῆς ψυχῆς ἐπιστήμην" δηλαδή προσφέρουσα ἀνθρωπίνως τό μέγιστον τῶν διανοητικῶν της δυνάμεων τῆς ἐπιστήμης καί τῆς σοφίας. Ἀφ’ ἑτέρου δέ νά εὑρίσκεται συνεχῶς καί ἀδιακόπως συνδιασκεπτομένη τῷ Ἁγίῳ Πνεύματι καί εἰσδεχομένη ὅλην τήν νοητήν λαμπηδόνα Αὐτοῦ, δηλαδή νά εὑρίσκεται εἰς κατάστασιν τοῦ μεγίστου τῆς δεκτικότητος ἐν ἀποδοχῇ τῆς διδακτικῆς καί φωτιστικῆς ἐνεργείας τοῦ Ἁγίου Πνεύματος, τοῦ Παρακλήτου ὁ Ὁποῖος κατά τήν διαβεβαίωσιν τοῦ Κυρίου εἶναι “*τό Πνεῦμα τῆς ἀληθείας*” ὁδηγοῦν “*εἰς πᾶσαν τήν ἀλήθειαν*” (Ἰωάν. 16, 13).

Εἴμεθα πιστοί καί ἀδιάλλακτοι εἰς τήν γραμμήν αὐτήν ὡς ἄνθρωποι τῆς Ἐκκλησίας καί ὡς ἔχοντες τήν μεγίστην καί ἱερωτάτην εὐθύνην τῆς διαφυλάξεως καί μεταδόσεως τῆς ἀπολύτου ἀληθείας τῆς ἐν Χριστῷ ἀποκαλυφθείσης; Ποῦ ἀκριβῶς εὑρίσκεται τό κήρυγμά μας, ἡ κατήχησίς μας, καί ἡ ἀδιάκοπος προσφορά ὀρθοδόξου διδαχῆς; Πόσην σημασίαν ἔχομεν ἀποδώσει εἰς τήν διάδοσιν τῆς Ὀρθοδόξου πίστεώς μας, μιᾶς μοναδικῆς πίστεως ταυτιζομένης μέ τό Εὐαγγέλιον καί τήν ἀποστολικήν παράδοσιν, δι’ ὅλων τῶν σήμερον προσφερομένων μέσων καί δυνατοτήτων ἐπικοινωνίας; Τί κάνομεν πρός ἀντιμετώπισιν τῶν ποικίλων ἀντιχριστιανικῶν καί ἀντιορθοδόξων εἰσβολέων εἰς τόν χῶρον τοῦ Διαδικτύου, τοῦ Internet, καί τῶν ἱστοσελίδων (web sites); Εἰς ποῖον ἐπίπεδον ταυτίσεως μέ τήν ἀλήθειαν τοῦ Εὐαγγελίου εὑρίσκεται ὁ ἔντυπος λόγος μας;

Τό περασμένον ἔτος πλησίον τῆς πόλεως τοῦ Los Angeles ἤρχισε νά λειτουργῇ ἕνα τεράστιον πανεπιστημιακόν συγκρότημα μέ 100 φοιτητάς, ἀλλά μέ προοπτικήν 10.000 φοιτητάς. Ἐκτίσθη ὑπό μιᾶς ὁμάδος κάποιας θρησκευτικῆς παραφυάδος ἐξ Ἰαπωνίας, ἐστοίχισε 300 ἑκατομμύρια δολλάρια καί ἐδημιουργήθη μέ ἀποκλειστικόν σκοπόν τήν διάδοσιν τῆς “θρησκευτικῆς ἀληθείας” τῆς ὁμάδος αὐτῆς. Ἀνά πᾶσαν ὥραν ἀναφύονται ἐν Ἀμερικῇ διά νά περιορισθῶ εἰς περιοχήν τήν ὁποίαν γνωρίζω, κέντρα διαδόσεως τῆς "ἀληθείας" τοῦ Ἰσλάμ. Ποῖος εἶναι ὁ ἀπολογισμός μας ἀπό πλευρᾶς πάθους, ζήλου καί ἐφευρετικότητος εἰς προσπαθείας δημιουργίας κέντρων προβολῆς τῆς ἀληθείας τῆς πίστεως; Τί ἀποτέλεσμα προκύπτει ἀπό τήν σύγκρισίν μας μέ τούς ποικίλους ἑτεροθρήσκους ἤ καί ἀθρήσκους εἰς τό ζήτημα αὐτό;

Πιθανῶς θεωροῦμεν ὡς δεδομένον καί ἐφησυχάζομεν μέ τήν πεποίθησιν ὅτι ἡ ἀλήθεια τῆς πίστεώς μας εἶναι ἀκατανίκητος καί τελικῶς ἐπικρατεῖ. Εἶναι ὅμως ἔτσι; Μήπως πρέπει νά ἐνθυμηθῶμεν τό φοβερόν ἐρώτημα τοῦ Κυρίου; "*Πλήν, ὁ υἱός τοῦ ἀνθρώπου ἐλθών ἆρα εὑρήσει τήν πίστιν ἐπί τῆς γῆς;*" (Λουκ. 18, 8). Τό ἐρώτημα προβάλλει τό τρομακτικόν ἐνδεχόμενον μιᾶς πλήρους ἐκλείψεως τῆς πίστεως ἐκ τοῦ πλανήτου γῆ. Οὐαί τοῖς ὑπευθύνοις δι' οἱανδήποτε μείωσιν, σχετικοποίησιν, καί, ὅ μή γένοιτο, ἔκλειψιν τῆς ἀληθείας τῆς πίστεως ἐκ τοῦ κόσμου μας.

2) Τό δεύτερον στοιχεῖον σχετίζεται μέ τόν σκοπόν τῆς Ἐκκλησίας νά εἶναι ἡ ζῶσα συνέχεια τῆς διακονίας τοῦ Κυρίου, τῆς θεραπευτικῆς τῶν ψυχικῶν καί σωματικῶν τραυμάτων καί πληγῶν τῶν ἀνθρώπων.

Ἐκεῖνος ὑπῆρξεν ὁ διακονῶν Θεός, ὁ Ὁποῖος ἐδήλωσεν ὅτι "*ἐγώ δέ ἐν μέσῳ ὑμῶν εἰμι ὡς ὁ διακονῶν*" (Λουκ. 22, 27) καί "*διῆλθεν εὐεργετῶν καί ἰώμενος*" (Πραξ. 10, 38). Ἀποτελεῖ γεγονός τεραστίας σημασίας διά τήν Ἐκκλησίαν, ἀπό πλευρᾶς σκοποῦ καί ἀποστολῆς, ἡ θεμελιώδης καί προγραμματική ἐντολή τοῦ Κυρίου πρός τούς ἀποστόλους: "*Πορευόμενοι δέ κηρύσσετε λέγοντες ὅτι ἤγγικεν ἡ βασιλεία τῶν οὐρανῶν. Ἀσθενοῦντας θεραπεύετε, νεκρούς ἐγείρετε, λεπρούς καθαρίζετε, δαιμόνια ἐκβάλλετε· δωρεάν ἐλάβατε, δωρεάς δότε*" (Ματθ. 10, 8). Τό κήρυγμα-ἀναγγελία τῆς βασιλείας τῶν οὐρανῶν συνοδεύεται ἀπαραιτήτως ἀπό διακονίαν θεραπευτικήν ψυχῶν καί σωμάτων, διακονίαν ἡ ὁποία καλύπτει εὐρύτατον φάσμα ἀνθρωπίνων καταστάσεων αἵτινες ἀπαιτοῦν συμπαράστασιν, προστασίαν, ὑποστήριξιν, παράκλησιν, ἴασιν. Εἰς τόν σύγχρονον κόσμον ἡ σπουδαιότης τῆς παρουσίας τῆς Ἐκκλησίας ὡς διακονούσης πραγματικότητος εἶναι τεραστία λόγῳ τοῦ τρομακτικοῦ ἀριθμοῦ καί τῆς ἀπιθάνου διαφοροποιήσεως περιπτώσεων ἐπειγουσῶν ἀνθρωπίνων ἀναγκῶν. Ἡ Ἐκκλησία δέν δύναται νά κηρύττῃ τό Εὐαγγέλιον τῆς Βασιλείας τοῦ Θεοῦ ὡς ὁ Κύριος ἐάν συγχρόνως δέν ζῇ πολιτεύεται καί διέρχεται, ἐν μέσῳ τοῦ κόσμου εὐεργετοῦσα, ἰωμένη καί διακονοῦσα ὡς Ἐκεῖνος.

Ποῦ εὑρισκόμεθα εἰς τό σημεῖον αὐτό ὡς Ἐκκλησία σήμερον; Ἀσφαλῶς γίνονται πολλά καί μάλιστα ἀξιοθαύμαστα εἰς πολλάς περιοχάς. Τό ἐρώτημα ὅμως εἶναι: Πόσον δυναμικόν εἶναι τό ἔργον τῆς Ἐκκλησίας καί εἰς πόσον βαθμόν συνυφασμένον μέ τό κηρυκτικόν της ἔργον; Ἡ διακονία τοῦ Κυρίου συνεδύαζε ἀνά πᾶν βῆμα κήρυγμα καί ἰάσεις, λόγον καί θεραπευτικήν τῶν ἀναγκῶν διακονίαν. Ἀποτελεῖ αὐτό συνείδησιν τῶν πιστῶν μας; Καί πῶς συμβαίνει εἰς πολλάς περιπτώσεις ἡ Ἐκκλησία ὡς διακονῶν ὀργανισμός νά περιορίζεται εἰς τήν λεγομένην φιλανθρωπίαν ὑπό τήν στενήν ἔννοιαν τοῦ ὅρου καί δή πραγματοποιουμένην κυρίως ὑπό γυναικῶν διά τῶν Φιλοπτώχων Ἀδελφοτήτων;

Τό ζήτημα δέν εἶναι ἁπλῶς νά αὐξήσωμεν ὡς σύνολον ἐκκλησιαστικόν καί ὡς ἐπί μέρους πιστοί τήν φιλανθρωπικήν μας δραστηριότητα. Τό ζήτημα εἶναι νά καταστήσωμεν τήν παντοειδῆ θεραπευτικήν διακονίαν τῆς Ἐκκλησίας ἀναπόσπαστον καί ζωτικήν συνιστῶσαν τῆς συνειδήσεώς της καί τοῦ ἔργου της. Τό ζήτημα εἶναι νά ἐμφυσήσωμεν εἰς τούς πιστούς μας τό πνεῦμα τῆς διακονίας ὡς θεμελιώδους χαρακτηριστικοῦ τοῦ ὀρθοδόξου ἤθους, τῆς γνησίας χριστιανικῆς προσωπικότητος, καί τῆς ὁλοκληρωμένης χριστιανικῆς ζωῆς. Ἐνταῦθα ἀπαιτεῖται συστηματική ἀγωγή, δημιουργία συναφῶν μορφωτικῶν εὐκαιριῶν, καλλιέργεια πνεύματος πρωτοβουλίας δι' ἔργα ἀγάπης καί προνοίας.

3) Τό τρίτον στοιχεῖον τοῦ σκοποῦ τῆς Ἐκκλησίας ὡς πραγματικοῦ σώματος Χριστοῦ, εἶναι ἡ βίωσις καί συνεχής προβολή τῆς θεμελιώδους Χριστολογικῆς πίστεως εἰς Ἰησοῦν Χριστόν σταυρωθέντα καί ἀναστάντα. Ἐάν ἡ Ἐκκλησία εἶναι ὁ Χριστός παρατεινόμενος εἰς τούς αἰῶνας ὡς ζῶσα, ψηλαφητή πραγματικότης, τότε ἡ Ἐκκλησία αὐτή πρέπει νά μεταγγίζῃ διά παντός τρόπου καί μέσου Σταυρόν καί Ἀνάστασιν. Αὐτό σημαίνει ἔντονον συνείδησιν μετοχῆς εἰς τήν λυτρωτικήν διαδικασίαν, τήν ἀπελευθέρωσιν ἀπό τήν ἐνοχήν καί τήν ἁμαρτίαν τήν πραγματοποιηθεῖσαν ἐν τῷ Σταυρῷ. Αὐτό ἐπίσης σημαίνει συνείδησιν τῆς ὑπερβάσεως τῆς φθορᾶς καί τοῦ θανάτου διά τῆς Ἀναστάσεως.

Ἡ κεντρική καί ἀποφασιστική σημασία τῆς συμβιώσεως καί συμπορείας μέ τόν παθόντα καί ἐκ νεκρῶν ἐγερθέντα Κύριον, ἐμφανίζεται κατά ὑπέροχον τρόπον εἰς τήν λειτουργικήν ζωήν τῆς Ἐκκλησίας. Τό φαινόμενον δέν εἶναι τυχαῖον. Δέν ὑπάρχει ἐκκλησιαστική ἀκολουθία εἰς τήν ὁποίαν νά μή γίνεται ἀναφορά εἰς τόν Σταυρόν καί τήν Ἀνάστασιν, διά νά μή ἀναφερθῶμεν εἰς τόν εἰκονογραφικόν, τόν διακοσμητικόν καί τόν ἀρχιτεκτονικόν χῶρον ἔνθα ὀπτικῶς ἡ κυριαρχία τοῦ Σταυροῦ εἶναι πρόδηλος. Ἡ ἰδία κυριαρχία εἶναι ἐπίσης προφανής εἰς τήν συνεχῆ χρῆσιν τοῦ σημείου τοῦ Σταυροῦ. Καί βεβαίως δέν εἶναι καθόλου τυχαῖον τό γεγονός ὅτι ἀπό τῶν ἀρχαϊκῶν ἁπλῶν συμβόλων πίστεως μέχρι τοῦ ὑπερόχου συμβόλου πίστεως Νικαίας-Κωνσταντινουπόλεως ἡ ὁμολογία "Κύριος Ἰησοῦς Χριστός σταυρωθείς καί ἀναστάς" ἀποτελεῖ θεμελιώδη διακήρυξιν πίστεως. Πέραν ὅμως τούτου τό ἐρώτημα εἶναι κατά πόσον οἱ πιστοί μας ζοῦν ἐκτός τῶν ἀκολουθιῶν τήν ἄρρητον χαράν τοῦ γεγονότος τοῦ Σταυροῦ καί τῆς Ἀναστάσεως. Τό ἐρώτημα εἶναι κατά πόσον ἡ προσοχή μας ὡς Ἐκκλησία ἑστιάζεται εἰς τό μοναδικόν αὐτό Χριστολογικόν γεγονός τό ὁποῖον ἀποτελεῖ τό κέντρον καί τήν οὐσίαν τῆς Ὀρθοδόξου πίστεως.

Ἐδῶ καί πάλιν πρέπει νά τονισθῇ ἡ ἀνάγκη συστηματικῆς διδαχῆς ἐπί τοῦ ζωτικοῦ αὐτοῦ θέματος Ὀρθοδόξου πίστεως. Ἴσως ἐνίοτε ἤ καί συχνάκις νά προβάλλεται ἡ ἀντίρρησις ὅτι "αὐτά εἶναι δογματικά θέματα, τά ὁποῖα εἶναι μᾶλλον θεωρητικά καί δέν ἀπασχολοῦν τόν σύγχρονον ἄνθρωπον." Εἶναι θεωρητικόν θέμα ἡ ἁμαρτία, ἡ ἐνοχή, ἡ ἀνθρωπίνη ἀποτυχία, ἡ δουλεία τοῦ κακοῦ καί τῆς φθορᾶς, ὁ θάνατος; Εἶναι δογματικόν θέμα ἡ ἐλευθερία καί ἡ λύτρωσις ἀπό τό ἄγχος τῆς ἁμαρτίας καί τῆς ἐγκοσμίου αἰχμαλωσίας καί ἡ βίωσις τῆς εἰρήνης τοῦ Θεοῦ, τῆς πάντα νοῦν ὑπερεχούσης (Φιλιπ. 4, 7), καί τῆς ἀφάτου χαρᾶς τῆς μετ' Αὐτοῦ κοινωνίας καί τῆς τελικῆς ἀναστάσεως; Δέν θά ἔπρεπε καί ἐνταῦθα νά ἀκολουθήσωμεν πιστῶς τούς μεγάλους Πατέρας τῆς Ἐκκλησίας μας, οἱ ὁποῖοι δέν ἔπαυσαν οὐδ' ἐπί στιγμήν νά ὁμιλοῦν καί νά ἀναλύουν ἀπό πάσης ἀπόψεως τήν πρωταρχικήν ἀλήθειαν τῆς ἐν Χριστῷ σωτηρίας διά τοῦ Σταυροῦ καί τῆς Ἀναστάσεως;

4) Τό τέταρτον στοιχεῖον τοῦ σκοποῦ τῆς Ἐκκλησίας σήμερον, ἀναφέρεται εἰς τήν λατρευτικήν προσφοράν. Εἴμεθα ὡς Ἐκκλησία ἡ συνεχής καί ζῶσα παρουσία τοῦ Χριστοῦ ὡς τοῦ μεγάλου Ἀρχιερέως. Κατ' οὐσίαν εἰς πᾶσαν λατρευτικήν σύναξιν Ἐκεῖνος εἶναι ὁ Λειτουργός, ὁ προσφέρων καί προσφερόμενος, ὁ ἀεί μεσιτεύων καί ἡγούμενος τῶν εὐχῶν καί δεήσεων ἡμῶν. Ἐντεῦθεν καί ἡ μοναδική σπουδαιότης τῆς λατρευτικῆς μας ζωῆς.

Τό κύριον αἴτημα ἐν προκειμένῳ δέν εἶναι ἁπλῶς νά προσφέρωμεν μίαν λογικήν καί εὐάρεστον λατρείαν, προσκυνοῦντες τόν ἐν Τριάδι Θεόν ἐν πνεύματι καί ἀληθείᾳ (Ἰωάν. 4, 24). Τό κύριον αἴτημα ἐνταῦθα εἶναι νά ἀναπτύξωμεν καί ἐμπεδώσωμεν τήν συνείδησιν ὅτι ἐν ἑκάστῃ λατρευτικῇ εὐκαιρίᾳ λειτουργοῦμεν ὡς συμπαριστάμενοι τῷ μοναδικῷ Ἀρχιερεῖ Ἰησοῦ Χριστῷ, ὅτι τελοῦμεν ἐπί γῆς ὅ,τι Ἐκεῖνος τελεῖ ἐν οὐρανῷ μεσιτεύοντες ὑπέρ παντός τοῦ κόσμου.

Ἡ ἰσχυρά συνείδησις τῆς Ἐκκλησίας ὅτι προσευχομένη καί λειτουργῶσα λειτουργεῖ ἐν κόσμῳ ὡς ὁ Χριστός θά βοηθήσῃ εἰς λύσιν πολλῶν λειτουργικῶν προβλημάτων διότι θά προσφέρῃ ὄντως ἐξόχους προοπτικάς τῆς λατρείας ὡς κέντρου ἀποκαλύψεως τοῦ μυστηρίου τοῦ ἐν Τριάδι προσκυνητοῦ Θεοῦ καί τῆς ἀρρήτου ἑνώσεως μετ᾽ αὐτοῦ. Δέν πρέπει νά λησμονῆται ὅτι τόσον ἐν τῇ ἱστορίᾳ ὅσον καί ἐν τῷ παρόντι, πλῆθος μεταστροφῶν καί ἀποδοχῆς τῆς Ὀρθοδόξου πίστεως συνέβησαν ἐν συναρτήσει πρός ἐμπειρίας συνδεομένας μέ παρακολούθησιν λατρευτικῶν ἐκδηλώσεων ἐν τῇ Ἐκκλησίᾳ. Ὁ μοναδικός ὄντως καί ἱερώτατος Ναός τῆς τοῦ Θεοῦ Σοφίας ἐν τῷ Οἰκουμενικῷ Πατριαρχείῳ ὑπῆρξε κατ᾽ ἐξοχήν ὁ χῶρος ἐντυπωσιακῶν μεταστροφῶν καί προσχωρήσεων εἰς τήν Ὀρθοδοξίαν ἐπί μακρούς αἰῶνας.

Ἐνταῦθα δέον νά ὑπογραμμισθοῦν δύο ζωτικά θέματα. Τό πρῶτον εἶναι ἡ ἀνάγκη μεθοδικῆς καί ὁλοπλεύρου λειτουργικῆς ἀγωγῆς τόσον διά τά παιδιά καί τούς νέους ὅσον καί διά τούς ὡρίμους. Εἶναι καιρός νά παύσωμεν νά θεωρῶμεν ὡς δεδομένον ὅτι τό πλῆθος τῶν ἐκκλησιαζομένων ἔχει τήν ἀπαιτουμένην λειτουργικήν γνῶσιν. Ἡ ἐν γνώσει καί συνειδήσει συμμετοχή εἰς τήν λειτουργικήν ζωήν ἀποτελεῖ ἕν ἐκ τῶν ὧν οὐκ ἄνευ συστατικῶν τοῦ ὀρθοδόξου ἤθους καί ἀληθοῦς χριστιανικοῦ φρονήματος. Ἀλλά δέν δημουργεῖται χωρίς ἐπίμονον καί οὐσιαστικήν λειτουργικήν ἀγωγήν.

Τό δεύτερον συναφές ζωτικόν θέμα εἶναι ἡ ἀναγκαιότης δημιουργίας καί διατηρήσεως συνθηκῶν λατρείας, αἱ ὁποῖαι βοηθοῦν εἰς ἀνάπτυξιν ἀνθηρᾶς λειτουργικῆς ζωῆς. Τό θέμα εἶναι πολυσύνθετον καί περιλαμβάνει ζητήματα ἀρχιτεκτονικῆς, εἰκονογραφίας, ἀκουστικῆς, μουσικῆς, γλώσσης, χρόνου τελετουργιῶν κ.ο.κ., καί ἀξίζει νά εὑρίσκεται πάντοτε εἰς τήν πρώτην γραμμήν ἐνδιαφέροντος τῶν Ἐνοριῶν μας.

Συμπερασματικαί τινες παρατηρήσεις

Τά μέχρι τοῦδε ἐκτεθέντα ὁδηγοῦν εἰς ὡρισμένα συμπεράσματα, ἐνδεχομένως βοηθητικά εἰς τόν προγραμματισμόν τοῦ ἀμέσου ἔργου μας. Ἐπιτρέψατέ μοι νά ὑπομνήσω ἐν συνόψει τινά ἐξ αὐτῶν.

1) Ὁ σκοπός τῆς Ἐκκλησίας καί τῆς χριστιανικῆς ζωῆς, παρά τήν μακράν ζωήν καί ἱστορικήν συνέχειαν ἐν τῷ βίῳ τῶν ἐνοριῶν μας, δέν εἶναι πάντοτε σαφής οὔτε ἐπαρκῶς γνωστός ἐν τῇ θαυμαστῇ πληρότητί του. Ὑπάρχει ζωτική καί ἄμεσος ἀνάγκη κατά Χριστόν παιδείας καί μορφώσεως τῶν πιστῶν μας. Ἡ ἐργασία κατηχήσεως μεταξύ τῶν παιδιῶν πρέπει νά ἐπεκταθῇ καί εἰς τούς ὡρίμους. Πρέπει νά γίνῃ μέλημα τοῦ ποιμαντικοῦ καί ἐκπαιδευτικοῦ ἔργου μας εἰς ἐπίπεδον κατ' ἀρχήν ἐνορίας καί περαιτέρω ἐπισκοπῆς.

2) Ὁ σκοπός τῆς Ἐκκλησίας τόσον καθ' ἑαυτήν ὅσον καί ὡς πρός τό πλήρωμά της εἶναι ἡ βίωσις, συνέχεια καί προβολή τοῦ ἔργου τοῦ Κυρίου (1) ὡς τοῦ Διδασκάλου τῆς ἀπολύτου ἀληθείας, (2) ὡς τοῦ διακονοῦντος Θεοῦ, τοῦ θεραπεύοντος τάς πληγάς καί τά τραύματα τῶν ἀνθρώπων, (3) ὡς τοῦ μεγάλου

Ἀρχιερέως τοῦ ἐν οὐρανοῖς ἀενάως μεσιτεύοντος ὑπέρ ἡμῶν, καί (4) ὡς τοῦ Σταυρωθέντος καί Ἀναστάντος ὑπέρ τῆς σωτηρίας τοῦ κόσμου Κυρίου. Εἶναι φανερόν ὅτι ἐνταῦθα γίνεται ἀναφορά εἰς τήν δογματικήν ἀλήθειαν τῆς πίστεως, εἰς τήν ποιμαντικήν δρᾶσιν τῆς Ἐκκλησίας εἰς τήν λατρευτικήν πρᾶξιν της καί τέλος εἰς τήν πίστιν τῆς Ἐκκλησίας εἰς τόν Σταυρωθέντα καί Ἀναστάντα Κύριον Ἰησοῦν Χριστόν, τόν χορηγόν τῆς σωτηρίας καί τοῦ ἁγιασμοῦ.

Ἡ Ἐκκλησία, ὡς συνέβη ἀνά τούς αἰῶνας, ὀφείλει νά καλλιεργῇ ἐν ἰσορροπίᾳ τά ἀνωτέρω βασικά δομικά στοιχεῖα τοῦ ἀληθοῦς ὀρθοδόξου ἤθους. Μονομερεῖς τονισμοί καί ἀπολυτοποιημέναι ἑστιάσεις εἴτε εἰς δογματικά θέματα, εἴτε εἰς ποιμαντικάς δραστηριότητας, εἴτε εἰς λειτουργικά ζητήματα, ὁδηγοῦν εἰς ἀνισορροπίας καί εἰς ἀπώλειαν τοῦ πολυτιμωτάτου χαρακτηριστικοῦ τοῦ ὀρθοδόξου ἤθους, τό ὁποῖον εἶναι ἡ ὁλοκληρία, ἡ ἁρμονία τῶν μερῶν, ἡ διατήρησις τῆς ἀκεραιότητος ὅλων τῶν πλευρῶν ὥστε, κατά τόν Ἀπόστολον Παῦλον, νά "*παραστήσωμεν πάντα ἄνθρωπον τέλειον ἐν Χριστῷ*" (Κολοσ. 1, 28), "*ἵνα ἄρτιος ᾖ ὁ τοῦ Θεοῦ ἄνθρωπος πρός πᾶν ἔργον ἀγαθόν ἐξηρτισμένος*" (2 Τιμοθ. 3, 17). Ἐάν δέν γίνῃ αὐτό τότε θά ἐξακολουθήσωμε νά ἔχωμε τό φαινόμενον τῶν θρησκευτικῶν ἀκροτήτων μέ ὑπερτονισμούς ὡρισμένων πλευρῶν καί παραγκονίσεις ἄλλων, μέ φανατισμούς καί ἀνοικείους προσκολλήσεις εἰς πρόσωπα καί ἰδέας ἐπί βλάβῃ τῆς ἀκεραιότητος τοῦ ὀρθοδόξου ἤθους καί σαφεῖ μειώσει τῆς πίστεως.

Ἀποτελεῖ πολύ μεγάλην εὐλογίαν τό γεγονός ὅτι ἀνήκομεν εἰς τό Οἰκουμενικόν Πατριαρχεῖον, τό ὁποῖον ἐπί μακρούς αἰῶνας καί μέχρι σήμερον διέδωσε καί ἐπιμελῶς ἐκαλλιέργησε τόν πολυτιμώτατον θησαυρόν τῆς δημιουργίας ἑνός προτύπου Ὀρθοδόξου χριστιανικοῦ ἤθους. Ἑνός προτύπου τό ὁποῖον ἐμφανίζει ἰσόρροπον ἀνάπτυξιν ὅλων τῶν πλευρῶν, ἀκεραιότητα πίστεως καί πράξεως, ἔντονον ἐνδοεκκλησιαστικήν καλλιέργειαν ἀλλά καί ἄνοιγμα μαρτυρίας πρός ὁλόκληρον τόν κόσμον.

Αὐτό τό πάνσεπτον Πατριαρχεῖον ἔζησε μετά πρωτοφανοῦς προσηλώσεως καί ἐμμονῆς τόν σκοπόν τῆς Ἐκκλησίας καί τήν οὐσίαν τοῦ Ὀρθοδόξου χριστιανικοῦ ἤθους ὡς διακηρύξεως τῆς ἀνοθεύτου καί ἀκριβοῦς ἀληθείας τῆς ἀποκαλυφθείσης ἐν Χριστῷ Ἰησοῦ καί σφραγισθείσης διά τοῦ Τιμίου Αὐτοῦ Αἵματος.

Αὐτό τό πάνσεπτον Πατριαρχεῖον τῆς Κωνσταντινουπόλεως, τῆς Βασιλίδος τῶν πόλεων, ἐβίωσεν ἐν συγκλονιστικῇ ἀφοσιώσει καί δημιουργικῇ πρωτοτυπίᾳ τόν σκοπόν τῆς Ἐκκλησίας καί τῆς χριστιανικῆς ζωῆς ὡς θεραπευτικῆς τῶν ἀνθρωπίνων πληγῶν καί τραυμάτων διακονίας τοῦ σαρκωθέντος Υἱοῦ καί Λόγου τοῦ Θεοῦ.

Αὐτό τό ἱερώτατον καί παγκόσμιον Κέντρον τῆς Ὀρθοδοξίας ἐν Κωνσταντινουπόλει ἐπραγματοποίησε κατά ἀριστουργηματικόν τρόπον τόν σκοπόν τῆς Ἐκκλησίας ὡς λειτουργούσης ἐν πνεύματι καί ἀληθείᾳ μετά τοῦ μεγάλου Ἀρχιερέως Ἰησοῦ Χριστοῦ. Οὕτω ἐδημιούργησε μίαν ἔξοχον λειτουργικήν παράδοσιν εἰς λατρείαν τοῦ ἐν Τριάδι προσκυνητοῦ Θεοῦ καί εἰς οὐσιαστικήν λειτουργικήν οἰκοδομήν τῶν πιστῶν.

Αὐτό τό Οἰκουμενικόν Πατριαρχεῖον ἐβίωσε διά τῆς συνεχοῦς προσφορᾶς, κόπου, πόνου καί θυσιῶν τόν σκοπόν τῆς Ἐκκλησίας ὡς παγκοσμίου μαρτυρίας τοῦ Σταυροῦ καί τῆς Ἀναστάσεως καί ὡς κιβωτοῦ τῆς ἐν Χριστῷ σωτηρίας δι' ὁλόκληρον τόν κόσμον, διά τήν κτίσιν πᾶσαν.

Τό σπουδαῖον εἶναι ὅτι τό Πατριαρχεῖον συνεδύασε τά ἀνωτέρω τέσσαρα στοιχεῖα ὡς ἐν ἁρμονίᾳ συνιστώσας τοῦ σκοποῦ τῆς Ἐκκλησίας καί τοῦ προτύπου καί γνησίου ὀρθοδόξου ἤθους. Μέ τόν τρόπον αὐτόν κατέθεσεν εἰς τήν παγκόσμιον ὀρθόδοξον κοινότητα ἕνα ὄντως πολυτιμώτατον καί ἀναντικατάστατον γνώμονα διακριβώσεως καί ἐκτιμήσεως τοῦ βαθμοῦ προσεγγίσεως τοῦ ὀρθοδόξου ἤθους καί τῆς χριστιανικῆς ἐν γένει ζωῆς πρός τό ἀπόλυτον πρότυπον καί μέτρον, δηλ. πρός τό "*μέτρον ἡλικίας τοῦ πληρώματος τοῦ Χριστοῦ*" (Ἐφεσ. 4, 13).

3) Τρίτον, δέον ὅπως κατανοηθῇ ὅτι σκοπός τῆς Ἐκκλησίας ὡς συνεχοῦς παρουσίας τοῦ Χριστοῦ εἶναι νά ἀποτελῇ κέντρον μεταμορφώσεως. Κατ' οὐσίαν τό Εὐαγγέλιον εἶναι παράγων συνεχοῦς ἀλλαγῆς: "Μετανοεῖτε" εἶναι ἡ λέξις ἐκφράζουσα τήν οὐσίαν τῆς ἀνθρωπίνης στάσεως ἔναντι τοῦ Εὐαγγελίου. Ἡ Ἐκκλησία δέν εἶναι χῶρος ἀδρανείας καί στασιμότητος. Ἡ οὐσία της καί ἡ παράδοσίς της εἶναι συνεχής ζωή δυναμισμοῦ καί μεταμορφώσεως. Ὁ σκοπός αὐτός ἦτο, εἶναι καί θά παραμείνῃ εἰς τό κέντρον τῆς ζωῆς της καί τῆς δράσεώς της. Ὁ σκοπός αὐτός θά πρέπει νά διαμορφώνῃ τά προγράμματα ζωῆς καί δράσεως τῆς Ἐκκλησίας.

4) Τό ἔργον τῆς Ἐκκλησίας μας, τόσον τοπικῶς ὅσον καί παγκοσμίως ὑπό τήν σοφήν καί πνευματέμφορον ἡγεσίαν τοῦ Οἰκουμενικοῦ ἡμῶν Πατριαρχείου, ὑπῆρξε ἀνέκαθεν, ἀλλά εἶναι πολύ περισσότερον σήμερον, ἔργον ἐξαιρετικῆς σπουδαιότητος, ἰδίως ἀπό πλευρᾶς μαρτυρίας τῆς Ὀρθοδόξου πίστεως. Ἡ σπουδαιότης καί ἱερότης τοῦ ἔργου αὐτοῦ καί ἡ ἀναγκαιότης τῆς μεταδόσεως "*τοῖς ἐγγύς καί τοῖς μακράν*" τοῦ χαρισθέντος ἡμῖν θησαυροῦ, δέν ἐπιτρέπουν φθοροποιούς ἐνδο-ορθοδόξους ἔριδας, νοσηρᾶς ἐνδοστρεφείας ἤ ἀρνήσεις τῆς κηρυκτικῆς ἀποστολῆς τῆς Ἐκκλησίας λόγῳ ἀπομονωτισμῶν μή συμβατῶν μέ τό Εὐαγγέλιον

τοῦ Θεοῦ "*ὅς πάντας ἀνθρώποις θέλει σωθῆναι καί εἰς ἐπίγνωσιν ἀληθείας ἐλθεῖν*" (1 Τιμ. 2, 4).

Ἔχομεν τήν ὄντως ἔξοχον καί ἱερωτάτην τιμήν νά εἴμεθα οἱ Ἱεράρχαι τοῦ Πανσέπτου Οἰκουμενικοῦ Θρόνου. Ἡ ἱστορία, τό παρόν καί τό μέλλον τοῦ Θρόνου αὐτοῦ μᾶς προσφέρουν μίαν ὑπέροχον προοπτικήν μαρτυρίας τοῦ Εὐαγγελίου καί συμβολῆς εἰς τήν σωτηρίαν τοῦ ἀνθρώπου καί τοῦ κόσμου.

The Challenges of Pluralism: The Orthodox Churches in a Pluralistic World

Holy Cross Greek Orthodox School of Theology[1]

Brookline, MA
October 3, 2002

Introduction

I offer my wholehearted thanksgiving to God for the joy and the blessing to be with you this evening and to begin this momentous Ecumenical Conversation on *The Orthodox Churches in a Pluralistic World*. For this significant event, I express my warmest thanks to the Reverend President of Hellenic College and Holy Cross, Fr. Nicholas Triantafilou, and to the Reverend Dean of the School of Theology, Dr. Emmanuel Clapsis, who has worked enthusiastically for this encounter which perhaps he has seen as an opportunity for a more elaborate and inclusive research and discussion on a cherished topic he dealt with in his recent book *Orthodoxy in Conversation, Orthodox Theologi-*

[1]This address was the Keynote Address for the conference "The Orthodox Churches in a Pluralistic World: An Ecumenical Conversation" sponsored by Holy Cross Greek Orthodox School of Theology and the World Council of Churches in cooperation with the Boston Theological Institute and Harvard Divinity School's Initiatives in Religion and Public Life. The address and the conference papers were recently published under the conference title, edited by Rev. Father Emmanuel Clapsis (Geneva and Brookline: WCC Publications and Holy Cross Orthodox Press, 2004), 1-10.

cal Engagements. I am also deeply grateful to Dr. Konrad Raiser and the World Council of Churches, to Dr. Rodney Petersen and the Boston Theological Institute, and to Professor David Little and the Center for the Study of Values in Public Life, Harvard Divinity School, for their substantive cooperation in producing this Ecumenical Conversation.

Sincere thanks belong also to the esteemed colleagues of the Faculty of the Holy Cross School of Theology and of the various universities from America and from Europe who were kind enough to participate as speakers in this meeting. Omission of thanks due to "ignorance, forgetfulness or multitude of names," to use Saint Basil's phrase, is of course, unintentional.

We are calling this conference a "conversation." But in the spirit of this conference on pluralism, we should not be too ready to take at face value our own label of "conversation." This conference is *more* than a conversation; it is more than just an exchange of words.

Let us recall from the field of linguistics the idea of *performative speech acts*. These are sentences which not only convey information, but also accomplish some action just in the process of being spoken. For example, the statement, "I apologize," not only conveys information about the speaker's mental state, but also performs the work of creating an apology; just as the use of the phrase "I promise" can bring about the existence of a promise, or the words "I thank you" effect an expression of gratitude.

What we do here this week in holding this Ecumenical Conversation on Orthodoxy and Pluralism is not simply the conveyance of information between one another. This conversation is itself a *performative speech act*, whereby we create the very thing we are talking about. We are living out, albeit in a small way, Orthodox values and priorities in a pluralistic world through this conversation with members of the wider American and international theological community. We are not merely talking theologically; to borrow a modern expression, we are truly "producing theology" by the words that we exchange here in a spirit of mutual respect, interest, and love.

But here, we are going to have more than a performative speech act. The Polish poet Czeslaw Milosz, a Nobel Laureate in 1980, wrote a remarkable poem under the title *Readings*. The text begins with the following five verses:

You asked me what is the good of reading the Gospels in Greek.
I answer that it is proper that we move our finger
Along the letters more enduring than those carved in stone,
And that, slowly pronouncing each syllable,
We discover the true dignity of speech.

We discover the true dignity of speech! This conversation on pluralism is also a terrific opportunity *to discover and to promote the true dignity of speech,* in addition to producing a performative speech act.

Let us then proceed with a few thoughts on "The Challenge of Pluralism for Orthodoxy." What follows could be called introductory comments. The program of the next two days is so rich and thorough that any attempt to offer something truly comprehensive in the form of a keynote address would certainly become an exercise in frustration and futility. Here, then, are some introductory comments, grouped around three themes: a) the challenge of pluralism for Orthodoxy, b) the context of our conversation, and c) suggestions for responding to the pluralistic challenge.

The Challenge of Pluralism for Orthodoxy

From the outset, we must be clear about the matter

before us. The issues of pluralism and globalization are intimately related to one another and are matters of profound interest, not only for Orthodox Christians in America, but in every place in the world. The effects of globalization are felt everywhere, especially through the means of the Internet, e-mail, cellular telephone technology, and the different forms of electronic media. Even in communities around the world which do not have the cultural or racial heterogeneity of the United States, there is nonetheless a sort of "pluralism by proxy," due to the power of modern technologies of communication to represent the wealth of human diversity across vast distances almost instantaneously.

What this means, then, is that a given society can be a cultural island no more. The marketplace of ideas is open to all, and geographic isolation is no longer an issue in the dissemination of ideology. No society is "immune," so to speak, from the possibility of influences from outside. The Orthodox Church in Greece, for instance, must take into account the same ideas and societal trends that are faced by the Orthodox Churches in America or in other places. With the advent of globalization, every community is a pluralistic community, even those societies which try to be closed to outside influences. Let us then speak more specifically about the dimensions of our pluralistic reality that, through globalization, are common to all civilized societies, and therefore common to all Orthodox Churches across the world.

In a period of rapid globalization, in a world community that is increasingly conscious of its pluralistic character, the Orthodox Churches meet a great *challenge*. The word "challenge", however, is not to be understood with negative connotations, but rather in the most positive and optimistic sense. The pluralistic world is not an *obstacle* to Orthodoxy; it is rather an *opportunity*. In a pluralistic global society, the Orthodox Church is challenged to match her Incarnational Christology with an equally Incarnational ecclesiology.

At this point, it is important to bring to our conversation a truly programmatic passage from Saint Paul's First Epistle to the Corinthians. In chapter nine, Paul speaks of his labors as a true Apostle of Christ, defining his Apostleship not in terms of rank or privilege, but in terms of servanthood and sacrifice. He says:

> *19. For though I am free from all men, I have made myself*
> *a slave to all, that I might win the more. 20. To the Jews*
> *I became as a Jew, in order to win Jews; to those under*
> *the law I became as one under the law—though not being*
> *myself under the law—that I might win those under the*
> *law. 21. To those outside the law I became as one outside*
> *the law—not being without law toward God but under*
> *the law of Christ—that I might win those outside the law.*
> *22. To the weak I became weak, that I might win the weak.*
> *I have become all things to all men, that I might by all*
> *means save some. 23. I do it all for the sake of the Gospel,*
> *that I may share in its blessings.*

> *19. Ἐλεύθερος γὰρ ὢν ἐκ πάντων πᾶσιν ἐμαυτὸν*
> *ἐδούλωσα, ἵνα τοὺς πλείονας κερδήσω· 20. καὶ*
> *ἐγενόμην τοῖς Ἰουδαίοις ὡς Ἰουδαῖος, ἵνα Ἰου-*
> *δαίους κερδήσω· τοῖς ὑπὸ νόμον ὡς ὑπὸ νόμον, μὴ*
> *ὢν αὐτὸς ὑπὸ νόμον, ἵνα τοὺς ὑπὸ νόμον κερδήσω·*
> *21. τοῖς ἀνόμοις ὡς ἄνομος, μὴ ὢν ἄνομος Θεοῦ ἀλλ᾽*
> *ἔννομος Χριστοῦ, ἵνα κερδάνω τοὺς ἀνόμους· 22.*
> *ἐγενόμην τοῖς ἀσθενέσιν ἀσθενής, ἵνα τοὺς ἀσθε-*
> *νεῖς κερδήσω· τοῖς πᾶσιν γέγονα πάντα, ἵνα πάντως*
> *τινάς σώσω. 23. πάντα δὲ ποιῶ διὰ τὸ εὐαγγέλιον,*
> *ἵνα συγκοινωνὸς αὐτοῦ γένωμαι.*

If we were to attach a label to Saint Paul's approach to evangelism, we might call it *personal pluralism;* the Apostle takes a positive approach to the pluralism that he finds in the Roman world of the first century A.D., by seeking to express, in the microcosm of his own personhood, the full panoply of human diversity: Jewish, Gentile, under the law, outside the law, strong, or weak.

And why does he exhibit this "personal pluralism?" The Apostle tells us: *"I do it all for the sake of the Gospel, that I may share in its blessings"* [πάντα δὲ ποιῶ διὰ τὸ εὐαγγέλιον, ἵνα συγκοινωνὸς αὐτοῦ γένωμαι] (1 Corinthians 9:23). We are not to understand by this statement that Saint Paul expects to earn the blessings of the Gospel through his pluralistic labors. Rather, by this statement we understand the Apostle as meaning that he enjoys the blessings of the Gospel *in and through* his work of being "all things to all people." The blessing is the pluralistic labor, directly related to the salvation of the people.

The reason for this statement is transparent if we understand correctly the Christology of Saint Paul. *Becoming all things to all people* requires an act of personal *kenosis,* a self-emptying, accomplished in order to accommodate the needs of the other, followed by a journey into the depths of one's humanity to discover the fullness and variety of our extraordinary nature as creatures who bear the image of an infinite God. And having found within himself the potential to become all things for all people, and having the true Apostolic freedom to become all things for all people, the Apostle shows himself an *imitator of Christ* [μιμητής Χριστοῦ] (cf. 1 Corinthians 11:1), *who took the form of a servant* [μορφὴν δούλου λαβών] (Philippians 2:7) in order to redeem our enslaved race, who condescended to come even *in the likeness of sinful flesh* [ἐν ομοιώματι σαρκὸς ἁμαρτίας] (Romans 8:3) in order to save sinners. For Saint Paul, therefore, the pluralistic encounters of his Apostolic ministry become a means for greater Christ-likeness within his own person. His work is a most existential and experiential way of living in union with Christ so that he might declare, *"It is no longer I who live, but Christ Who lives in me"* [*ζῶ δὲ οὐκέτι ἐγώ, ζῇ δὲ ἐν ἐμοὶ Χριστός*] (Galatians 2:20).

This then is the challenge of a pluralistic society for our Orthodox Church: to encounter the contemporary world as Saint Paul did in imitation of Christ the God who became a human being. The more pluralistic encounters we effect for the sake of the Gospel, the more opportunities we have to become all things to all people, in the Pauline sense, sharing in the blessings of the Gospel.

The Context of our Conversation

It would be wise for us, at the beginning of our conversation on pluralism, to take a moment to consider the context in which we find ourselves. This is a necessary exercise to examine thoughtfully our present situation, the historical antecedents, and the trends leading into the future for our global society.

There would seem to be a general consensus among Americans that we are living in an increasingly pluralistic society and in a world that is rapidly evolving towards greater and greater diversity. Objectively, however, quite the opposite might be true. If anything, the standard cultural markers point to the fact that the world is also rapidly growing more *homogeneous*. If we speak in terms of languages, for instance, we observe a rapid dying-off of indigenous languages around the world, and even of whole language groups in some places. Linguists predict that the number of distinct languages in the world will have shrunk from about 6000 to around 3000 by the end of this century—a loss of some thirty languages *each year*.

In conjunction with this trend is the increasing loss of biodiversity in the ecological sphere, with a concomitant change in the lifestyle of indigenous peoples. Wetlands are being drained and paved. Desert communities are converted into lakeside resorts through the damming of rivers. Rain forests are rapidly being turned into grazing land for cattle. This trend goes hand in hand with the global spread of Western cultural expressions in terms of music, dress, cuisine, entertainment, and most recently, electronic communications via the Internet.

Sometimes, phenomena related to globalization and diversity might be misleading. Let me cite a pertinent example. Here in the United States of America, many Americans are able today to receive a Spanish-language television channel through their local cable system. Twenty years ago this would not have been possible. Some would point to this as proof of a greater diversity in America in 2002 than in 1982. But the argument is weak. The United States has always been an ethnically diverse country, even from its very inception and up until the imposition of immigration quotas. Moreover, Spanish-speaking communities have been a significant part of many American cities for most of the nation's existence. The fact that they have their own television stations now is only proof that these communities are more visible to their neighbors than before, but not that they are part of a trend towards a more diverse society. In fact, in terms of content and appearance, the game shows, soap operas, movies and news programming of the Spanish channels on TV appear to borrow more from standard American network fare than to be an expression of authentic Hispanic-American culture. Therefore, in spite of the appearances, the phenomena of Spanish language TV channels in America could be a pointer to homogenization rather than to diversity.

So while on the one hand, it is certainly true that America is becoming more *conscious* of its pluralistic make-up, it is certainly not the case that America is necessarily becoming a more diverse society. America has always been home to a wide range of ethnic, linguistic, cultural, and religious communities. If anything, one might argue rather that America is losing its diversity as the grandchildren of immigrants become more "Americanized," as the traditional ethnic neighborhoods of towns and cities are transformed, as the Greek-towns and Chinatowns of our major cities shrink and change, and as electronic media promulgate the Hollywood standards for dress, behavior, and speech habits.

It is paradoxical, then, that in this period of increasing homogenization, America and many countries in the world find within themselves a growing conflict of cultural polarization. By cultural we mean here a large spectrum of components including religion. But this perhaps is the main area of diversification. The so-called "Culture Wars" have been escalating year after year, and the battlefields are the school board meetings, the radio call-in shows, the sidewalks around women's health clinics, the jury rooms, and the voting booths. From the vast relevant literature let me mention as an example the book, *Culture Wars: The Struggle to Define America*, by James Davidson Hunter.[2] In this book the author describes the combatants most actively engaged in the struggle: the advocates from both sides are deeply patriotic, committed to the founding values of America, profoundly moralistic, fully engaged in their religion (or philosophy of life), well-read and well-spoken, and open to forming nontraditional alliances to further their cause. Hunter also documents the fact that the lines of

[2]James Davison Hunter, *Culture Wars: The Struggle to Define America* (New York: BasicBooks/HarperCollins Publishers, Inc., 1991).

today's cultural struggles do not fall along any of the old societal boundaries like race or creed, but rather cut across them. Catholics oppose Catholics at the abortion clinic picket lines, Jews vilify Jews in the media, and Protestants lambaste Protestants at the town meeting. In this sense, the pluralism of contemporary America and several modern countries is quite different from the diversity of the past. Increasingly, America is becoming a neighborhood of "houses divided" so to speak. The new diversity of America is not in the variety of languages spoken at the marketplace, but in the use of a common vocabulary of words, symbols, myths, and meanings to express radically different visions of national life. And this has a tremendous importance for our conversation.

This, in fact, is the chief battleground of the culture wars: a semantic tug-of-war to impose a particular set of definitions and a particular narrative and interpretation of national history on the population as a whole. As specialists say (Hunter p. 184): "The battle will be nearly over when the linguistic preferences of one side of the cultural divide become the conventions of society as a whole."

What this means for our conversation here is that we must be sensitive to the fact that pluralism is often obscured by common speech habits. In former times, the pluralism of American society was a visible and audible property, observed in differences in skin color and language. Today, however, the most authentic pluralism seems to be ideological rather than racial, and this pluralism is often invisible and inaudible, unless one knows how to decode the shared keywords of the various parties on the ideological spectrum. This challenges us as Orthodox Christians, therefore, to be extremely careful and sensitive in our use of language. It forces us to reassess what we truly intend to mean by our theological speech, to examine how it is likely to be understood by our fellow citizens in this society. It is not enough to say the right thing objectively. In many cases, we will need to discover fresh metaphors and narratives to articulate our beliefs in this pluralistic society of ours. This task is facilitated by our classical cultural Hellenic heritage, which is in essence transcultural and favors creative usage of language and expression of ideas and beliefs. To use the metaphor of the Gospel, we need *new wineskins*, in terms of communication and language, for the *new wine* of our Orthodox Faith in America (cf. Matthew 9:17).

This, in short, is a simplified overview of the context in which we conduct our conversation of this weekend. We are mistaken, however, if we think ourselves to be inhabiting an entirely novel cultural milieu, unlike any seen before. A quick look at the cultural setting of first-century Palestine will reveal to us several affinities with our own time. Jesus Christ was born into a society that was struggling with the frictions of an uncomfortable pluralism. In the mix was a Jewish ruling class with accommodationist attitudes towards the regime of Caesar, Hellenized Jews, conservative Sadducees, progressivist Pharisees, isolationist Essenes, along with Samaritans, Gentiles, and Roman overlords. One could not have predicted that from within this cultural chaos and ideological diversity would emerge a way of life that would unite men and women of every social class, nation, tribe, and tongue, and ultimately even the fractured Roman Empire itself. And yet this was precisely the power of the Gospel in that ancient reflection of our own times. And, by the grace of God, it can have this same power again in our own times as well.

Responding to the Pluralistic Challenge: Three Suggestions

Within this cultural-ideological diversification, within this pluralistic context, what can we as Orthodox Churches offer to contemporary society? In the course of the following two days of our *Ecumenical Conversation*, we are going to hear numerous suggestions and propositions worth considering.

In this closing part of my introductory comments, allow me to submit three, I suppose, well known suggestions, which might be useful to remember in our discussions.

a) The first is a suggestion related to the story of Pentecost and to the practice of the Early Church. The central event in Pentecost was the fact that the Apostles were empowered by the Holy Spirit to speak the good news in all the languages of the multitude gathered that day in Jerusalem.

It is noteworthy that the miracle of Pentecost was *not* that the assembled crowd was made to understand the speech of a single man in a single language, regardless of the native tongue of the hearers. Rather, the miracle was that the one Gospel was expressed equally in a variety of languages. Anyone who recognizes the intimate link of language to culture must also recognize the bold statement that Pentecost makes: the truth of Christ can be embodied in more than one or two cultural-linguistic systems. The work of the Church is not to construct a single universal culture; instead, the Kingdom of God created by the One Holy Spirit contains many languages, many cultures. In the words of Fr. Emmanuel Clapsis, Pentecost tells us about "the active presence of God in all cultures."[3] This is a strong Orthodox view of the Kingdom, and for it we can lay claim to a long-standing tradition of insisting that "the Christian faith must become incarnated (or indigenized) in order to produce authentic fruits of dynamic human cooperation with God" (Clapsis, 8).

[3]Fr. Emmanuel Clapsis, "Gospel and Cultures—An Eastern Orthodox Perspective," in *Orthodoxy and Cultures*, edited by Ioan Sauca (Geneva: World Council of Churches 1996), 21.

In this instance, let us consider the practice of the Early Church. How did the Church treat the Holy Scriptures? The Greek language was still the *lingua franca* of the Roman world even into the era of the Church Fathers, and for most Greek speakers of the time around the Mediterranean Sea who employed the variety known as *koine*, the language of most of the New Testament would have been accessible and understandable in the original.

And yet, very early on in the life of the Church, we find a significant commitment to the work of translating the Scriptures into the various local vernaculars: Syriac, Ethiopic, Georgian, Armenian, the Vulgate of Saint Jerome, Coptic in both the Sahidic and Bohairic dialects, and Gothic. What does this multiplicity of Bible versions demonstrate, if not a strong sense among the early Christian Fathers that the faith of Christ must be indigenized, so to say, to the greatest extent possible?

We all know that translation is an inexact science, that the difficulty of finding equivalent renderings can introduce unintended meanings to a text, or conversely limit the range of purposeful ambiguities. We know also that in the face of the Gnostic movements, early Christianity was deeply concerned about *the form of sound words* (2 Timothy 1:13), about vocabulary and nuances of meaning. Nevertheless, despite the risks inherent in the translator's art, the Early Church responded to its mission in a pluralistic world by deliberately advancing her own linguistic pluralism in the core expression of the Faith, the Holy Scriptures. This diversity was matched as well by a diversity of liturgical expressions, and an openness to variety in other facets of life for the Christian communities of the Eastern Empire, so that even in the "globalized" environment of the ancient Roman world, the Church never neglected the particular and specific cultural elements of local parishes, never overlooked the sociocultural or ethnic pluralism.

b) The second suggestion refers to our Orthodox notion of *personhood*, and the importance that this idea has in our dealing with the challenge of the pluralistic world of today. With the theological term *person*, we express a complexity of ideas and values. Among persons there is a fundamental commonality of essence, while at the same time an indelible distinction of uniqueness. Personhood, at one and the same time, implies the existence of the other through the shared nature, and yet also upholds the primacy of the individual as significant and precious in his or her own right.

Modern society has a tendency to reduce persons to the description of their external characteristics. How often, for example, do we see reports in the media that present demographic information solely in terms of the categories of race, gender, or social class? How much of our political rhetoric is shaped by the notion that the nation is simply a collection of constituencies: blacks, whites, senior citizens, or blue-collar workers? This sort of reductionism is offensive to the anthropological sensibilities of Orthodox theology, and as loyal citizens of our society we should resist it. By no means should the pressures of modern globalization be allowed to define the emerging global community simply in terms of focus groups and market targets.

As Metropolitan John Zizioulas of Pergamon has written in his book *Being as Communion*: "Uniqueness is something absolute for the person. The person is so absolute in its uniqueness that it does not permit itself to be regarded as an arithmetical concept, to be set alongside other beings, to be combined with other objects, or to be used as a means, even for the most sacred goals. The goal is the person itself."[4] Our Orthodox insistence on the uniqueness of personhood is strongly evident even in our liturgical practice. To mention an example, every sacrament is personalized by the recitation of the name of the Christian who has been given a renewed personhood and a new name in Christ.

And yet our Orthodox notion of personhood is altogether distinct from the American idea of "individualism." This is because personhood is fulfilled only in community, only in the relationship of love and openness to the other, as different as the other might be. Thus, no matter how advanced is the state of globalization, no matter what forms pluralism will take in the near or the distant future, our Orthodox notion of personhood will be of paramount importance and has to be constantly emphasized in any and every pluralistic context.

c) The third and final suggestion connects the pluralistic challenge to the Eucharistic community, to the Orthodox parish. Whereas the Apostle Paul practiced a kind of personal pluralism, our parishes should be the proponents of *a parish pluralism*, being all things to all people, by their makeup and their outlook and above all by their communal mode of life, instantiating constructively a "unity in diversity" that could be a model for our whole society. This idea has been articulated in the past years by Christos Yannaras, among others, in his book *The Freedom of Morality* (cf. especially chapter 11), where he identfied the Eucharistic community—the local parish—as the startingpoint for an Orthodox program of a more comprehensive social engagement, an emphasis on personal relationships within the Eucharistic community and a fostering of strong communal and Eucharistic life among our people. The spiritual reconstruction of the local parish into an authentic community is, then, not simply one of the priorities for Orthodoxy in this era, but the "priority program." As we conduct our conversation on plural-

[4]John Zizioulas, *Being As Communion* (Crestwood, NY: Saint Vladimir's Seminary Press, 1985), 47.

ism this weekend, let us be mindful about how our ideas and proposals can be translated into the concrete actions of community church life, leading our parishes into offering some sort of a parish pluralism. Such a parish pluralism, saving the uniqueness and integrity of the person and the unity and vitality of the community, could serve as a superb model for our globalized and pluralistic society.

Conclusion

At the very beginning of this presentation, we mentioned, as a guiding text, the declaration of Saint Paul in First Corinthians 9:22: *"I have become all things to all people, that I might by all means save some."* We end with the same phrase: "I have become all things to all people that I might by all means save some."

An adequate theology of pluralism is not simply a philosophical nicety for our Orthodox Churches of the twenty-first century. It is the necessary tool for our accomplishment of the work set before us by the Lord in His Great Commission to go forth into all the world to preach the Gospel. Unless we understand how we, as a Church and as local parishes and as theologians and clergy and laity, can become "all things to all people" in an appropriate, authentic, and Orthodox way, unless we understand how to *live* our pluralism while still holding fast to the one truth of the one Lord Jesus Christ, and one Church, we will by no means save any. And we will by no means respond to the sublime mandate of the same Lord telling us: *"As the Father has sent me, even so I send you"* (John 20:21).

Η ΟΡΘΟΔΟΞΗ ΕΚΚΛΗΣΙΑ ΚΑΙ ΘΕΟΛΟΓΙΑ ΣΤΗΝ ΑΜΕΡΙΚΗ ΣΗΜΕΡΑ: ΠΕΝΤΕ ΠΡΟΚΛΗΣΕΙΣ

ARISTOTELIAN UNIVERSITY*

THESSALONIKI, GREECE
NOVEMBER 19, 2002

Ἐκφράζω τίς θερμότατες εὐχαριστίες μου γιά τήν ἐξαιρετική τιμή πού γίνεται πρός τήν ἐλαχιστότητά μου μέ τήν ἀναγόρευσή μου σέ Ἐπίτιμο Διδάκτορα τοῦ Τμήματος Θεολογίας τοῦ Ἀριστοτελείου Πανεπιστημίου Θεσσαλονίκης.

Εὐχαριστῶ τόν ἐλλογιμώτατο Πρόεδρο τοῦ Τμήματος, Καθηγητή κ. Μιλτιάδη Κωνσταντίνου, τά μέλη τοῦ Τμήματος, τόν Κοσμήτορα τῆς Θεολογικης Σχολῆς Καθηγητή Ἰωάννη Ταρνανίδη. Ἰδιαιτέρως εὐχαριστῶ τόν ἐλλογιμώτατο Πρύτανι τοῦ Ἀριστοτελείου Πανεπιστημίου Θεσσαλονίκης γιά τήν οὐσιαστική προσωπική συμμετοχή του στήν διαδικασία τῆς τιμητικῆς ἀναγορεύσεως.

Εὐχαριστῶ τούς παρόντας στήν ἀποψινή ἐκδήλωση, ἰδιαζόντως δέ τόν ἐκλεκτό φίλο Καθηγητή κ. Ἰωάννη Καραβιδόπουλο γιά τόν ἔπαινο πού εἶχε τήν καλωσύνη νά ἑτοιμάση, καί στόν ὁποῖο εἴχαμε τήν δυνατότητα

*This address was given on the occasion of the acceptance of an honorary Doctorate from the School of Theology of the Aristotelian University of Thessaloniki.

νά θαυμάσουμε τήν ἑρμηνευτική του δεινότητα, ἐφ᾽ ὅσον μπόρεσε νά ἑρμηνεύσῃ περιωρισμένα μᾶλλον δεδομένα, μέ τρόπον πού νά δημιουργήσῃ μιά εἰκόνα πού μέ ἀφήνει ἀπολύτως καί συντριπτικῶς ἔκπληκτο. Τοῦ εἶμαι εὐγνώμων γιά τόν κόπο τῆς πολλῆς ἀγάπης καί ὑπερβαλλούσης τιμῆς. Ἡ σημερινή ἐκδήλωση ἀποτελεῖ τμῆμα μιᾶς μακρᾶς ἱστορίας, πού μέ συνδέει μέ τό Πανεπιστήμιο Θεσσαλονίκης ἤδη ἀπό τά παιδικά μου χρόνια. Μιᾶς ἱστορίας ἡ ὁποία τονίζει τούς ἰσχυροτάτους δεσμούς μου μέ τό Πανεπιστήμιο αὐτό καί τήν ἐντονότατη συγκίνησή μου γιά τό σημερινό γεγονός τό ὁποῖο, μέ ἐντάσσει ὀργανικά στό Ἀριστοτέλειο Πανεπιστήμιο Θεσσαλονίκης. Γι᾽ αὐτή τήν ὄντως τιμητικώτατη ἔνταξη ἐκφράζω τήν βαθύτατη εὐγνωμοσύνη μου πρός τόν Θεό τοῦ φωτός καί πάσης γνώσεως, καί πρός ὅλους τούς ἀνθρώπους συντελεστάς. Θά παρουσιάσω ἐν συντομίᾳ πέντε πλευρές τῆς σημερινῆς Ὀρθοδόξου Θεολογίας καί Ἐκκλησίας στήν Ἀμερική: Πέντε Προκλήσεις.

Ἡ Πρόκληση τῆς Μειονότητος

Ἡ Ὀρθόδοξη Θεολογία καί Ἐκκλησία στήν Ἀμερική σήμερα βρίσκονται σέ μιά ἐντελῶς εἰδική θέση ἀπό πολλές ἀπόψεις. Μιά ἀπό τίς κύριες ἀπόψεις εἶναι ὅτι, ἡ Ὀρθόδοξη Θεολογία καί Ἐκκλησία στήν Ἀμερική ἀνήκουν σέ μειονότητα ἀπό πλευρᾶς πληθυσμιακῆς σέ μιά τεράστια χώρα 300 ἑκατομμυρίων ἀνθρώπων, ὅπου οἱ Ὀρθόδοξοι εἶναι πιθανῶς περί τά 5 ἑκατομμύρια. Ἡ μεγάλη πλειονότητα ἐντός τῶν 5 αὐτῶν ἑκατομμυρίων εἶναι φυσικά οἱ Ἕλληνες Ὀρθόδοξοι πού εἴμεθα περί τά 2 ἑκατομμύρια. Αὐτό σημαίνει ὅτι ὡς Ἕλληνες Ὀρθόδοξοι ἀποτελοῦμε μόλις τό 0.7% τοῦ συνολικοῦ ἀμερικανικοῦ πληθυσμοῦ καί ὡς Ὀρθόδοξοι μόλις τό 1.7%. Εἴμεθα σαφέσταστα μειονότητα.

Μιά μειονότητα, λόγω ἀκριβῶς τοῦ γεγονότος ὅτι εἶναι μειονότητα, συνήθως ζεῖ καί κινεῖται ὑπό εἰδικές ψυχολογικές, πνευματικές, καί πολιτιστικές συνθῆκες. Στίς πλεῖστες τῶν περιπτώσεων αὐτό εἶναι ἕνα στοιχεῖο μᾶλλον δυσμενές. Εἶναι φυσικό ἐνδεχόμενο μιά μειονότητα νά ἀναπτύξῃ ἰσχυρά αἰσθήματα ἀνασφαλείας, ἰσχυρά αἰσθήματα μειονεξίας καί νά ἐμπλακῇ σέ μιάν ὑπέρμετρη προσπάθεια ἀναγνωρίσεως, ἡ ὁποία μέ τή σειρά της πιθανώτατα θά προκαλέσῃ χαρακτηρολογικές καί ἄλλες ἀρνητικές ἀλλαγές.

Ἐν τούτοις, στήν Ἀμερική τό δεδομένο τοῦ νά ἀνήκῃ κανείς σέ μειονότητα εἶναι δεδομένο πού διαφέρει σημαντικά ἀπό παρόμοια φαινόμενα σέ ἄλλες περιοχές. Καί διαφέρει σημαντικά διότι κατ' ἀρχήν ἡ Ἀμερική ἔχει μεγάλο ἀριθμό μειονοτήτων. Βεβαίως πρέπει νά ἀναγνωρισθῇ ὅτι στό θρησκευτικό θεολογικό πεδίο εἴμεθα στατιστικά μικρός ἀριθμός.

Ἐπειδή ὅμως ἡ Ἀμερική εἶναι μιά χώρα ὅπου ὑπάρχει ἀπόλυτη ἄνεση κινήσεως, ἐν τελευταίᾳ ἀναλύσει ἡ ἔννοια μειονότητα δέν ἐπηρεάζει τόσο ἔντονα. Ἐπί πλέον, στήν Ἀμερική ὑπάρχει μιά ἐμπειρία πλήρους θρησκευτικῆς ἐλευθερίας. Ἀξίζει νά σημειωθῇ ὅτι στίς Η.Π.Α. ἐνῶ ἰσχύει σαφής διαχωρισμός κράτους καί θρησκείας ὁ διαχωρισμός αὐτός δέν εἶναι ἐχθρικός πρός τήν θρησκεία διότι ἔγινε γιά νά δώσῃ τήν δυνατότητα στήν θρησκεία νά κινηθῇ ἐλεύθερα καί νά μή δεσμεύεται ἤ ἐπηρεάζεται ἀπό τό κράτος. Ἡ ἀρχική ἐπιλογή αὐτῆς τῆς ἔντονης διαχωριστικῆς γραμμῆς σχετίζεται ἀκριβῶς μέ αὐτό τό πνεῦμα, καί ἑπομένως ὁ λόγος τοῦ διαχωρισμοῦ δέν ἦτο λόγος ἐχθρικότητος, ἀλλά μᾶλλον προστασίας τῆς θρησκείας ἀπό ἐξωτερικές ἐπιδράσεις καί ἐπεμβάσεις καί δή τοῦ κράτους. Γι' αὐτό καί ὁ χαρακτήρας καί ἡ λειτουργία μιᾶς θρησκευτικῆς καί ἐκκλησιαστικῆς μειονότητος στήν Ἀμερική, ὅπως εἶναι ἡ δική μας, δέν ἐξαρτᾶται ἀπό τό γεγονός ὅτι ἀποτελοῦμε μειονότητα.

Ἐπί πλέον στήν περίπτωση τῆς Ὀρθοδόξου Θεολογίας καί Ἐκκλησίας στήν Ἀμερική, ἐν σχέσει πρός τήν ἔννοια τῆς μειονότητος, λειτουργεῖ καί ἕνας ἄλλος παράγων, ὁ ὁποῖος εἶναι πολύ σημαντικός. Ὁ παράγων αὐτός εἶναι τό ὅτι, ἡ Ὀρθόδοξη Ἐκκλησία στήν Ἀμερική ἔχει ἰσχυρότατες καί ἄμεσες συνδέσεις μέ τίς Ὀρθόδοξες Μητρικές Ἐκκλησίες, κατά βάσιν τῆς Εὐρώπης, καί συγκεκριμένα τῶν τεσσάρων ἀρχαίων καί τῶν ὑπολοίπων νεωτέρων Πατριαρχείων καί Αὐτοκεφάλων Ἐκκλησιῶν. Τό γεγονός αὐτό μάλιστα ἐτονίσθη σέ διάφορες περιπτώσεις πού εἶχαν σχέση μέ γενικώτερες ἐνέργειες, ὅπως ἡ ἀναγνώριση τῆς ἐκλογῆς τοῦ Πατριάρχου Ἱεροσολύμων ἀπό τήν Ἰσραηλινή Κυβέρνηση, γιά νά ἀναφέρω ἕνα παράδειγμα. Καί ἐτονίσθη διότι κατέστη γνωστό ὅτι δέν εἴμεθα μία οἱαδήποτε Ἐκκλησία ἤ χριστιανική παραφυάδα, ἡ ὁποία ζεῖ ἐν ἀπομονώσει στήν Ἀμερική μέ 2 ἤ 3 ἤ 5 ἑκατομμύρια πιστούς, ἀλλά συνδεόμεθα ἄμεσα καί ὀργανικά μέ τό ἀνά τήν Οἰκουμένη σῶμα τῆς Ὀρθοδοξίας, τό ὁποῖο ἀριθμεῖ ἐπισήμως πλέον τῶν 250 ἑκατομμυρίων ἀνθρώπων.

Αὐτομάτως λοιπόν, ἡ αὐτοσυνειδησία μας ἐν Ἀμερικῇ ὡς ἐκκλησιαστικῆς καί θεολογικῆς μειονότητος ἀποκτᾶ ἰδιαίτερο βάθος καί πλάτος καί ὁ ἄρρηκτος δεσμός, συγκεκριμένα στή δική μας περίπτωση μέ τήν Μητέρα Ἐκκλησία, τό Οἰκουμενικό Πατριαρχεῖο, καί παράλληλα μέ τήν Ἐκκλησία τῆς Ἑλλάδος, δίνει μιά πολύ ἰσχυρότερη βάση στήν ὅλη ζωή τῆς Ἐκκλησίας καί στήν θεολογική της παραγωγή. Θά λέγαμε λοιπόν συμπερασματικά, ὅτι τά ἀρνητικά στοιχεῖα τά συνδεόμενα μέ τήν ἰδέα τῆς μειονότητος εἶναι στήν περίπτωσή μας πολύ μειωμένα, ἄν ὄχι ἀνύπαρκτα. Τό γεγονός αὐτό ἐξουδετερώνει τήν ἀνάγκη μιᾶς ἀγχώδους προσπαθείας γιά ἐπιβίωση καί ἀναγνώριση, ἐνῶ ταὐτοχρόνως παρέχει τήν εὐχέρεια στήν Θεολογία μας καί στήν Ἐκκλησία μας, νά κινηθοῦν ἐλεύθερα καί δημιουργικά σ' ἕνα τεράστιο γεωγραφικά καί ἀνθρωπολογικά χῶρο, γιά νά δώσουν τό πολύτιμο μήνυμα τῆς Ὀρθοδοξίας. Αὐτό σημαίνει ὅτι, ἡ Θεολογία καί ἡ Ἐκκλησία μας ἐν Ἀμερικῇ δέν εἶναι σέ κατάσταση μειονεξίας, ἐπιβιώσεως καί ἀμύνης λόγῳ μειονότητος, ἀλλά σέ κατάσταση εἰδικῆς ἀποστολῆς εὐαγγελισμοῦ "*τοῖς μακράν καί τοῖς ἐγγύς*" (Ἐφεσ. 2, 17).

Ἡ αἴσθηση, ἡ ἐμπειρία, ἡ αὐτοσυνειδησία μιᾶς Θεολογίας καί μιᾶς Ἐκκλησίας πού εἶναι σέ κατάσταση ἀποστολῆς, διότι ἔχει τελικά νά δώσῃ οὐσιαστική μαρτυρία περί τοῦ Εὐαγγελίου, παρέχουν ἀμέσως σ' αὐτή τήν Ἐκκλησία καί σ' αὐτή τήν Θεολογία, τεράστιες δυνατότητες μιᾶς προσφορᾶς ὄντως μοναδικῆς. Ἡ πρόκληση τῆς μειονότητος μεταβάλλεται σέ κλήση ἀποστολῆς.

Ἡ Πρόκληση τῆς Ἀγγλικῆς Ὀρθοδόξου Θεολογικῆς Γλώσσης

Ἡ δεύτερη πρόκληση σχετίζεται μέ τήν ηὐξημένη σέ ἀριθμό καί ἀξιοσημείωτη σέ ποιότητα Ὀρθόδοξη Θεολογική παραγωγή στήν Ἀμερική. Ἡ ζωή σέ μιά χώρα στήν ὁποία βασική γλῶσσα εἶναι ἡ ἀγγλική, ἡ ὕπαρξη μεγάλου ἀριθμοῦ νέων ἐπιστημόνων δευτέρας ἤ τρίτης γενεᾶς, καί τό φαινόμενο μεγάλου ποσοστοῦ μικτῶν γάμων, ἐτόνισαν τήν ἀνάγκη παραγωγῆς καί διαθέσεως κατηχητικοῦ, πνευματικοῦ, λειτουργικοῦ, καί ἐκπαιδευτικοῦ ὑλικοῦ στήν ἀγγλική γλῶσσα. Ἐπί πλέον ἡ συμμετοχή τῶν Ὀρθοδόξων σέ διαλόγους καί κοινές προσπάθειες μέ ἄλλες χριστιανικές ὁμολογίες, ὡδήγησε κατ᾽ ἀνάγκην στήν δημιουργία καί τήν προσφορά καταλλήλου λεξιλογίου, καί λεπτεπιλέπτων διατυπώσεων νοημάτων, τά ὁποῖα ἐκφράζουν μέ ἀκρίβεια καί πληρότητα τό ὀρθόδοξο πνεῦμα καί τήν ὀρθόδοξη ὁμολογία πίστεως. Αὐτά ἔπρεπε νά διατυπωθοῦν πλέον στά ἀγγλικά, μέ ἀποτέλεσμα, ἀφ᾽ ἑνός μέν τό ὀρθόδοξο γλωσσικό ὄργανο στά ἀγγλικά νά ἀναπτυχθῇ σέ μεγάλο βαθμό, ἀφ᾽ ἑτέρου δέ νά ἐμφανισθῇ μιά πολύ σημαντική θεολογική παραγωγή. Ὁ μελετητής τῆς ὀρθοδόξου θεολογικῆς παραγωγῆς στήν Ἀμερική στίς δεκαετίες τοῦ 1960, τοῦ 1970, τοῦ 1980, τοῦ 1990 καί τοῦ 2000, μένει κατάπληκτος ἀπό τήν ραγδαία αὔξηση βιβλίων, κειμένων καί γενικά γραπτῶν ἐκφράσεων τῆς Θεολογίας μας στά ἀγγλικά ἀπό δεκαετία σέ δεκαετία. Σήμερα, γιά νά ἀναφέρω ἕνα παράδειγμα, ὑπάρχουν βιβλιοπωλεῖα στήν Ἀμερική πού διαθέτουν ἀποκλειστικά καί μόνον ὀρθόδοξα βιβλία. Αὐτό σημαίνει μιά αὐξανομένη ζήτηση ὀρθοδόξων βιβλίων, ἡ ὁποία δέν παρατηρεῖται μόνο μεταξύ ὀρθοδόξων, ἀλλά καί μεταξύ ἑτεροδόξων.

Ἐπί πλέον στό ὅλο θέμα τῆς αὐξανομένης παραγωγῆς Ὀρθοδόξου λόγου στά ἀγγλικά πρέπει νά ὑπολογισθοῦν ὄχι μόνο τά ἔντυπα ἀλλά καί τά σύγχρονα ἠλεκτρονικά μέσα, οἱ ἱστοσελίδες τοῦ διαδικτύου, τά videos καί τά DVDs. Γιά νά ἀναφέρω ἕνα χαρακτηριστικό παράδειγμα ἀπό τήν Ἀρχιεπισκοπή μας, ἡ ἱστοσελίδα στό διαδίκτυο τῆς δικῆς μας Ἑλληνικῆς Ὀρθοδόξου Ἀρχιεπισκοπῆς Ἀμερικῆς εἶναι μιά ἱστοσελίδα πού παρέχει πλουσιώτατο ὑλικό ὀρθοδόξου λόγου στά ἀγγλικά. Ἄς μοῦ ἐπιτραπῇ νά παρατηρήσω ἐνδεικτικά ὅτι, τό ὑλικό πού προσέφερε ἡ ἱστοσελίδα μας ἀμέσως μετά τήν 11η Σεπτεμβρίου, ἦτο ἐπιπέδου καί ἐκτάσεως τήν ὁποία λίγες ἱστοσελίδες ἀριθμητικά μεγάλων θρησκευτικῶν ὁμολογιῶν τῆς Ἀμερικῆς προσέφεραν.

Εἶναι χαρακτηριστικό ὅτι στήν ἐπέτειο τῆς 11ης Σεπτεμβρίου ἡ ὁποία ἔγινε πρό δύο μηνῶν, κατά τήν διάρκεια μόνο δύο ἡμερῶν, δηλαδή τῆς 10ης καί 11ης Σεπτεμβρίου, ἡ ἱστοσελίδα τῆς Ἀρχιεπισκοπῆς μας ἐδέχθη τίς "ἐπισκέψεις" 50.000 ἀτόμων, μέ μέσον ὅρον παραμονῆς καί ἐρεύνης τοῦ σχετικοῦ ὑλικοῦ στό διαδίκτυο ἐπί 11 λεπτά. Πρόκειται γιά ἀριθμό ὄντως ἐντυπωσιακό. Περί τίς 50.000 ἄνθρωποι, ὄχι μόνο Ὀρθόδοξοι, ἀλλά ἄτομα πάσης θρησκείας καί προελεύσεως, χρησιμοποίησαν τήν ἱστοσελίδα μας γιά νά προμηθευθοῦν ὑλικό τό ὁποῖο προσφέρει ὀρθόδοξη θεολογία, ἐκκλησιολογία, ποιμαντική, ἀκόμη καί λειτουργικά στοιχεῖα στήν ἀγγλική γλῶσσα.

Στίς ἀρχές τῆς δεκαετίας τοῦ 70 τά βιβλία τά ὁποῖα ἀναφέρονται στήν ὀρθόδοξη θεολογία, δογματική, λειτουργική, ποιμαντική ἦταν λίγα σέ ἀριθμό. Σήμερα ὑπάρχει ἕνας τεράστιος ἀριθμός βιβλίων τά ὁποῖα καλύπτουν ὅλα τά ἀνωτέρω θεολογικά πεδία. Ἐπί πλέον ἔχει γίνει μιά πάρα πολύ μεγάλη μεταφραστική ἐργασία γιά νά μεταφερθῆ ὁ ὑμνολογικός, λατρευτικός, καί λειτουργικός πλοῦτος στά ἀγγλικά. Ἐδῶ δημιουργεῖται μία ὁλόκληρη φιλολογία, μία γλῶσσα, μία εἰδική ὁρολογία, ἕνα καινούργιο λεξικό χρήσεως μεταφορᾶς ὅρων ἀπό τά πρωτότυπα κείμενα στά ἀγγλικά, μέ ὅσο τό δυνατόν μεγαλύτερη πιστότητα καί καλλιέπεια. Ἡ προσφορά εἶναι ἐξαιρετικά μεγάλη, ἄν, ἐκτός τῶν ἄλλων, λάβουμε ὑπ' ὄψιν ὅτι σημαντικός ἀριθμός ἀνθρώπων πού μετεστράφησαν καί εἰσῆλθαν στήν ὀρθοδοξία, τό ἔκαμαν διότι εἶχαν τήν δυνατότητα νά διαβάσουν κείμενα ὀρθόδοξα. Τό ἀξιόλογο σέ πολλές περιπτώσεις ἐκδόσεως μεταφράσεων λειτουργικῶν κειμένων εἶναι ὅτι οἱ ἀνωτέρω ἐκδόσεις εἶναι δίγλωσσες, μέ τήν προσφορά μαζί μέ τήν ἀγγλική μετάφραση καί τοῦ ἑλληνικοῦ πρωτοτύπου. Μέσῳ τῶν διγλώσσων αὐτῶν βιβλίων πολλοί κατά κυριολεξία ἀνεκάλυψαν σπουδαῖες βασικές ἀκολουθίες ὅπως τούς καθ' ἡμέραν ὄρθρους καί ἑσπερινούς καθώς καί τό πλουσιώτατο ἁγιολογικό ὑμνολογικό ὑλικό.

Δέν ὑπάρχει ἀμφιβολία ὅτι ἡ Ὀρθόδοξη Ἐκκλησία καί Θεολογία στήν Ἀμερική σήμερα ἔχει τήν θεόσταλτη δυνατότητα δημιουργίας μιᾶς ὑψηλοῦ ἐπιπέδου Θεολογικῆς καί ἐκκλησιαστικῆς ὀρθοδόξου γλώσσης στά ἀγγλικά, διά τῆς αὐξανομένης παραγωγῆς ὀρθοδόξου λόγου διά παντός προσφερομένου μέσου ἐντύπου ἤ ἠλεκτρονικοῦ. Μέ ἄλλα λόγια εἶναι σέ κατάσταση παραγωγῆς, ἡ ὁποία δέν ἀποβλέπει μόνο στήν οἰκοδομή ἑνός δεδομένου ποιμνίου, ἀλλά ἐν τελευταίᾳ ἀναλύσει ἀποβλέπει στήν οἰκοδομή καί στήν προβολή τῆς Ὀρθοδοξίας σέ πολύ εὐρύτερα στρώματα στό Δυτικό Ἡμισφαίριο. Ἡ δημιουργία πλούσιας θεολογικῆς παραγωγῆς σέ ἀγγλική γλῶσσα ἀποτελεῖ ἀσφαλῶς πρόκληση. Καί στήν περίπτωση ὅμως αὐτή ἡ πρόκληση γίνεται κλήση ἀποστολῆς.

Ἡ Πρόκληση τῶν Μειζόνων Θεολογικῶν Πεδίων

Ἡ τρίτη πρόκληση γιά τήν Ὀρθόδοξη Θεολογία καί Ἐκκλησία στήν Ἀμερική αναφέρεται σέ μείζονα θεολογικά πεδία τά ὁποῖα ἐμφανίζονται ὑπό εἰδικές συνθῆκες καταστάσεις καί γλωσσικές διαμορφώσεις στήν Ἀμερική. Ἀναφέρω ἐνδεικτικά τρία τέτοια πεδία.

Τό πρῶτο εἶναι ἡ Ἐκκλησιολογία. Στήν Ἀμερική ὑπάρχει ἕνα ἰσχυρότατο, μονίμως ἐνεργό ρεῦμα, μιά σταθερή τάση πού τονίζει καί καλλιεργεῖ ἐντόνως τήν ἀτομικότητα, καί ἑπομένως παρέχει τήν εὐχέρεια νά δημιουργοῦνται εὐκολώτατα νέες θρησκευτικές ὁμάδες διά ἀποκοπῆς, κατά ὁποιονδήποτε τρόπο, ἀπό προϋπάρχουσες κοινότητες. Ἔτσι παρατηρεῖται συχνά ἕνα φαινόμενο συνεχοῦς διασπάσεως, συνεχοῦς διαλύσεως, εὐρυτέρων συνόλων σέ μικρότερα σύνολα. Γι᾽ αὐτό καί σήμερα στήν Ἀμερική εἶναι δηλωμένες ὑπό τό ὄνομα διαφοροποιημένων θρησκευτικῶν ὁμάδων περί τίς 22.000 θρησκευτικές ὁμολογίες. Μέσα στίς 22.000 περιλαμβάνονται καί μείζονες χριστιανικές Ἐκκλησίες, ὅπως ἡ Ρωμαιοκαθολική μέ 60 περίπου ἑκατομμύρια, καί ἡ Ὀρθόδοξη μέ σύνολο 5 περίπου ἑκατομμύρια, ἀλλά περιλαμβάνονται καί ποικίλες αὐτόνομες θρησκευτικές κοινότητες μέ ἑκατό ἤ διακόσια μέλη πού ἀποτελοῦν ἰδιαίτερα σώματα μέ ἰδιαίτερη θρησκεία. Αὐτή ἡ ἀποσπασματικότητα, αὐτή ἡ κατάτμηση ὀφείλεται σέ μιά ἐκκλησιολογία, ἡ ὁποία εἶναι κατά κυριολεξία δεσμία μιᾶς ἄκρατης ἀτομοκρατίας.

Σ᾽ αὐτή τήν περίπτωση ἡ Ὀρθόδοξη Ἐκκλησία μας στήν Ἀμερική ἀντιμετωπίζει μιά πρόκληση, ἡ ὁποία μεταβάλλεται σέ κλήση γιά μιά ζωτική ὄντως ἀποστολή νά προβάλῃ καί νά ἐγκαθιδρύσῃ μιά ἐκκλησιολογία ἑνότητος καί ὑγιοῦς ἰσορροπίας, ἡ ὁποία ἀκριβῶς τονίζει τήν ἔννοια τῆς Ἐκκλησίας ὡς ἀδιασπάστου, ἀδιαιρέτου καί ἑνιαίου σώματος Χριστοῦ. Ἑνός σώματος μέσα στό ὁποῖο τά ἄτομα ἀναπτύσσονται ἁρμονικά καί ἔτσι ἀποφεύγονται τά θλιβερά φαινόμενα κατατμήσεων, σχισμάτων, παραφυάδων ἤ παρασυναγωγῶν.

Ἡ Χριστολογία εἶναι τό δεύτερο πεδίο. Πολλές Ἐκκλησίες καί Ὁμολογίες στήν Ἀμερική ἐμφανίζουν μία ἔκδηλη Χριστοκεντρικότητα. Ἡ Χριστοκεντρικότητα αὐτή σέ ἀρκετές περιπτώσεις ἔχει δώσει σχετικῶς ἀξιόλογα κείμενα, ἀλλά σέ πάρα πολλές περιπτώσεις εἶναι μία Χριστοκεντρικότητα, ἡ ὁποία φαίνεται νά λειτουργῇ ἀσχέτως πρός τό Τριαδικό δόγμα. Γιά ὡρισμένες ἀπό τίς Χριστολογίες, οἱ ὁποῖες εὐνοοῦν τήν Χριστοκεντρικότητα ἀπό πλευρᾶς κεντρικοῦ ἐκκλησιαστικοῦ βιώματος, ὑπάρχει ἀπόσταση καί ἐν πολλοῖς κατ' οὐσίαν ἄγνοια τῆς μοναδικῆς διασυνδέσεως Χριστολογίας καί Τριαδολογίας. Ἐδῶ δημιουργεῖται μιά πρόκληση γιά τήν Ὀρθοδοξία.

Στήν πρόκληση αὐτή ἡ Ὀρθόδοξη Θεολογία καί Ἐκκλησία στήν Ἀμερική ἀπαντᾶ μέ τήν παρουσίαση μιᾶς Χριστολογίας μέ ἐντονώτατη Χριστοκεντρικότητα, ἀλλά Χριστοκεντρικότητα ἡ ὁποία εἶναι σαφέστατα Τριαδολογική καί Τριαδοκεντρική. Ἡ θεμελιώδης αὐτή ἀλήθεια προβάλλεται ἀνά πᾶσαν στιγμήν διά τῶν θεολογικῶν κειμένων, διά τῆς λειτουργικῆς πράξεως καί διά τοῦ Ὀρθοδόξου ἤθους ὥστε νά ἐξασφαλίζεται μιά ἁρμονία Χριστολογίας καί Τριαδολογίας, ἡ ὁποία ἐμποδίζει τήν ἀνάπτυξη ὑπερμέτρων πλευρῶν τῆς α ἤ β δογματικῆς ἀληθείας, μέ συνέπειες τήν μειωμένη παρουσίαση ἄλλων στοιχείων καί τήν ἀνισορροπία στό περιεχόμενο τῆς πίστεως. Ἐδῶ λοιπόν ἡ Ὀρθόδοξος Θεολογία καί Ἐκκλησία τῆς Ἀμερικῆς ἔχει τόν μοναδικό ρόλο τῆς προβολῆς, διδασκαλίας καί ἐμπεδώσεως μιᾶς Χριστοκεντρικότητας καί μιᾶς Χριστολογίας ἡ ὁποία ἐναρμονίζεται μέ τίς ἄλλες βασικές πλευρές τοῦ δόγματος.

Ἡ Πνευματολογία εἶναι τό τρίτο πεδίο. Σέ πολλά σημεῖα τοῦ κόσμου, ἀλλά ἰδιαιτέρως στήν Ἀμερική συναντοῦμε ἕνα φαινόμενο τό ὁποῖο παρουσιάζεται μέ δύο ἀντίθετες μορφές προκλήσεως. Ἡ μία μορφή εἶναι μιά Πνευματολογία, πού εἶναι σέ ἀπόσταση ἀπό τό Τριαδολογικό δόγμα, καί μᾶλλον ἀγνοεῖται στή ζωή τῆς Ἐκκλησίας. Πρόκειται γιά μιάν ἀντίληψη κατά τήν ὁποία τό Ἅγιον Πνεῦμα δέν βιοῦται ὡς τό "Πνεῦμα τῆς Ἀληθείας", ὡς "ὁ Παράκλητος", "ὁ πανταχοῦ παρών καί τά πάντα πληρῶν". Πρόκειται δηλαδή γιά μιάν ἀντίληψη πνευματολογικῆς ἀναιμίας ἤ ἀνεπαρκείας.

Ἡ ἄλλη, διαμετρικά ἀντίθετη μορφή τῆς Πνευματολογικῆς προκλήσεως συναντᾶται σέ ὁμολογίες καί σύνολα στήν Ἀμερική, στά ὁποία κυριαρχεῖ μιά πνευματολογία τοῦ πεντηκοστιανοῦ τύπου. Στήν περίπτωση αὐτή οἱ ἄνθρωποι ἰσχυρίζονται ὅτι λαμβάνουν κατ' εὐθεῖαν καί αἰσθητῶς τό Ἅγιο Πνεῦμα ἀνά πᾶσαν στιγμήν καί κατά βούλησιν, καί ζοῦν ἐκστατικές καταστάσεις μέ γλωσσολαλίες καί συναφῆ φαινόμενα.

Ἀπό τά ἀνωτέρω καθίσταται φανερό ὅτι εὑρισκόμεθα ἀφ' ἑνός μέν ἐνώπιον μιᾶς ἀντιλήψεως μετρίας ἕως πλήρους παραγνωρίσεως καί ἀποστασιοποιήσεως τοῦ Ἁγίου Πνεύματος ἀπό τήν ζωή μιᾶς συγκεκριμένης ὁμολογίας, ἀφ' ἑτέρου δέ ἐνώπιον μιᾶς πλήρους ἀπορροφήσεως οὐσιαστικῶν δογματικῶν στοιχείων ἀπό μιά Πνευματολογία, ἡ ὁποία ἔχει ἀναπτυχθῆ ὑπερμέτρως.

Ἡ Ὀρθοδοξία στήν Ἀμερική ἔχει ἕνα τεράστιο ρόλο νά ἀντιτάξῃ καί στήν Πνευματολογική πρόκληση τήν ἀληθινή καί πλήρη Πνευματολογία καί νά μεταδώσῃ τήν περί τοῦ Ἁγίου Πνεύματος πραγματικότητα καί ὄχι ἁπλῶς διδασκαλία. Πρόκειται γιά ἕνα ἐξαιρετικά πολυσύνθετο ἔργο διά τοῦ ὁποίου ἑκατομμύρια ἀνθρώπων θά γνωρίσουν τήν πλήρη περί τοῦ Ἁγίου Πνεύματος ἀλήθεια καί θά ἔχουν τήν δυνατότητα νά ζήσουν τήν πραγματικότητα τῆς σκηνώσεως τοῦ Παρακλήτου στίς ψυχές των.

Ἡ Πρόκληση τῆς Ἑλληνικῆς Πολιτιστικῆς Κληρονομίας

Ἡ τετάρτη πρόκληση πού ἀντιμετωπίζει ἡ Ὀρθόδοξη Θεολογία καί Ἐκκλησία στήν Ἀμερική συνδέεται μέ τήν ἑλληνική πολιτιστική κληρονομιά. Ἡ Ἑλληνική Ὀρθόδοξη Ἐκκλησία τῆς Ἀμερικῆς προσφέρει Ὀρθοδοξία, ἀλλά προσφέρει αὐτομάτως, λόγῳ ὀργανικῆς σχέσεως, καί οὐσιαστικά στοιχεῖα τῆς ἑλληνικῆς πολιτιστικῆς κληρονομιᾶς, εἴτε κλασσικοῦ, εἴτε ἑλληνιστικοῦ, εἴτε βυζαντινοῦ τύπου. Αὐτή ἡ προσφορά εἶναι ἀναπόσπαστο στοιχεῖο ἐκφράσεως τῆς ζωῆς τῆς Ἐκκλησίας, τό ὁποῖο σέ χώρους ὅπως ὁ ἑλληνικός, εἶναι αὐτονόητο καί λειτουργεῖ κατά κάποιο τρόπο αὐτομάτως, ἀλλά σέ χώρους ἐκτός τῆς Ἑλλάδος, δέν εἶναι καθόλου αὐτονόητο οὔτε λειτουργεῖ αὐτομάτως.

Χρειάζεται νά ἐξηγηθῇ στόν πολύ κόσμο, τόν ἐντός καί ἐκτός τῆς Ἑλληνικῆς Ὀρθοδόξου Ἐκκλησίας τῆς Ἀμερικῆς, ὅτι τό στοιχεῖο τῆς Ἑλληνικῆς πολιτιστικῆς κληρονομιᾶς δέν ἀναφέρεται σέ κάποιον ἄκρατον ἐθνικισμό, δέν ἔχει σχέση μέ οἱονδήποτε σωβινισμό, ἀλλά ἀποτελεῖ ὄντως ἕνα πολυτιμότατο θησαυρό, ὁ ὁποῖος πλουτίζει καί διευκολύνει ποικιλοτρόπως τό ἔργο τῆς προσφορᾶς τοῦ Εὐαγγελίου. Στήν περίπτωση αὐτή γίνεται ἕνα ἄνοιγμα, τό ὁποῖο θεωροῦμε ἐκ τῆς πείρας καί ἐκ τῶν πραγμάτων ὅτι εἶναι ἄνοιγμα τό ὁποῖο δίδει προοπτικές προσβάσεως σέ ὄντως θαυμαστούς κόσμους. Σέ μιά πρόσφατη μνημειώδη ἔκδοση, ἀφιερωμένη στήν Ἑλληνική κλασική διανόηση, οἱ ἐκδότες Καθηγηταί J. Brunschwig καί G.E.R. Lloyd σημειώνουν χαρακτηριστικά στόν πρόλογο ὅτι τά Ἑλληνικά κλασσικά κείμενα "δημιούργησαν καί ἔθρεψαν τήν ὅλη παράδοση τῆς Δυτικῆς σκέψεως. Ἐδῶ τά αἰσθήματα οἰκειότητος καί ἀποστάσεως συνυφαίνονται. Εἴμεθα σέ οἰκεῖο ἔδαφος σέ μακρυνή χώρα. Ταξιδεύουμε χωρίς νά ἐγκαταλείπουμε τό δωμάτιό μας. Ἡ ὅλη διανόησή μας κατά τόν ἕνα ἤ τόν ἄλλο τρόπο περνάει μέσα ἀπό τήν διανόηση τῶν Ἑλλήνων" (J. Brunschwig and G.E.R. Lloyd: *Greek Thought: A Guide to Classical Knowledge.* Cambridge, MA and London: The Belknop Press of Harvard University Press, 2000, page IX).

Βαρυσήμαντες διακηρύξεις ὅπως ἡ ἀνωτέρω δείχνουν μιά ἀναγνώριση ὅτι, τό στοιχεῖο τῆς ἑλληνικῆς πολιτιστικῆς κληρονομιᾶς δέν εἶναι κάτι τό ὁποῖο περιορίζεται ἐθνολογικά, ἀλλά κάτι τό ὁποῖο ἀνήκει σέ ὁλόκληρη τήν ἀνθρωπότητα, γι' αὐτό καί ἐξακολουθεῖ νά λειτουργῆ σέ ὅλα τά γεωγραφικά μήκη καί πλάτη. Ὅταν σήμερα στό κέντρο τῆς Νέας Ὑόρκης, στό νευραλγικότερο σημεῖο μιᾶς γιγαντιαίας κοσμοπόλεως, ὅπως εἶναι ἡ Νέα Ὑόρκη, εἴχαμε μιά ἔκθεση κυκλαδικῆς τέχνης πού μᾶς πήγαινε πίσω στό ἔτος 3200 πρό Χριστοῦ, καί ἐν συνεχείᾳ στό ἴδιο σημεῖο μιά ἔκθεση μεταβυζαντινῆς τέχνης, ἐνῶ προετοιμάζεται γιά τήν ἄνοιξη τοῦ 2004 μιά ἄλλη μεγάλη ἔκθεση βυζαντινῶν εἰκόνων στό Μητροπολιτικό Μουσεῖο τῆς Νέας Ὑόρκης, δέν μποροῦμε νά ἀμφιβάλλουμε γιά τόν τεράστιο ρόλο πού παίζει ἐντός τοῦ συγχρόνου κόσμου ἡ ἑλληνική πολιτιστική κληρονομιά.

Ἐν ὄψει αὐτῆς τῆς παγκόσμιας ἀναγνωρίσεως τοῦ Ἑλληνικοῦ Πολιτιστικοῦ στοιχείου, ὡς Ἑλληνική Ὀρθόδοξη Ἐκκλησία καί Θεολογία στήν Ἀμερική, εὑρισκόμεθα σέ κατάσταση ἀποστολῆς, διότι ἔχουμε τήν ἐξαιρετικά λεπτή, ἀλλά καί εὐλογημένη ὑποχρέωση νά δώσουμε αὐτό τό γνήσιο ἑλληνικό στοιχεῖο μέ τόν καλύτερο τρόπο. Μέ τρόπο πού δέν εἶναι ἐθνοκεντρικός καί σωβινιστικός, ἀλλά διαχρονικός καί πανανθρώπινος. Καί ἐδῶ λοιπόν γιά μιά ἀκόμη φορά εἴμεθα ἐνώπιον μιᾶς προκλήσεως τήν ὁποία καλούμεθα νά μεταμορφώσουμε σέ ἀποστολή.

Ἡ Πρόκληση τῆς Τεχνολογίας, τοῦ Πλουραλισμοῦ καί τῆς Παγκοσμιοποιήσεως

Τελειώνω μέ ἀναφορά σέ μιά πέμπτη πρόκληση, ἡ ὁποία εἶναι ἐπίσης ἐξαιρετικά ἐνδιαφέρουσα καί εἶναι ἰδιαίτερα χαρακτηριστική τῆς Ἀμερικῆς. Πρόκειται γιά τήν πρόκληση πού ἐμφανίζεται μέσῳ τῆς συνδυασμένης παρουσίας τῆς ἁλματώδους τεχνολογικῆς ἀναπτύξεως, τοῦ ἐντόνου πολιτιστικο-θρησκευτικοῦ πλουραλισμοῦ καί τῆς ραγδαίας παγκοσμιοποιήσεως. Ἐν ὄψει τῆς τεράστιας καί πολυσύνθετης αὐτῆς πραγματικότητος, πραγματικότητος πού συνιστᾶ ἐντονώτατη πρόκληση γιά τήν Ἐκκλησία καί τήν Θεολογία, ἐμεῖς στήν Ἀμερική εἴμεθα κατ' ἀνάγκην στήν πρώτη γραμμή. Καί τοῦτο διότι ζοῦμε σέ μιά χώρα τεχνολογικά ἀναπτυγμένη σέ ὑπέρτατο βαθμό, καί διότι ἀντιμετωπίζουμε τό φαινόμενο μιᾶς κυριαρχούσης πλουραλιστικῆς ἐξελίξεως, ἡ ὁποία συμβαδίζει μέ τό γεγονός μιᾶς παγκοσμιοποιήσεως πού δέν ἀναχαιτίζεται εὔκολα. Ἐδῶ ἔχουμε τόν πολύ εἰδικό ἀλλά καί δύσκολο ρόλο τῆς διατηρήσεως τῶν ἰσορροπιῶν καί τῆς διαμορφώσεως κριτηρίων καί παραμέτρων πού προλαμβάνουν ἀνισόρροπες ἀναπτύξεις. Πῶς θά βιωθῇ μιά γνήσια Ὀρθόδοξη πνευματικότητα ἐντός τῶν καταστάσεων ζωῆς πού δημιουργοῦνται ἀπό τό τρίπτυχο τεχνολογία-πλουραλισμός-παγκοσμιοποίηση; Πῶς θά ἀναπτυχθῇ ἕνα ὑγιές Ὀρθόδοξο ἦθος τό ὁποῖο ἐνῶ θά εὑρίσκεται σέ ὀργανική συνέχεια μέ τήν μακραίωνα παράδοση καί ἐμπειρία τῆς Ἐκκλησίας θά μπορῇ ταὐτόχρονα νά λειτουργῇ πλήρως καί ἀποτελεσματικῶς ἐντός τῆς ἀμέσου ἀμερικανικῆς πραγματικότητος; Πῶς θά καλλιεργηθῇ τό Ὀρθόδοξο φρόνημα ὑπό συνθῆκες πού μᾶλλον εὐνοοῦν τήν ἀπουσία φρονήματος λόγῳ ἀκριβῶς ἐπικρατήσεως ἄλλων ὑπαρξιακῶν προτεραιοτήτων;

Τό πεδίο πού διανοίγεται ἐνώπιόν μας εἶναι εὐρύτατο καί ἀπαιτεῖ ἐργασία τόσο στό θεωρητικό, ὅσο καί στό πρακτικό ἐπίπεδο. Ἀπαιτεῖ ἐργασία καί συνεχῆ προσπάθεια τόσο στούς Θεολογικούς Πανεπιστημιακούς χώρους ὅσο καί στήν πρακτική ζωή τῶν ἐνοριῶν. Ἡ καθαρῶς θεωρητική θεολογική ἔρευνα καί ἀνάλυση τῶν συναφῶν θεμάτων πρέπει νά συνοδεύεται ἀπό πρακτικές ποιμαντικές ἐφαρμογές γιά τίς κοινότητές μας καί τούς ἀνθρώπους μας. Τελικός σκοπός τῆς σύνθετης αὐτῆς προσπαθείας εἶναι ἡ σύν Θεῷ διαμόρφωση καί παρουσία κοινοτήτων καί ἀνθρώπων πού θά ἐκφράζουν γνήσιο ὀρθόδοξο ἦθος καί θά εἶναι φορεῖς ἀληθινοῦ ὀρθοδόξου φρονήματος ἐντός τῆς ἔντονης τεχνολογικῆς, πλουραλιστικῆς καί παγκοσμιοποιημένης ἀμερικανικῆς κοινωνίας. Φυσικά τό ἔργο εἶναι τεράστιο, ἀλλά πραγματοποιεῖται μέ τήν ἰσχύ καί τήν χάρη τοῦ Θεοῦ. Ἑνός "*Θεοῦ ποιοῦντος θαυμάσια καί γνωρίσαντος ἐν τοῖς λαοῖς τήν δύναμιν αὐτοῦ*" (Ψαλμ. 76, 15).

Παρουσιάσαμε σέ ἁδρές γραμμές πέντε πλευρές-προκλήσεις πού συνδέονται μέ τήν Θεολογία μας καί τήν Ἐκκλησία μας στίς Ἡνωμένες Πολιτεῖες σήμερα: Τήν πρόκληση πού ἀπορρέει ἀπό τό γεγονός ὅτι εἴμεθα μειονότης σέ μιά ἀχανῆ χώρα· Τήν πρόκληση πού σχετίζεται μέ τήν ἀνάγκη δημιουργίας ὑψηλοῦ ἐπιπέδου ὀρθοδόξου ἀγγλικῆς γλώσσης ἐκφραστικῆς τῆς ὑπέροχης Θεολογίας μας· Τήν πρόκληση πού δημιουργεῖται ἀπό τήν ἀνάγκη προσφορᾶς, μέ συγκεκριμένο ἀλλά καί ἰσορροπημένο τρόπο, βασικῶν δογματικῶν ἀληθειῶν στίς περιοχές τῆς Ἐκκλησιολογίας, τῆς Χριστολογίας καί τῆς Πνευματολογίας· Τήν πρόκληση πού ἀναφέρεται στήν Ἑλληνική πολιτιστική μας κληρονομιά καί τήν διατήρηση καί παρουσίασή της μέ τόν ὡραιότερο καί πληρέστερο τρόπο· καί Τήν πρόκληση τῆς βιώσεως τῆς Ὀρθοδοξίας καί τῆς δυναμικῆς προβολῆς τῆς Ὀρθοδόξου πίστεως στόν τεχνολογικό, πλουραλιστικό καί παγκοσμιοποιημένο χῶρο τῆς Ἀμερικῆς.

Οἱ προκλήσεις αὐτές τονίζουν τό γεγονός τῶν μεγάλων εὐθυνῶν καί ὑποχρεώσεών μας ὡς Ἑλληνικῆς Ὀρθοδόξου Ἀρχιεπισκοπῆς Ἀμερικῆς. Ἐν τελευταίᾳ ἀναλύσει μᾶς θέτουν σέ κατάσταση ἀποστολῆς, σέ κατάσταση μιᾶς μόνιμης εἰδικῆς κλήσεως ἀπό τόν Θεό νά εἴμεθα οἱ Ἀπόστολοι τῆς Ὀρθοδοξίας στό Δυτικό Ἡμισφαίριο. Ἔχουμε δεχθῆ μέ βαθύτατη εὐγνωμοσύνη τήν κλήση αὐτή. Καί εἴμεθα ὑπόχρεοι στούς ἁπανταχοῦ τῆς γῆς ἀδελφούς μας πού συμπαρίστανται στήν ἱερή προσπάθειά μας, ἰδιαίτερα στούς ἀδελφούς μας τῆς Θεολογικῆς Σχολῆς τοῦ Ἀριστοτελείου Πανεπιστημίου Θεσσαλονίκης, πού μέσῳ τῶν γραμμῶν αὐτῶν ἔγιναν κοινωνοί τῶν προκλήσεων πού ἀντιμετωπίζουμε καί τῶν ἀγώνων στούς ὁποίους, τοῦ Θεοῦ συνεργοῦντος καί εὐλογοῦντος ἔχουμε ἀποδυθῆ.

As Poor, Yet Making Many Rich: Orthodoxy in the American Context

Yale Divinity School

New Haven, Connecticut
April 29, 2003

Introduction

In this Resurrection season of glory and jubilation, I greet you all in the Orthodox manner with the traditional salutation of Pascha: *Christos Anesti*! Christ is Risen!

It is with particular joy that I find myself here today, at the famous Yale University, an international center for research and knowledge, answering a truly honorific invitation by my good friend and distinguished colleague Dean Harold Attridge of the Yale Divinity School. I am deeply touched by the present occasion of being together with beloved and esteemed friends like Dean Attridge, sharing memories of an unforgettable past and visions of a promising future.

Thinking of the past, I cannot help but remember "the Game," the notorious athletic competition between Yale and Harvard which was a permanent yearly feature throughout our years at Harvard. Here, today, we do not have "the Game," but we certainly have some sort of an invasion of Harvard into the Yale territory if you look at the group comprising Dean Attridge, Professors John Collins and Adela Yarbro Collins, and myself. This, of course, is a happy invasion; in fact, this is no invasion at all, and no game at all. This is some sort of a repetition of the annual exchange visits between the Harvard and Yale New Testament Departments in the late sixties and early seventies. This is simply an opportunity, if I may use the inspirational passage from the Epistle to the Hebrews, *to have consideration for one another with an aim of provoking love and good works* [κατανοῶεν ἀλλήλους εἰς παροξυσμὸν ἀγάπης καὶ καλῶν ἔργων] (Hebrews 10:24), and to *love one another with brotherly affection and to outdo one another in showing honor* [τῇ φιλαδελφία εἰς ἀλλήλους φιλόστοργοι, τῇ τιμῇ ἀλλήλους προηγούμενοι] as Saint Paul said in Romans 12:10.

On the occasion of this wonderful academic and ecumenical encounter, my thoughts turn to the words of a specific biblical text, namely Saint Paul's Second Epistle to the Corinthians. His words throughout are words of humility, words of brotherly affection and of a yearning for concord and peace. So many phrases and passages in this epistle could be fitting slogans for Christian ecumenical activities. Especially in the sixth chapter, we find what might even be a basic guideline for the work of inter-Christian dialog.

Following that particular chapter, addressing each other as *"fellow laborers with God"* (2 Corinthinas 6:1), we might go on to exhort and encourage one another to receive God's help fruitfully and not in vain. We might offer one another a firm resolve not to put obstacles in anyone's way (6:3), but to commend ourselves to each other in the work of ministry (6:4) through *purity, knowledge, forbearance, kindness, genuine love, truthful speech, and the power of God* (6:6-7a). Above all, we might declare our purpose to have hearts wide open for one another in Christ, unrestricted in affection and reciprocal respect. As Saint Paul states: *"Our mouth is open to you Corinthians; our heart is wide. You are not restricted by us, but you are restricted in your own affection. In return - I speak as to children – widen your hearts also"* (2 Corinthians 6:11-13).

It is in this spirit of openness and brotherly affection that I come to speak to you today on the subject of Orthodoxy in the American context. My purpose is to facilitate and further the work of ecumenical dialog by creating among you some familiarity with the spirit and outlook of Orthodox Christianity as you encounter it here in the New World.

The Church of Paradox

For many Americans, the movie *My Big Fat Greek Wedding* seemed to contain the sum and substance of their exposure to the Orthodox faith, encapsulated in a rather awkward scene of an adult baptism and a highly hilarious sequence of a wedding ceremony. Such scenes projected back to the American public some of its own vaguely formulated presuppositions about Orthodox Christianity. Here you have an image of Orthodoxy as a rather antiquated and inscrutable set of religious ideas and customs that are practiced without full understanding, in small ethnic enclaves, by homesick immigrants clinging to their vestige of a distinctive identity.

But this is not an accurate image of Orthodoxy in the New World. We clearly are in need of a more realistic and meaningful picture of this community of an ancient Christian faith such as the Orthodox community in the United States. This, however, is not to be done by a statistical reportage of facts and figures. Instead, as a kind of prolegomenon to further ecumenical conversations between Christians, I will try to give you a sense of what the essence and mission of Orthodoxy presently is and may be in the coming years of the twenty-first century.

My starting point is a reference again to chapter 6 of Paul's Second Epistle to the Corinthians. In this chapter Saint Paul presents an astonishing and intriguing series of paradoxes that he has joined together (2 Corinthians 6:6b-10):

> *We are treated as impostors, and yet are true; as unknown, and yet well known; as dying, and behold we live; as punished, and yet not killed; as sorrowful, yet always rejoicing; as poor, yet making many rich; as having nothing, and yet possessing everything.*

These paradoxes, *mutatio mutandis* in the case of Orthodoxy, are the starting point of my thoughts this afternoon. In many ways, the Orthodox Church is the Christian Church of paradox, a paradox epitomized in the phrase *as poor yet making many rich, as having nothing and yet possessing everything,* a phrase used as the title of my presentation. We can go immediately and directly to the substance of the paradox just by considering the fact that the central dogmas of the ancient Orthodox faith to which Orthodoxy passionately and unyieldingly adheres are deep and paradoxical mysteries.

Let me mention a few: the oneness of the Triune God; the divine and human person of Jesus Christ; His birth from a virgin mother; the synergy between divine grace and human freedom in salvation; the real death of Christ on the Cross and His Resurrection with a fully human yet incorruptible body, and so on. But it is precisely these dogmas that give form and life to the Orthodox way of being, with all of the sense of paradox and wonder that they inspire.

An illustration at this juncture will be appropriate and useful. If one observes the Orthodox icons of the Eucharistic Supper on the one hand and of the Holy Trinity, or, as it is more accurately called, the Hospitality of Abraham on the other, one notices a striking similarity in the composition of the two: the table, the setting, the postures and positioning of the persons in the two icons. This is no mere coincidence. Insofar as the Eucharist is the constitutive sacrament of the *Ecclesia*, the Church thereby becomes a living icon of the life and fellowship of the Holy Trinity. Hence, there are striking, basic similarities in the two icons. And if our God is a God of paradox, it should be no surprise that the Church too, in an iconic fashion, reflects the paradoxical nature of the divine, living in a mode of being that surpasses human intellect and becomes a crux for worldly understanding.

The Orthodox Church, then, lives constantly in a paradox, in a creative tension between the various poles of its existence as a human earthly entity that is indwelt by the divine transcendent Spirit of God. To one who is encountering Orthodoxy from a different Christian perspective, there may be a temptation towards *reductionism*—the impulse to assess the Church in terms of familiar analytical categories that do not correspond to the realities of living Orthodoxy. This tendency is all the more pronounced in our American context, where Orthodoxy has appeared as a latecomer on the scene, and finds itself in a sociopolitical milieu that is quite different from the traditional homelands of Orthodox Christianity. If reductionism, however, is applied in the case of Orthodoxy, then inevitably a wrong picture will emerge which does not represent Orthodoxy.

Orthodoxy in the American Context

Orthodoxy in the American context, in order to be properly and adequately understood, has to be viewed as a Church living in the paradox of the true faith. We constantly experience in a plethora of variations the Pauline paradox of being *unknown and yet well known, sorrowful, yet always rejoicing, poor, yet making many rich, having nothing and yet possessing everything*. I will proceed with the presentation of five basic areas in which the paradoxical nature of the Orthodox Church in America is depicted. But before that, let me speak briefly about the history of the arrival and the settling of the Orthodox people in America. This is necessary in order to avoid any reductionism or offhand classification of Orthodoxy within the American socioreligious environment. It is important for our Protestant and Catholic brothers and sisters to be aware of an important fact, namely, that the arrival of Orthodox Christianity in the Western Hemisphere was relatively late compared to the other Christian communities, and that the impetus for its arrival was somewhat different. For example, the first sizable waves of immigration from Greece to the New World began in the 1880's, and continued until the imposition of quotas in the twentieth century. Similar patterns of immigration hold for persons belonging to other traditional Orthodox ethnicities, such as those who emigrated from Russia, Romania, Serbia, and the Middle East.

The reason for this delay, so to speak, in coming to America had to do with conditions in the homelands, and in particular in those areas where the Ottoman occupation made freedom of movement problematic.

The motivation for migration was also rather different. Unlike the Pilgrims and Puritans who came to the New World to avoid religious persecution, or the Catholic missionaries who came to convert a continent, Orthodox immigrants left their homes largely for economic reasons. This fact is of a significance which cannot be overstated. While the Greeks and Russians brought their faith with them to America and Canada, by and large they did not bring their church with them at first. That is to say, the arrival of clergy, the founding of Orthodox parishes, and the establishment of organized ecclesiastical bodies occurred well after the emigrating laity had set down roots in their communities across the United States.

From the point of view of Old World Orthodoxy, the result has been an ecclesiastical situation in America that is somehow irregular, and has even been described as non-canonical, as somehow a bending of the norms and rules of Orthodox Church governance. For instance, it is not the norm for Orthodoxy to have multiple jurisdictions with overlapping territories, or multiple hierarchs in a single city. And yet this is the status quo in America from the nineteenth century up to the present, such that Greek, Russian, Albanian, Lebanese, Jordanian, Romanian, Serbian, and Ukrainian Orthodox faithful can live in the same neighborhoods, and yet have separate parishes along ethnic lines, answering to different bishops, but all in the same locale. The Orthodox in this land have become somewhat used to this situation as yet another element of the American melting pot, and yet according to the ideals of Orthodox ecclesiology, such a condition is neither normal nor desirable.

But as problematic as the status quo can be administratively and organizationally, it is not ultimately a failure *theologically*. The Orthodox of America remain united in faith despite the diversity of their ethnic heritage or linguistic and cultural expressions.

United though not Uniform

And this leads me to the first key point, the first area of paradox, if you will, of American Orthodoxy. The Orthodox Church in the New World is *united* though not *uniform*. In a Protestant understanding especially, the diversity of Orthodox Churches—Greek Orthodox, Russian Orthodox,

Antiochian Orthodox, Carpatho-Russian Orthodox, and so on—looks like a variety of Christian denominations. This is decidedly not the case. Despite the diversity of names, Orthodoxy is one in terms of creed, sacraments, Canon Law, ecclesiastical ethos, and ethics. This unity, however, does not result in any kind of top-down imposition of uniformity.

For example, even within the Greek Orthodox Archdiocese of America, there is a marvelous diversity of languages spoken in worship, including Greek, English, Spanish, and so on, according to the needs of the local community and the abilities of the assigned clergy. The same holds true of our sister Orthodox jurisdictions. Where uniformity of practice or expression exists, it has its source in a conscious faithfulness to the wellspring of our common Holy Tradition, and to the movement of the Holy Spirit. But unity is the essence, *the unity of the Spirit in the bond of peace* (Ephesians 4:3).

It should be noted, however, that this unity has also clear administrative expressions and manifestations of uniformity. The strongest evidence is SCOBA, an acronym for the Standing Conference of the Canonical Orthodox Bishops in the Americas. SCOBA is a coordinating agency uniting the various Orthodox jurisdictions in this country in common projects and actions. Two of them are worth mentioning: IOCC and OCMC. IOCC, the International Orthodox Christian Charities, is a philanthropic organization that deals with offering assistance (medical supplies, food, etc.) to needy areas outside the United States of America. OCMC, the Orthodox Christian Mission Center, serves the needs of areas in Africa, the Far East, and elsewhere where the local Orthodox Churches are developing and need special care. SCOBA with its agencies of IOCC and OCMC is a visible expression of unity and uniformity in action within the body of the Orthodox Church in America.

Conservative without being Fundamentalist

This leads me to the second key point, the second paradox of Orthodoxy in America. Orthodoxy is *conservative* without being *fundamentalist*. Without a doubt, on the spectrum of Christian churches, the Orthodox Church falls on the right side, as a Church that is careful to maintain unchangingly the form and content of its theological and liturgical life. Orthodoxy has little by way of analogue in its history to the earthshaking events of the Protestant Reformation or the Second Vatican Council. Moreover, the modifications of church life from Old World to New are relatively few and minor, and this is again by conscious choice.

And yet, despite its conservative nature, Orthodoxy does not fit well in the category of other better-known conservative bodies, inasmuch as it does not project the same fundamentalist impulse. The Orthodox take Scripture seriously, but not always literally. At this point an example coming from a basic Orthodox understanding of the biblical texts, namely Patristic exegesis and interpretation, will be illuminating. Take, for instance, four major biblical exegetes like John Chrysostom, Cyril of Alexandria, Eusebius of Caesarea and Theodoret of Cyrrhus, and study their exegesis of the book of the Prophet Isaiah. You will immediately see a pronounced diversity in terms of emphasis on historical or allegorical exegesis, on the literary, theological or messianic interpretative tendencies. The respect for the Isaiahnic text is unlimited but the exegesis offered by the specific Fathers has nothing to do with any fundamentalist approach.[1] The Orthodox apply the an-

[1]See more on this subject in Metropolitan Demetrios Trakatellis, "The-

cient canonical traditions rigorously, but not rigidly. The Orthodox receive their dogmatic heritage conservatively, but also creatively. In general, the characteristics of American-style fundamentalism are quite lacking in the ethos of Orthodox Christianity, making it a *tertium quid*, a third entity in the liberal and conservative mix of modern religiosity.

No doubt, this is due in large part to the strongly apophatic character of Orthodox theology. The teachers of the Church have always been careful to avoid overstepping the bounds of revealed knowledge, or tainting divine truths with human speculations or interpolations. As Saint Gregory the Theologian, the well known fourth century Father of the Church, once wrote of God (*Oration* 28.4): "To define Him in words is an impossibility." Human language fails to serve adequately early on in the spiritual quest for divine knowledge. If there is a "fundamental" core of Orthodox dogma, it is precisely this apophaticism. It is for this reason that in comparison to Western confessions and catechisms, Orthodox creedal statements, though linguistically precise, seem positively minimalistic.

To many in America, these apophatic and mystical qualities of Orthodox thought and worship, these paradoxes are termed "Eastern" and possibly viewed as exotic, ornate to the point of extravagance, or even foreign to the simplicity of the Gospel. This again is a reductionist view, making the adjective "Eastern" a catch-all term for more than a continent and a half of human diversity. If "Eastern" means everything from the Straits of the Bosporus to the Bering Sea, from the Aegean Greek Islands to San Francisco Bay,

odoret's Commentary on Isaiah: A Synthesis of Exegetical Traditions", in *New Perspectives on Historical Theology*, edited by Bradley Nassif (Grand Rapids: Eerdmans, 1996), 313-342.

from the Mediterranean Sea to the Baltic Sea, then it means nothing, except perhaps "non-Western."

Orthodoxy is not merely "Eastern," but is truly "catholic" in the original sense of the Greek word, "καθολικός," conveying the concept of totality, worldwide universality. That which should be perceived as "Eastern" about Eastern Orthodoxy is not any limitation to a particular geographical or cultural setting, but rather an embracing inclusivity. What makes Eastern Christianity "Eastern" is precisely this all inclusive and at the same time eclectic spirit—part of the legacy of our Hellenistic roots—which incorporates "τὸ καλὸν κἀγαθόν" [the good and the beautiful], wherever it may be found. Richness, not simplicity, is a *desideratum* in the so-called "Eastern" mindset. This eclecticism has made Orthodoxy rich in terms of its liturgical and theological expressions. By comparison, some of the more parochial expressions of "Western" Christianity seem somewhat sterile and limited.

Genuinely Orthodox and Truly American

And so we come to observe the third paradox of Orthodoxy in the American context: Orthodoxy can be both genuinely *Orthodox* in the all-inclusive and eclectic sense and yet also truly *American*. Orthodox Christianity is not in any sense incompatible with the ideals of American freedom, democracy, and self-determination. On the contrary, our Orthodox theological notions of personhood and the *imago Dei* fit quite comfortably with the leading ideas of the founding fathers of this nation. Orthodox Christians participate wholeheartedly in the democratic processes of the United States and Canada. Indeed, for the first generations of Greek immigrants, voting on Election Day was treated almost with the respect of a divine commandment!

Orthodox Christians inhabit the entire spectrum of political affiliation, from the left to the right. They are avid consumers of the free press here in America and are enthusiastic about voicing their opinions on the issues of the day. They are interested in having their Orthodox values and interests shape the policy of our leaders, and they work toward this goal.

But more than that, Orthodox Christians in America have also worked to have the influence run in the opposite direction as well. American democratic and majoritarian ideals have been brought into the sphere of the Church and her life, and have shaped the very way that our Archdiocese is administered. The result has been a successful marriage of clerical and lay oversight of the Church at every level—in the parish, the diocese, and in the Archdiocese. This cooperation of clergy and laity in the governance of the Church is strikingly different from the mainly clerical administrations of the Orthodox Church in its Old World homelands. It stands as yet another example of the eclectic and authentically "catholic" nature of the Orthodox Church.

Ancient yet Maturing

And this consideration brings us to the fourth paradox. Orthodoxy in the American context is on the one hand a contemporary expression of a very *ancient* Christian faith, and yet on the other hand is a community that is *still in the process of maturation*. Orthodoxy is old, but it is not ossified; it continually experiences growth and change and—perhaps the best word is—renewal. This word is particularly apt as we gather here in the week after Orthodox Pascha, the so-called "Διακαινίσιμον Ἑβδομάδα" (Bright Week), or more technically, the "Week of Renewal." In the Resurrection of Christ, all things enter into a possibility for renewal and transformation, and as the Church whose focus is the Resurrection, Orthodoxy remains open to renewal in every context.

There is much that the Orthodox community of America needs to work out as it sinks its roots in American soil. One of the greatest challenges will be resolving the difficulties that were caused by the immigration patterns of the Orthodox. There is much to be done to produce a fully American and genuinely Orthodox expression of our Church life—liturgically, canonically, organizationally, academically, and so on. For this, we depend crucially on two sources of good counsel: on the wisdom and direction of the ancient mother churches of Orthodoxy, Churches with a life of almost 2000 years, and on our brothers and sisters in Christ from the other Christian communions in the American context, such as yourselves.

For instance, the Orthodox in America are profiting from their fellow Christians in the realm of biblical scholarship and related theological disciplines. We are on our way to producing our own "homegrown" Orthodox scholars and seminary professors. We, likewise, are learning how to communicate more effectively the good news of our faith by means of the electronic and print media that are available. Here again, we have often profited from our fellow Christian churches for effective techniques and ways of evangelism in the American setting. At the same time, our churches are heavily involved in educating our faithful on the necessity and programs of stewardship, so that the ministries of our Archdiocese may grow and progress. In this case, too, we look to our Christian brethren for extensively tested and successfully applied methods of educating the faithful.

Conclusion

So finally we arrive at the fifth key point, the fifth paradox which characterizes Orthodoxy in the American context. This is the fact revealed in the Pauline phrase from Second Corinthians: *As poor, yet making many rich* (2 Corinthinas 6:10).

I have mentioned already that the prime motivation for immigrants from the Orthodox homelands of Eastern Europe and the Middle East was the motivation of economic progress. Often the Orthodox came to this land in a condition of relative poverty. In comparison to other ethnic groups and religious affiliations, their numbers have been small, and their visibility in society has been low.

And yet, by God's grace, they have been granted the grace to be contributors in a significant way to the health and welfare of American society at large. It would be redundant to recount the role of the Orthodox Church: socially, in the Civil Rights movement of the 1950's; or academically, as living proponents of the Hellenistic legacy from which Western culture has blossomed; or philanthropically, in the efforts of our charitable organizations; or artistically, in cinema, literature, and the performing arts; or patriotically, in terms of the service that Orthodox Christians have offered to defend this nation and her freedoms; or culturally, in the positive ways that the traditional Orthodox ethnicities have advanced the cause of diversity in their adopted hometowns across the nation, in the Northeast, in the Far West, in the Deep South, and in the Midwest. Even though poor, they have been given the grace to make many rich, in many ways.

And when, by God's favor, several Orthodox believers became rich, they offered generously to the cultural, educational and scientific advancement of American society. The pertinent examples are many. I am thinking of the numerous endowed chairs at various universities. I am also thinking of two recent indicative cases. The first of these cases is the following. In the last seven years the Metropolitan Museum in New York inaugurated seven totally new, spacious galleries, centrally located, exhibiting items from the classical and the Byzantine period. All of the galleries are full donations of three Greek Orthodox families. The second case concerns two universities in Boston, Tufts and Northeastern, which, last November, saw the inauguration of two huge, ultramodern and state of the art centers for research related to biomedical, nutritional and health related sciences. Both are generous offerings exceeding one hundred million dollars by two members of our Orthodox Church, both first generation Greek Americans.

But these contributions are only a characteristic part of the particular spiritual bequest of Orthodoxy in America which can have a tremendous impact. For in coming to America, the Orthodox brought with them something new and unique to the American setting. They brought a spirit of Christian brotherhood that transcended the old and sometimes bitter rivalries between Catholicism and Protestantism. For in the Orthodox, both Catholics and Protestants find both a reflection of the image of themselves and of the other, but without the negative and probably rancorous associations of past history. And so, in the Orthodox, they find a point of contact with none of the barriers of old grudges or prejudices.

Here we come to the ultimate, all-inclusive paradox of Orthodoxy in the American context: The Orthodox as they simply are themselves—united but not uniform, conservative but not fundamentalist, Eastern but also Western, ancient but always being renewed. As they remain faithful to their Orthodox heritage of Trinitarian communion of unity in diversity, they can become for other Christians an opportunity to behold their own potential and their own future through the continued work of ecumenical dialog. The more the Orthodox are distinctively themselves, the more they can become an image of the whole of American Christianity.

The essence and mission of Orthodoxy in the American context, then, is to continue to hold forth the paradoxical wonders of God's grace that have brought us together in this blessed country, so that through our erstwhile poverty, many may be made rich in innumerable ways. This is my prayer for our ecumenical encounters in the years and decades to come. After all, it is not a small thing to be able to use the language of the great Apostle Paul and to dare to declare humbly and joyfully with him: "*As servants of God we commend ourselves in every way… As poor, yet making many rich, as having nothing and possessing everything*" (2 Corinthians 6:4-10).

Sacred Text and Interpretation: Perspectives in Orthodox Biblical Studies

A Conference in Honor of Professor Savas Agourides

Keynote Address*

Holy Cross Greek Orthodox School of Theology

Brookline, MA

October 29, 2003

It is a joy to be in fellowship with you throughout this very important theological conference. I say that this conference is important, foremost, because of its topic: "Sacred Text and Interpretation: Perspectives in Orthodox Biblical Studies." Biblical interpretation has been a central function in the life of the Church, and a conference focused upon it is vital indeed. Second, this present gathering is important because it deals with biblical interpretation from an Orthodox angle, pointing to future developments and to truly promising perspectives for Orthodox biblical studies. Third, this is an important conference because its participants come from various theological schools from America and Europe, bringing with them a wealth of exegetical interpretation and an impressive personal contribution to the biblical field, thus creating the proper condi-

*This address was delivered at an international conference of Orthodox biblical and patristic scholars. The conference was a tribute to Professor Savas Agourides, Professor Emeritus of the University of Athens, for his immense scholarly contributions to Orthodox biblical studies.

tions for an exciting exchange of insights and ideas during the four days of our colloquium. The honoree of the Conference, Professor Savas Agourides, adds to its significance since he is an internationally recognized Orthodox New Testament scholar, untiringly and constantly producing biblical exegesis of prime quality, and decisively promoting initiatives that advance the publication of a large amount of books and articles of biblical introduction and interpretation.

In view of all the above, I feel the need to express my deep gratitude to the President of Hellenic College and Holy Cross Greek Orthodox School of Theology, Fr. Nicholas Triantafilou; to the Dean, Fr. Emmanuel Clapsis; and to the entire Faculty of the School of Theology for organizing this important conference. Particular thanks belong to the biblical professors of the School, and especially to Fr. Theodore Stylianopoulos, a bright and creative Orthodox New Testament scholar, who is highly regarded by both Orthodox and non-Orthodox, even Jewish biblical scholars in the United States and abroad. I also offer words of warm thanks to the esteemed colleagues who come to our conference from various parts of the country, and even more from Athens and Thessaloniki.

In my opening remarks to such a stimulating symposium as the present one, I should like to offer some thoughts and comments on the topic, "The Four Gospels: Text as Interpretation." Here, the main thought is that the four Gospels constitute not only a sacred text, but also the interpretation of this very text. To put it differently, the four Gospels present not only the revealed truth of God, but they are, at the same time, the first uniquely and genuinely *biblical* commentaries. Allow me to start with some basic facts:

We have before us the four canonical Gospels of the New Testament, namely, the Gospel of Matthew, the Gospel of Mark, the Gospel of Luke, and the Gospel of John. These are four different texts which, nonetheless, deal with the same fundamental theme: the person of Jesus Christ, Son of God and Son of Man, pre-existing God who for us and for our salvation became man and took the form of a servant [μορφὴν δούλου λαβών] (Philippians 2:7), the one who was crucified, who died on the cross and was buried, who was resurrected from the dead and ascended into heaven, and who will come again to judge the living and the dead. Furthermore, the very same four Gospels narrate the deeds and words of Jesus Christ the Lord as the proclaimer and establisher of the Kingdom of God, who invites all people to a radical change through repentance, since the Kingdom of God is now at hand [*Μετανοεῖτε*, ἤγγικεν γὰρ ἡ βασιλεία τῶν οὐρανῶν] (Matthew 3:2).

Consequently, it has been pointed out that the four Gospels, although different, project one and the same Lord Jesus Christ, His unique ministry and His one Gospel message. Here numerous contemporary books and articles constituting a pertinent contemporary bibliography on this subject could be mentioned, as for instance the article by Helmut Koester, "One Jesus and Four Primitive Gospels" (*Harvard Theological Review*, 1966); the book by Martin Hengel, *The Four Gospels and the One Gospel of Jesus Christ* (Harrisburg: Trinity Press, 2000); the book by Larry Hurtado, *Lord Jesus Christ: Devotion to Jesus in Earliest Christianity* (Grand Rapids: Eerdmans, 2003); the book by James D.G. Dunn, *Jesus Remembered* (Grand Rapids: Eerdmans, 2003); the book by Rudolf Schnackenburg, *Jesus in the Gospels: Biblical Christology* (Louisville: Westminster, 1995); and the book by Marcus Borg and N.T. Wright, *The Meaning of Jesus: Two Visions* (San Francisco: Harper, 1999).

The topic of this quite contemporary bibliography is ancient, reaching back to the early Christian period, and is a topic that has been dealt with by various authors of antiquity in diversified ways. In this instance, we could cite Justin Martyr, Tatian, Clement of Alexandria, Saint Irenaeus, and, later, Saint Athanasios the Great and Eusebius of Caesarea. Tatian needs special mention here because he is the author who, as we know, attempted around the middle of the second century to combine the texts of the four canonical Gospels and create one continuous narrative. This work known as "Diatessaron" [Διά Τεσσάρων] survived in the Syrian Church until the fifth century A.D., but it finally gave way to the four canonical Gospels, dying away as a text in Church usage.

Tatian's attempt to synthesize the four Gospel texts reveals a tacit assumption: that the four Gospels proclaim one and the same Jesus Christ regardless of their stylistic differences and variations in content. It is, however, extremely significant that Tatian's attempt found formidable literary and theological opponents in the persons of prominent theologians of the early Church like Irenaeus, Tertullian, Clement of Alexandria, Hippolytus, and Origen. These early exegetes knew well that the four Gospels were not only accounts of the one Gospel of Jesus Christ, His person and ministry, but simultaneously were also interpretations of the one Gospel. They simply read the four Gospels as both texts and interpretations that projected the inexhaustible wealth of the one divine revelation in astonishing, fascinating, and brilliant variations.

I shall now proceed with more specific data that shows the four Gospels as interpretive texts, as biblical commentaries, so to speak. For obvious restrictions of time, allow me to present two relevant series of examples:

The first of these examples is shown in the very opening of each of the four Gospels, which indicates the interpretative approach of the Evangelists. What exactly do we encounter here?

We start with the Gospel of Matthew. Even a passing acquaintance with the genealogical material presented in Matthew 1:1-17, will suffice to convince the reader that this presentation of the lineage of Jesus Christ is a work of theological interpretative art, not of genealogical science. The very first verse of the Gospel of Matthew, *Βίβλος γενέσεως Ἰησοῦ Χριστοῦ, υἱοῦ Δαβείδ, υἱοῦ Ἀβραάμ* [*The book of the genealogy of Jesus Christ the son of David the son of Abraham*], solemnly announces and firmly establishes in a declaratory way the Davidic and Abrahamic origin of Jesus the Messiah. Thus, the birth of Christ is interpreted in the frame of a genealogical retrospective that includes the figures of David and Abraham, two who guarantee the messianic identity of Jesus.

The genealogy then itself serves the same purpose. Choices clearly have been made by the Evangelist to include certain elements, for instance four "fallen" women, and to exclude others so that the genealogy works out to three sets of fourteen generations. Fourteen, nonetheless, is the double of seven, a sacred number, so that here a numerological cue is offered that the birth of Jesus is by a divine plan that has been preordered and has been brought to its full consummation in His Nativity. Here, we have a textual reference to an event, i.e. the Nativity of Christ, and a concurrent offering of a messianic interpretation of this event through a brilliantly presented genealogy.

We move to the opening chapter of the Gospel of Mark. Mark does not start with the Nativity of Christ but with the preaching of John the Baptist. The first sentence, however is of a declaratory nature: *Ἀρχὴ τοῦ εὐαγγελίου Ἰησοῦ Χριστοῦ, Υἱοῦ τοῦ Θεοῦ* (Mark 1:1) [*The beginning of the Gospel of Jesus Christ the Son of God*]. Having established the context of what is going to follow, i.e. the Evangelion and Christ as the Son of God, Mark introduces John the Baptist. The introduction is made by a lengthy quotation from the Old Testament which combines a passage from Exodus 23:20 and Isaiah 40:3. The combination presents an ingenious merging of the idea of a messenger of the Messiah and the idea of such an event happening in the desert. This is a clear specimen of a Markan interpretation of the Christological role of John the Baptist based on two Old Testament passages which in their original settings were not Christological.

The Markan opening demonstrates an important consideration of the Gospel text as interpretation, which is two-fold: the Gospel not only and most obviously interprets the events of Christ's life in the terms of Old Testament revelation, but also interprets the Old Testament literature in the context of the events surrounding the appearance of Christ.

In the opening chapter of the Gospel of Luke, we encounter yet another eloquent example of the Gospel both as text and as interpretation. The two stories narrated in chapter 1, namely the birth of John the Forerunner and the Annunciation to the Virgin Mary, are cast in the form of Old Testament typological events: the child of the promise, born to barren and aging parents, as in the case of John the Forerunner, is clearly reflective of the well-known cases of Abraham-Sarah, Isaac and Hannah-Samuel. On the other hand, the narrative of the Annunciation to the Virgin Mary displays characteristics of the so-called "call" narratives of God's anointed servants (cf. Moses, Isaiah, Jeremiah), marked by the sequence of divine call—human objection—divine retort— human acquiescence.

The narrative in the first chapter of Luke is a masterpiece of narrative, combining typological interpretation of the Old Testament model stories and extensive hymnological expansions with direct reference to the Incarnation and Nativity of Christ. Here again, as in the Gospels of

Matthew and Mark, the work of the Evangelist as both narrator and interpreter is apparent.

Coming to the fourth Gospel, the Gospel of John, we encounter the same phenomenon in a considerable variation. Chapter 1 of this Gospel begins with the famous prologue in which elements of Old Testament reference are easily discernible in the introduction of John the Baptist as a decisive witness for Jesus, the promised and expected Messiah. At the same time, the prologue of the Gospel, instead of offering a narrative of the birth of Christ in the form of the Matthean or Lucian narratives, offers an amazing statement of pre-existence incarnation. This statement constitutes a bold interpretation of the birth of the Messiah in a language which is an astonishing amalgamation of phrases from Genesis 1:1, Proverbs 8:22, the Wisdom of Solomon 9:1, Psalms 33:6, and common Hellenistic religious terminology.

Just the description of the birth of Christ in John 1:1-5 and 1:14 constitutes a superb example of the Gospel text as simultaneously event and its interpretation. This text is worth quoting:

> 1. Ἐν ἀρχῇ ἦν ὁ λόγος καὶ ὁ λόγος ἦν πρὸς τὸν
> θεόν, καὶ θεὸς ἦν ὁ λόγος. 2. οὗτος ἦν ἐν ἀρχῇ
> πρὸς τὸν θεόν. 3. πάντα δι᾽ αὐτοῦ ἐγένετο, καὶ
> χωρὶς αὐτοῦ ἐγένετο οὐδὲ ἕν. ὃ γέγονεν, 4. ἐν αὐτῷ
> ζωὴ ἦν, καὶ ἡ ζωὴ ἦν τὸ φῶς τῶν ἀνθρώπων· 5. καὶ
> τὸ φῶς ἐν τῇ σκοτίᾳ φάνει, καὶ ἡ σκοτία αὐτὸ οὐ
> κατέλαβεν.
> 14. Καὶ ὁ λόγος σὰρξ ἐγένετο καὶ ἐσκήνωσεν ἐν
> ἡμῖν, καὶ ἐθεασάμεθα τὴν δόξαν αὐτοῦ, δόξαν ὡς
> μονογενοῦς παρὰ πατρός, πλήρης χάριτος καὶ ἀλ-
> ηθείας. 15. Ἰωάννης μαρτυρεῖ περὶ αὐτοῦ καὶ κέ-
> κραγεν λέγων, Οὗτος ἦν ὃν εἶπων, Ὁ ὀπίσω μου
> ἐρχόμενος ἔμπροσθέν μου γέγονεν.

> *1. In the beginning was the Word, and the Word was with God, and the Word was God. 2. He was in the beginning with God; 3. all things were made through him, and without him was not anything made that was made. 4. In him was life and the life was the light of men. 5. The light shines in the darkness and the darkness has not overcome it.*
> *14. And the Word became flesh and dwelt among us, full of grace and truth; we have beheld his glory, glory as of the only Son from the Father. 15. (John bore witness to him, and cried, "This was he of whom I said, 'He who comes after me ranks before me...)'"*

I close here the series of examples based on the first chapter of each of the four Gospels and proceed with a second series of examples of a different nature. They are indicative of the same phenomenon, namely the Gospel text as interpretation.

As already stated, the four Gospels present in essence the one Jesus Christ. The Lord is depicted by all four Evangelists as a divine teacher, as a miracle worker, as healer, as heavenly revealer of the ultimate divine plan for man and the universe, as crucified and risen, as true God and true man. The emphases and the nuances, however, in the above Christological image are different to each Evangelist, and this is precisely a matter of interpretative choices by each one of them.

In Matthew, for instance, Jesus Christ the Lord is depicted as the true, incomparable and absolute Teacher, the divine Rabbi. It is in this context that Matthew has preserved the unique sermon on the Mount in three long chapters, 5,6,and 7, in which we encounter the solemn declarations of the type *"You have heard that it was said 'an eye for an eye and a tooth for a tooth,' but I say to you…"* (Matthew

5:38-39). Here the authority of Christ as the Teacher of the new law is clearly placed above the authority of the Old Testament Mosaic Law. Matthew, throughout his Gospel, consistently projects the same image by offering extensive pericopes containing the teachings of Jesus. The message is clear: Christ is *the* Teacher of the *absolute Truth* superseding Moses and the Old Testament in general. But this is text and interpretation because it shows that Matthew selects from the available Christological material of the initial Church the data which emphasize Jesus as *the* Teacher.

The Evangelist Mark follows a different way, showing other interpretative preferences, although dealing with the same material. He has limited pericopes depicting Christ as teacher but plenty of cases painting Him as an amazing miracle worker. He presents Him as having the authority to perform mighty deeds that only God can perform, while at the same time He is, from the very beginning of His ministry (cf. chapter 3), the target of a deadly plot against Him by the religious leaders. Mark consistently presents Christ under the scheme of authority and passion, showing Him concurrently as the almighty Son of God and as the humble Son of Man constantly attacked by His opponents and finally crucified. One needs to only read chapters 8 through 10 of the Markan Gospel to see there a masterpiece of a text, presenting a fascinating narrative interpreted in the light of the Christological scheme of authority and passion. The Evangelist simultaneously records facts and accompanies them with a subtle interpretation.

In the Gospel of Luke, we come across another exegetical option. This Evangelist displays elements common to Matthew and Mark. He, like them, works on the basis of the main Christological scheme of public ministry (teaching, miracles) Cross and Resurrection. He interprets, however, Christ's person and ministry in the light of an immense love and tender care for the suffering, the rejected, and the poor. It is not accidental that Luke has preserved for the Church the parables that have been characterized as "Gospel within the Gospel," namely the parables of the Good Samaritan, the Prodigal Son, the Tax Collector and the Pharisee at prayer.

Also, it is not accidental that Luke offers a version of the Beatitudes in chapter 6 with striking characteristics differing from the parallel Beatitudes in Matthew, chapter 5. Luke has preserved the variation *Μακάριοι οἱ πτωχοί, ὅτι ὑμετέρα ἐστὶν ἡ βασιλεία τοῦ θεοῦ* while Matthew has *Μακάριοι οἱ πτωχοὶ τῷ πνεύματι*. Christ, in Luke 6, speaks about the poor; whereas in Matthew 5, Christ speaks about the humble. The same holds true for another Beatitude in the same passage: *μακάριοι οἱ πεινῶντες νῦν, ὅτι χορτασθήσεσθε*, the reference being simply to people who are deprived of food; whereas in Matthew, the Beatitude reads *μακάριοι οἱ πεινῶντες καὶ διψῶντες τὴν δικαιοσύνην*. Luke, by offering the variation on the poor and hungry, interprets Christ's saying as a saying displaying love and concern for the poor and hungry. This is text and interpretation.

The Gospel of John opens to us an immense world of text and interpretation. Christ the Logos and Son of God is in this case, as in the three synoptic Gospels, the teacher revealing heavenly plans; He is the miracle worker, although John is very selective in the number and kind of miracles; and He is the crucified and risen Lord. But the Gospel of John offers in addition the picture of Jesus as the preexisting God and Logos through whom everything was created. John depicts Jesus as engaged in deep theological debates and discussions, during which supernatural truths were revealed. John preserved for the incarnation the language of καταβαίνων, coming down, and, for the return to the heavenly Father after the Resurrection, the language of ἀναβαίνων, of going up. He used for the crucifixion the verb ὑψοῦμαι, to be lifted up, and even the verb δοξάζομαι, to be glorified. The Gospel of John saved for us also the superb formula ἐγώ εἰμί, I am, used by the Lord in conjunction with fundamental concepts like the concepts of the light of the world, the way, the truth, and the life. All this amazing wealth of special terminology is a genuine and accurate record of the words of Christ; but the inclusion of such a terminology in the Gospel of John, is undoubtedly the result of an interpretative decision. The text of the Gospel of John is text and interpretation dictated by Christological presupposition, and serves the need of the Church to which the Evangelist addressed His Evangelion.

ΕΞΕΖΗΤΗΣΑ ΤΟ ΠΡΟΣΩΠΟΝ ΣΟΥ (ΨΑΛΜ. 26, 8): ΒΙΒΛΙΚΕΣ ΠΑΡΑΛΛΑΓΕΣ ΣΤΟ ΘΕΜΑ ΤΗΣ ΑΝΑΖΗΤΗΣΕΩΣ ΤΟΥ ΘΕΟΥ

ACADEMY OF ATHENS*

ATHENS, GREECE
NOVEMBER 14, 2003

Μακαριώτατε,
Σεβασμιώτατε ἐκπρόσωπε τοῦ Παναγιωτάτου Οἰκουμενικοῦ Πατριάρχου,
Ἀξιότιμε Κύριε Πρόεδρε τῆς Ἀκαδημίας Ἀθηνῶν,
Ἐξοχώτατε Κύριε Πρόεδρε τῆς Βουλῆς τῶν Ἑλλήνων,
Ἀξιότιμοι Κυρίες καί Κύριοι Ἀκαδημαϊκοί,
Ἐπίσημοι προσκεκλημένοι,
Κυρίες καί Κύριοι,

Χάριν δίδωμι Κυρίῳ τῷ Θεῷ ἐπί τῇ εὐσήμῳ ταύτῃ τελετῇ.

Ἐκφράζω τίς θερμότατες εὐχαριστίες μου γιά τήν ὄντως ἐξαιρετική τιμή τῆς ἐκλογῆς μου ὡς ἀντεπιστέλλοντος μέλους τῆς Ἀκαδημίας Ἀθηνῶν καί

*This address was given on the occasion of the official induction of Archbishop Demetrios of America "as an abroad-residing member of the Academy of Athens in the Discipline of Theology in the areas

γιά τήν παροῦσα ἐπίσημη ὑποδοχή. Ἡ εἴσοδός μου στό κορυφαῖο καί περίλαμπρο αὐτό τέμενος τῆς ἐπιστήμης, τῆς φιλοσοφίας, καί τῆς τέχνης, μέ συγκινεῖ βαθύτατα καί μέ πληροῖ εὐγνωμοσύνης τόσο πρός τά ἐκλεκτά μέλη τῆς Ἀκαδημίας, ὅσο καί πρός τόν Θεό τῆς σοφίας καί Πατέρα τῶν φώτων.

Ἰδιαιτέρως εὐχαριστῶ τόν ἀξιότιμο φίλο Πρόεδρο τῆς Ἀκαδημίας Ἀθηνῶν Καθηγητή Κύριο Γρηγόριο Σκαλκέα γιά τήν εὐμενέστατη ἐναρκτήρια προσφώνησή του, ἐνδεικτική τῆς εὐγενείας, τῆς ὀξυνοίας, καί τῆς γενναιοδωρίας τοῦ πνεύματός του. Ἐπίσης ἰδιάζουσες εὐχαριστίες ἐκφράζω καί πρός τόν Σεβασμιώτατο ἀδελφό Μητροπολίτη Περγάμου Κύριο Ἰωάννη γιά τήν εἰσαγωγική του παρουσίαση, μιά παρουσίαση ἀποκαλυπτική τῆς ἀσυνήθους θεολογικῆς του παιδείας, τῆς λαμπρότητος τῆς σκέψεώς του καί τοῦ βάθους τῆς πνευματικότητός του. Οἱ θερμές εὐχαριστίες μου ἀπευθύνονται καί πρός τούς ἐκλεκτούς καί ἀγαπητούς Ὁμογενεῖς, οἱ ὁποῖοι εἶχαν τήν πολλή καλωσύνη νά ἔλθουν ἀπό τήν Ἀμερική γιά νά παραστοῦν στήν σημερινή ἐπίσημη τελετή.

Καί ἤδη ἔχω τήν ἐξαιρετική τιμή, στόν συνεπτυγμένο χρόνο μιᾶς σύντομης ὁμιλίας, νά παρουσιάσω ὡρισμένες βασικές σκέψεις ἐπί τοῦ προαναγγελθέντος θέματος ὑπό τόν τίτλο, "'Ἐξεζήτησα τό πρόσωπόν Σου' (Ψαλμ. 26, 8): Βιβλικές παραλλαγές στό θέμα τῆς ἀναζητήσεως τοῦ Θεοῦ."

of Ethics and Political Sciences." The election to the Academy of Athens was held on November 28, 2002, and was ratified by a Presidential Decree of the President of the Hellenic Republic and published in the official Government Gazette (no. 29) of February 12, 2003.

Εἰσαγωγικά

Ἡ ἀναζήτηση τοῦ Θεοῦ ἀπό τόν ἄνθρωπο κάθε ἐποχῆς, κάθε πολιτισμοῦ καί κάθε γεωγραφικῆς περιοχῆς, ἀποτελεῖ θεμελιῶδες θρησκειολογικό φαινόμενο. Φαινόμενο πού ἐμφανίζεται σέ ποικίλες μορφές, πού ἐκφράζεται συχνά μέ διαμετρικά διαφοροποιημένους τρόπους, πού ἐμπλέκει τήν γλῶσσα, τήν τέχνη, τήν ἐπιστήμη, τήν πολιτική, τήν οἰκονομία καί γενικά τήν διανόηση τόσο τοῦ πρωτόγονου ἀνθρώπου τῶν ἀρχικῶν αἰώνων τῆς ἀνθρώπινης ἱστορίας, ὅσο καί τῶν προχωρημένων διανοητῶν τῆς σύγχρονης ἐποχῆς.

Ἡ ἀναζήτηση τοῦ Θεοῦ ὡς στοιχειῶδες θρησκειολογικό φαινόμενο, μπορεῖ τελικά νά ἀναχθῆ σέ μιά ἁπλῆ ἀλλά οὐσιαστική κίνηση τοῦ ἀνθρωπίνου ἐγώ πρός τό θεῖο Σύ, σέ μιά δυναμική φορά τῆς ἐγκόσμιας ὑπάρξεως τοῦ ἀνθρώπου πρός τήν ὑπερβατική ὕπαρξη τοῦ Θεοῦ. Μιά τέτοια ὅμως ἁπλουστευτική ἀναγωγή δέν πρέπει νά δημιουργήση τήν ἐντύπωση ὅτι πρόκειται γιά ἁπλό καί εὐκολονόητο φαινόμενο. Ἡ ἀπέραντη καί συνεχῶς διογκουμένη παγκόσμια βιβλιογραφία ἐπί τοῦ θέματος τονίζει ἀμέσως τήν πολυσύνθετη καί δυσερεύνητη φύση τοῦ φαινομένου τῆς ἀναζητήσεως τοῦ Θεοῦ ἀπό τόν ἄνθρωπο. Θαυμάσιο παράδειγμα ἐν προκειμένῳ μᾶς προσφέρουν τά βιβλικά κείμενα. Τά κείμενα αὐτά ἐνῶ ἀποκαλύπτουν τόν λόγο τοῦ Θεοῦ, ἀποκαλύπτουν ταὐτοχρόνως καί τόν ἀνθρώπινο λόγο περί Θεοῦ. Ἐνῶ κατ᾽ οὐσίαν φανερώνουν τό θέλημα τοῦ Θεοῦ ἀναζητοῦντος τόν ἄνθρωπο, φανερώνουν ἐπίσης καί τήν ἀσίγαστη ἐπιθυμία τοῦ ἀνθρώπου πού εὑρίσκεται ὑπαρξιακά σέ κατάσταση ἀναζητήσεως τοῦ Θεοῦ. Εἶναι χαρακτηριστικός στήν περίπτωση αὐτή ὁ στίχος 8 τοῦ 26ου ψαλμοῦ, ἀπό τό βιβλίο τῶν Ψαλμῶν τῆς Παλαιᾶς Διαθήκης: "*Σοί εἶπεν ἡ καρδία μου, ἐξεζήτησα τό πρόσωπόν Σου, τό πρόσωπόν Σου Κύριε ζητήσω.*" Πρόκειται γιά τόν στίχο πού ἀποτελεῖ μέρος τοῦ τίτλου τῆς παρούσης ὁμιλίας. Ὁ στίχος αὐτός ὡς ὀργανικό μέλος ἑνός θεοπνεύστου κειμένου ἀνήκει φυσικά στήν εὐρύτερη σφαῖρα τῆς ἀποκαλύψεως τοῦ Θεοῦ. Εἶναι ὅμως προφανές ὅτι ὁ ἴδιος στίχος ἐκφράζει μέ ἀπόλυτη σαφήνεια καί ἀδιαμφισβήτητο πάθος μιά καθαρῶς ἀνθρώπινη κατάσταση καί τάση τοῦ ἀνθρωπίνου ὄντος πρός τό θεῖον. Θά μποροῦσε ἐπομένως κάλλιστα νά μελετηθῆ καί ὡς κείμενο ἐνδεικτικό τῆς ἀναζητήσεως τοῦ Θεοῦ ἀπό τόν ἄνθρωπο.

Κάτι παρόμοιο συμβαίνει καί μέ πολλά ἄλλα βιβλικά κείμενα στά ὁποῖα μέ εὔγλωττο καί συναρπαστικό τρόπο, ἄλλοτε ἄμεσα, ἄλλοτε ἔμμεσα ἐμφανίζεται τό θέμα αὐτό τῆς ἀναζητήσεως τοῦ Θεοῦ σέ ἐξαιρετικά ἐνδιαφέρουσες διαφοροποιημένες μορφές. Ἡ διαφοροποίηση ἀναφέρεται κυρίως στό ποιός εἶναι ὁ ἀναζητούμενος Θεός καί ποιές οἱ προεξάρχουσες ἰδιότητές Του. Θά προσπαθήσω μέ ἄκρως συνοπτικό τρόπο νά παρουσιάσω μερικές ἀπό τίς παραπάνω διαφοροποιημένες μορφές πού συνιστοῦν οὐσιαστικές βιβλικές παραλλαγές στό ζωτικό ὑπαρξιακό φαινόμενο τῆς ἀναζητήσεως τοῦ Θεοῦ ἀπό τόν ἄνθρωπο.

Πρώτη Παραλλαγή:
Ἀπό τό μηδέν, τό χάος καί την ἀμορφία στήν τάξη καί στήν ἔλλογη διακυβέρνηση τοῦ κόσμου

Ἡ πρώτη παραλλαγή ἐμφανίζεται στό ἀρχικό κεφάλαιο τῆς Γενέσεως, δηλ. τοῦ πρώτου βιβλικοῦ κειμένου τῆς Παλαιᾶς Διαθήκης. Ἰδού ἐπιλεκτικά μερικοί στίχοι ἀπό τό πρῶτο κεφάλαιο τῆς Γενέσεως:

Ἐν ἀρχῇ ἐποίησεν ὁ Θεός τόν οὐρανόν καί τήν γῆν. Ἡ δέ γῆ ἦν ἀόρατος καί ἀκατασκεύαστος, καί σκότος ἐπάνω τῆς ἀβύσσου, καί πνεῦμα Θεοῦ ἐπεφέρετο ἐπάνω τοῦ ὕδατος (Γεν. 1, 1).

Καί εἶπεν ὁ Θεός· Γενηθήτω φῶς. Καί ἐγένετο φῶς (Γεν. 1, 3).

Καί εἶπεν ὁ Θεός· Γενηθήτω στερέωμα ἐν μέσῳ τοῦ ὕδατος καί ἔστω διαχωρίζον ἀνά μέσον ὕδατος καί ὕδατος. Καί ἐγένετο οὕτως (Γεν. 1, 6).

Καί εἶπεν ὁ Θεός· Συναχθήτω τό ὕδωρ τό ὑποκάτω τοῦ οὐρανοῦ εἰς συναγωγήν μίαν, καί ὀφθήτω ἡ ξηρά. Καί ἐγένετο οὕτως (Γεν. 1, 9).

Καί εἶπεν ὁ Θεός· Βλαστησάτω ἡ γῆ βοτάνην χόρτου, σπεῖρον σπέρμα κατά γένος καί καθ' ὁμοιότητα, καί ξύλον κάρπιμον ποιοῦν καρπόν, οὗ τό σπέρμα αὐτοῦ ἐν αὐτῷ κατά γένος ἐπί τῆς γῆς. Καί ἐγένετο οὕτως (Γεν. 1, 11).

Καί εἶπεν ὁ Θεός· Γενηθήτωσαν φωστῆρες ἐν τῷ στερεώματι τοῦ οὐρανοῦ εἰς φαῦσιν ἐπί τῆς γῆς, τοῦ διαχωρίζειν ἀνά μέσον τῆς ἡμέρας καί ἀνά μέσον τῆς νυκτός· καί ἔστωσαν εἰς σημεῖα καί εἰς καιρούς καί εἰς ἡμέρας καί εἰς ἐνιαυτούς· καί ἔστωσαν εἰς φαῦσιν ἐν τῷ στερεώματι τοῦ οὐρανοῦ ὥστε φαίνειν ἐπί τῆς γῆς. Καί ἐγένετο οὕτως (Γεν. 1, 14-15).

Καί εἶπεν ὁ Θεός· Ἐξαγαγέτω τά ὕδατα ἑρπετά ψυχῶν ζωσῶν καί πετεινά πετόμενα ἐπί τῆς γῆς κατά τό στερέωμα τοῦ οὐρανοῦ. Καί ἐγένετο οὕτως (Γεν. 1, 20).

Καί εἶπεν ὁ Θεός· Ἐξαγαγέτω ἡ γῆ ψυχήν ζῶσαν κατά γένος, τετράποδα καί ἑρπετά καί θηρία τῆς γῆς κατά γένος. Καί ἐγένετο οὕτως (Γεν. 1, 24).

Καί εἶπεν ὁ Θεός· Ποιήσωμεν ἄνθρωπον κατ' εἰκόνα ἡμετέραν καί καθ' ὁμοίωσιν, καί ἀρχέτωσαν τῶν ἰχθύων τῆς θαλάσσης καί τῶν πετεινῶν τοῦ οὐρανοῦ

καί τῶν κτηνῶν καί πάσης τῆς γῆς καί πάντων τῶν ἑρπετῶν τῶν ἑρπόντων ἐπί τῆς γῆς. Καί ἐποίησεν ὁ Θεός τόν ἄνθρωπον, κατ' εἰκόνα Θεοῦ ἐποίησεν αὐτόν, ἄρσεν καί θῆλυ ἐποίησεν αὐτούς (Γεν. 1, 26-27).
Καί εἶδεν ὁ Θεός τά πάντα ὅσα ἐποίησε, καί ἰδού καλά λίαν (Γεν. 1, 31).

Τί ἀκριβῶς παρατηροῦμε στήν περίπτωση αὐτή; Ἐδῶ ἔχουμε μιά περιγραφή τῆς δημιουργίας τοῦ σύμπαντος μέ ἰδιαίτερη ἔμφαση στόν πλανήτη Γῆ, τόν πλανήτη μας. Ἡ περιγραφή εἶναι ἀπολύτως μεθοδική, καί προχωρεῖ μέ διαδοχικές φάσεις πού ὁρίζονται μέ βασικούς ἐπαναλαμβανόμενους ὅρους (π.χ. "*καί εἶπεν ὁ Θεός*", "*καί ἐγένετο οὕτως*", "*ἡμέρα μία*", "*ἡμέρα δευτέρα*" κ.λ.π.), γιά νά δηλωθῆ ἡ συστηματική καί ἰσόρροπη ἀκολουθία τῶν μειζόνων γεγονότων τῆς δημιουργίας. Τά γεγονότα καλύπτουν ἕνα εὐρύ φάσμα δημιουργικῶν ἐνεργειῶν πού πραγματοποιοῦνται μέσῳ τοῦ παντοδύναμου λόγου τοῦ Θεοῦ Δημιουργοῦ. Στό τέλος τῶν ἕξι χρονικῶν περιόδων, στή διάρκεια τῶν ὁποίων πραγματοποιοῦνται τά μείζονα γεγονότα τῆς δημιουργίας, ἡ εἰκόνα πού ἀναδύεται εἶναι ἡ ἑξῆς: ἀπό τήν ἀρχική μηδενική κατάσταση ἀνυπαρξίας δημουργεῖται ἕνα σύμπαν, τό ὁποῖο θεωρούμενο ἀπό τήν ἀνθρώπινη σκοπιά χαρακτηρίζεται ὅπως εἶναι φυσικό ἀπό μιά γεωκεντρική ἄποψη. Σύμφωνα μέ τήν ἄποψη αὐτή ἡ γῆ εἶναι *ἀόρατος καί ἀκατασκεύαστος, καί σκότος ἐπιφέρεται ἐπάνω τῆς ἀβύσσου*. Ἡ ὁρολογία εἶναι ὁρολογία χάους, ἀμορφίας καί σκότους. Στή συνέχεια ὅμως, τό σκότος ὑποχωρεῖ, ἡ γῆ παίρνει σαφῆ μορφή μέ τόν διαχωρισμό θαλάσσης καί ξηρᾶς, ὁ φυτικός, ὁ ζωϊκός καί ὁ ἀστρικός κόσμος κάνουν τήν ἐμφάνισή των ὁπότε καί δημιουργεῖται ὁ ἄνθρωπος. Δημιουργεῖται *κατ' εἰ-*

κόνα καί καθ' ὁμοίωσιν Θεοῦ, μέ ἐντολή, αὐξάνεσθε καί πληθύνεσθε καί πληρώσατε τήν γῆν καί κατακυριεύσατε αὐτῆς (Γεν. 1, 28).

Τό ὑπέροχο αὐτό κείμενο μπορεῖ νά ἀναγνωσθῆ καί νά ἑρμηνευθῆ ὄχι μόνο ὡς θεολογική βιβλική περιγραφή τῆς δημιουργίας τοῦ κόσμου ἀλλά καί ὡς ἔκφραση τῆς εἰδικῆς ἀναζητήσεως τοῦ Θεοῦ. Στήν περίπτωση αὐτή ἡ ἀναζήτηση ἀποβλέπει σέ ἕνα Θεό ὁ ὁποῖος αἴρει τήν ἀνυπαρξία τοῦ κόσμου, δηλαδή δημιουργεῖ ἐκ τοῦ μηδενός τό σύμπαν, καί ἐν συνεχείᾳ μεταμορφώνει τό ἀρχικό χάος σέ κόσμο, εἰσάγει στό ἀρχέγονο σκότος τό φῶς, ἐναρμονίζει τό σύστημα τῶν θαλασσῶν μέ τήν ξηρά, παράγει τήν ζωή καί ἐν τέλει δημιουργεῖ τόν ἄνθρωπο στόν ὁποῖο χορηγεῖ τόν ἔλεγχο ἐπί πάντων. Ἡ ἀναζήτηση ἐδῶ τοῦ Θεοῦ συνδέεται μέ ὑπέρβαση τοῦ κοσμικοῦ φόβου, μέ ὑπέρβαση ἀφ' ἑνός μέν τοῦ τρόμου τῆς ἀνυπαρξίας, τοῦ χάους καί τῆς ἀταξίας τῶν στοιχείων τῆς φύσεως, ἀφ' ἑτέρου δέ τῆς ἀπειλῆς ἐκ τοῦ ζωϊκοῦ καί φυτικοῦ βασιλείου. Ἐπί πλέον ἡ δημιουργία τοῦ κόσμου διά μόνου τοῦ λόγου μέ τά διαδοχικά *καί εἶπεν ὁ Θεός*, τά ὁποῖα διαστίζουν τήν σχετική περιγραφή, προβάλλει τήν παντοδυναμία καί τό ἔλλογο τοῦ Θεοῦ αὐτοῦ ἐφ' ὅσον ὁ ἀναζητούμενος Θεός χορηγεῖ στόν ἄνθρωπο τήν κυριαρχία ἐπί τοῦ πλανήτου γῆς.

Ὁ ἀναζητούμενος Θεός τοῦ πρώτου κεφαλαίου τῆς Γενέσεως εἶναι Θεός δημιουργός οὐσιαστικῆς ὑπάρξεως ἔναντι μηδενικῆς ἀνυπαρξίας, τάξεως ἔναντι χάους, καί ἐλλόγου προνοίας ἔναντι ἀλόγου καί τυχαίας φορᾶς τῶν πάντων. Δέν ὑπάρχει ἀμφιβολία ὅτι ἕνας τέτοιος Θεός ἀποτελεῖ τόν ἀναζητούμενο Θεό πολλῶν συγχρόνων ἀνθρώπων.

Δεύτερη Παραλλαγή: Ἀπό τό θανάσιμο τραῦμα καί τήν πτώση στήν ἀποκατάσταση

Ἡ δεύτερη βιβλική παραλλαγή στό θέμα τῆς ἀναζητήσεως τοῦ Θεοῦ προέρχεται ἀπό ἕνα ἄλλο σπουδαιότατο παλαιοδιαθηκικό κείμενο, τό τρίτο κεφάλαιο τοῦ βιβλίου τῆς Γενέσεως. Πρόκειται γιά τήν περιγραφή τῆς πτώσεως τῶν πρωτοπλάστων, γιά τό λεγόμενο προπατορικό ἁμάρτημα τοῦ πρώτου ἀνθρωπίνου ζεύγους, τοῦ Ἀδάμ καί τῆς Εὔας. Ἰδού καί πάλιν ἐπιλεκτικά μερικοί στίχοι ἀπό τό κεφάλαιο 3 τῆς Γενέσεως πού περιγράφουν γραφικά τήν τραγική πτώση τοῦ πρώτου ἀνθρώπινου ζεύγους:

> *Ὁ δέ ὄφις ἦν φρονιμώτατος πάντων τῶν θηρίων τῶν ἐπί τῆς γῆς, ὧν ἐποίησε Κύριος ὁ Θεός. Καί εἶπεν ὁ ὄφις τῇ γυναικί· τί ὅτι εἶπεν ὁ Θεός, οὐ μή φάγητε ἀπό παντός ξύλου τοῦ παραδείσου; Καί εἶπεν ἡ γυνή τῷ ὄφει· ἀπό καρποῦ τοῦ ξύλου τοῦ παραδείσου φαγούμεθα, ἀπό δέ τοῦ καρποῦ τοῦ ξύλου, ὅ ἐστιν ἐν μέσῳ τοῦ παραδείσου, εἶπεν ὁ Θεός, οὐ φάγεσθε ἀπ' αὐτοῦ οὐδέ μή ἅψησθε αὐτοῦ, ἵνα μή ἀποθάνητε. Καί εἶπεν ὁ ὄφις τῇ γυναικί· οὐ θανάτῳ ἀποθανεῖσθε· ᾔδει γάρ ὁ Θεός, ὅτι ἐν ᾗ ἄν ἡμέρᾳ φάγητε ἀπ' αὐτοῦ, διανοιχθήσονται ὑμῶν οἱ ὀφθαλμοί καί ἔσεσθε ὡς θεοί, γινώσκοντες καλόν καί πονηρόν. Καί εἶδεν ἡ γυνή ὅτι καλόν τό ξύλον εἰς βρῶσιν καί ὅτι ἀρεστόν τοῖς ὀφθαλμοῖς ἰδεῖν καί ὡραῖόν ἐστιν τοῦ κατανοῆσαι, καί λαβοῦσα ἀπό τοῦ καρποῦ αὐτοῦ ἔφαγε· καί ἔδωκε καί τῷ ἀνδρί αὐτῆς μετ' αὐτῆς, καί ἔφαγον. Καί διηνοίχθησαν οἱ ὀφθαλμοί τῶν δύο, καί ἔγνωσαν ὅτι γυμνοί ἦσαν,*

καί ἔρραψαν φύλλα συκῆς καί ἐποίησαν ἑαυτοῖς περιζώματα.
Καί ἤκουσαν τῆς φωνῆς Κυρίου τοῦ Θεοῦ περιπατοῦντος ἐν τῷ παραδείσῳ τό δειλινόν, καί ἐκρύβησαν ὅ τε Ἀδάμ καί ἡ γυνή αὐτοῦ ἀπό προσώπου Κυρίου τοῦ Θεοῦ ἐν μέσῳ τοῦ ξύλου τοῦ παραδείσου. Καί ἐκάλεσε Κύριος ὁ Θεός τόν Ἀδάμ καί εἶπεν αὐτῷ. Ἀδάμ, ποῦ εἶ; Καί εἶπεν αὐτῷ· τῆς φωνῆς σου ἤκουσα περιπατοῦντος ἐν τῷ παραδείσῳ καί ἐφοβήθην, ὅτι γυμνός εἰμι, καί ἐκρύβην. Καί εἶπεν αὐτῷ ὁ Θεός· τίς ἀνήγγειλέ σοι ὅτι γυμνός εἶ, εἰ μή ἀπό τοῦ ξύλου, οὗ ἐνετειλάμην σοι τούτου μόνου μή φαγεῖν, ἀπ᾽ αὐτοῦ, ἔφαγες; Καί εἶπεν ὁ Ἀδάμ· ἡ γυνή, ἥν ἔδωκες μετ᾽ ἐμοῦ, αὕτη μοι ἔδωκεν ἀπό τοῦ ξύλου, καί ἔφαγον. Καί εἶπε Κύριος ὁ Θεός τῇ γυναικί· τί τοῦτο ἐποίησας; Καί εἶπεν ἡ γυνή· ὁ ὄφις ἠπάτησέ με, καί ἔφαγον. Καί εἶπε Κύριος ὁ Θεός τῷ ὄφει· ὅτι ἐποίησας τοῦτο, ἐπικατάρατος σύ ἀπό πάντων τῶν κτηνῶν...καί τῇ γυναικί εἶπε· πληθύνων πληθυνῶ τάς λύπας σου καί τόν στεναγμόν σου· ἐν λύπαις τέξῃ τέκνα.... Τῷ δέ Ἀδάμ εἶπεν· ὅτι ἤκουσας τῆς φωνῆς τῆς γυναικός σου καί ἔφαγες ἀπό τοῦ ξύλου, οὗ ἐνετειλάμην σοι τούτου μόνου μή φαγεῖν, ἀπ᾽ αὐτοῦ ἔφαγες, ἐπικατάρατος ἡ γῆ ἐν τοῖς ἔργοις σου· ἐν λύπαις φαγῇ αὐτήν πάσας τάς ἡμέρας τῆς ζωῆς σου....(Γεν. 3, 1-17).

Τό ἀνωτέρω περιγραφόμενο βασικό γεγονός τῆς πτώσεως τῶν *πρωτοπλάστων*, ἕνα βαθύτατα τραυματικό γεγονός, ἀναφέρεται κατ᾽ οὐσίαν στήν διάσπαση τῆς σχέσεως μέ τό Θεό. Μιᾶς σχέσεως, ἡ ὁποία εἶχε ἀμεσότητα καί πληρότητα ἐπικοινωνίας, πλήρη ἐλευθερία ἐπιλογῆς ἤ μή, ἀπό πλευρᾶς ἀνθρώπου, τῶν ὁδηγιῶν τοῦ Θεοῦ καί ἀρχέγονη ἀθωότητα καί καθαρότητα.

Ἡ παραπάνω περιγραφή, κλασσική στό εἶδος της καί στό θέμα της, ἀποκαλύπτει σημαντικά στοιχεῖα ἀναφερόμενα στήν ἀναζήτηση τοῦ Θεοῦ. Ἐδῶ, χωρίς ἀμφιβολία, ἐκφράζεται ἡ ἀπέραντη ὀδύνη γιά τήν ἀνθρώπινη πτώση, καί ἡ βαθύτατη νοσταλγία καί ὁ ἀσίγαστος πόθος γιά μίαν ἀποκατάσταση τῆς ἀρχικῆς σχέσεως, ὡς σχέσεως ἀμεσότητος καί πληρότητος ἐπικοινωνίας, πού συνοδεύεται ἀπό τήν ἀνάκτηση τῆς ἀπωλεσθείσης ἀθωότητος καί τήν δυνατότητα σωστῆς λειτουργίας τῆς ἀνθρώπινης ἐλευθερίας ὡς ζωτικῆς λειτουργίας ἐπιλογῆς τοῦ καλοῦ ἔναντι οἱασδήποτε προκλήσεως.

Τά δομικά στοιχεῖα τῆς περιγραφῆς τῆς πτώσεως τῶν πρωτοπλάστων στό τρίτο κεφάλαιο τοῦ βιβλίου τῆς Γενέσεως, ἀποκαλύπτουν μιά μορφή ἀναζητήσεως τοῦ Θεοῦ ὡς τοῦ ἀπολύτου Σύ, ἑνός Σύ πρός τό ὁποῖο ὑπάρχει ἄμεση πρόσβαση, ἑνός Σύ τό ὁποῖο μπορεῖ νά διορθώση ἔστω καί θανάσιμα ἀνθρώπινα λάθη καί νά ἐξαφανίση ἀρχέγονες ἐνοχές. Ἐδῶ ἡ ἀναζήτηση τοῦ Θεοῦ εἶναι ἀναζήτηση τῆς τέλειας προπτωτικῆς σχέσεως Θεοῦ καί ἀνθρώπου, σχέσεως ἡ ὁποία ἔχει ὑπερβῆ τήν τραυματική μεταπτωτική διάσπαση, καί καλύπτει τόν βαθύτατο ἀνθρώπινο πόθο γιά τό τέλειο Σύ, γιά τόν ἀπόλυτα σημαντικό Ἄλλο μέ τόν Ὁποῖο ὑπάρχει ἄμεση κοινωνία. Ἕνας τέτοιος ἀνθρώπινος πόθος, μιά τέτοια ἀναζήτηση τοῦ Θεοῦ εἶναι εὐδιάκριτη στόν κόσμο τοῦ 2003.

Τρίτη Παραλλαγή:
Ἡ θεοφανική ἐμπειρία

Ἡ τρίτη βιβλική παραλλαγή στό θέμα τῆς ἀναζητήσεως τοῦ Θεοῦ συναντᾶται σέ μιά σειρά ἀπό περικοπές τόσο στό βιβλίο τῆς Γενέσεως, ὅσο καί στό βιβλίο τῆς Ἐξόδου. Πρόκειται γιά περικοπές στίς ὁποῖες περιγράφονται ἐμφανίσεις τοῦ Θεοῦ σέ σημαντικά βιβλικά πρόσωπα ὅπως ὁ Ἀβραάμ, ὁ Ἰακώβ, ὁ Μωϋσῆς καί ἄλλοι. Τέτοιες θεοφανικές ἐμφανίσεις συναντοῦμε μεταξύ πολλῶν ἄλλων στό κεφάλαιο 18 τῆς Γενέσεως (περίπτωση τοῦ Ἀβραάμ παρά τήν δρῦν Μαμβρῆ), στά κεφάλαια 28 καί 32 τῆς Γενέσεως (περιπτώσεις τοῦ Ἰακώβ στίς περιοχές Μπεθέλ καί Πενιέλ), καί στά κεφάλαια 3, καί 32-34 τοῦ βιβλίου τῆς Ἐξόδου (περίπτωση τοῦ Μωϋσέως στήν καιομένη βάτο καί στο ὄρος Σινᾶ).

Ἡ περίπτωση Ἀβραάμ, εἰσάγεται στό κεφάλαιο 18 τῆς Γενέσεως μέ τήν χαρακτηριστική φράση *Ὤφθη δέ αὐτῷ* (δηλ. τῷ Ἀβραάμ) *ὁ Θεός πρός τῇ δρυί τῇ Μαμβρῇ καθημένου αὐτοῦ ἐπί τῆς θύρας τῆς σκηνῆς αὐτοῦ μεσημβρίας* (Γεν. 18, 1). Ἡ συνέχεια τῆς περιγραφῆς δέν ἀφήνει ἀμφιβολία ὅτι ἐδῶ πρόκειται περί θεοφανείας εἰδικοῦ τύπου. Ἡ θεοφανική αὐτή φανέρωση δέν εἶναι στιγμιαία οὔτε ἁπλῆ καί περιλαμβάνει προαναγγελίες σοβαρῶν ἐξελίξεων τόσο στήν ζωή τοῦ Ἀβραάμ ὡς γενάρχου, ὅσο καί στήν ἐπικείμενη καταστροφή τῶν Σοδόμων. Οὐσιῶδες μέρος τῆς θεοφανείας εἶναι ἕνας ἐκπληκτικός διάλογος μεταξύ Ἀβραάμ καί Θεοῦ. Λόγῳ τῆς σημασίας του, ὁ διάλογος αὐτός παρατίθεται κατωτέρω στήν πληρότητά του (Γεν. 18, 22-23). Πρόκειται γιά μιά περίπτωση παρεμβάσεως τοῦ Ἀβραάμ ὑπέρ τῆς σωτηρίας τῶν Σοδόμων:

Ἀβραάμ δέ ἔτι ἦν ἑστηκώς ἐναντίον Κυρίου. Καί ἐγγίσας Ἀβραάμ εἶπε· μή συναπολέσῃς (ἐν Σοδόμοις) δίκαιον μετά ἀσεβοῦς καί ἔσται ὁ δίκαιος ὡς ὁ ἀσεβής; Ἐάν ὦσι πεντήκοντα δίκαιοι ἐν τῇ πόλει, ἀπολεῖς αὐτούς; Οὐκ ἀνήσεις πάντα τόν τόπον ἕνεκεν τῶν πεντήκοντα δικαίων, ἐάν ὦσιν ἐν αὐτῇ; Μηδαμῶς σύ ποιήσεις ὡς τό ῥῆμα τοῦτο, τοῦ ἀποκτεῖναι δίκαιον μετά ἀσεβοῦς, καί ἔσται ὁ δίκαιος ὡς ὁ ἀσεβής. Μηδαμῶς· ὁ κρίνων πᾶσαν τήν γῆν, οὐ ποιήσεις κρίσιν; Εἶπε δέ Κύριος· ἐάν εὕρω ἐν Σοδόμοις πεντήκοντα δικαίους ἐν τῇ πόλει, ἀφήσω ὅλην τήν πόλιν καί πάντα τόν τόπον δι' αὐτούς. Καί ἀποκριθείς Ἀβραάμ εἶπε· νῦν ἠρξάμην λαλῆσαι πρός τόν Κύριόν μου, ἐγώ δέ εἰμι γῆ καί σποδός· ἐάν δέ ἐλαττονωθῶσιν οἱ πεντήκοντα δίκαιοι πέντε, ἀπολεῖς ἕνεκεν τῶν πέντε πᾶσαν τήν πόλιν; Καί εἶπεν· οὐ μή ἀπολέσω, ἐάν εὕρω ἐκεῖ τεσσαράκοντα πέντε. Καί προσέθηκεν ἔτι λαλῆσαι πρός αὐτόν καί εἶπεν· ἐάν δέ εὑρεθῶσιν ἐκεῖ τεσσαράκοντα; Καί εἶπεν· οὐ μή ἀπολέσω ἕνεκεν τῶν τεσσαράκοντα. Καί εἶπεν· μή τι, Κύριε, ἐάν λαλήσω· ἐάν δέ εὑρεθῶσιν ἐκεῖ τριάκοντα; Καί εἶπεν· οὐ μή ἀπολέσω, ἐάν εὕρω ἐκεῖ τριάκοντα. Καί εἶπεν· ἐπειδή ἔχω λαλῆσαι πρός τόν Κύριον· ἐάν δέ εὑρεθῶσιν ἐκεῖ εἴκοσι; Καί εἶπεν· οὐ μή ἀπολέσω ἕνεκεν τῶν εἴκοσι. Καί εἶπεν· μή τι, Κύριε, ἐάν λαλήσω ἔτι ἅπαξ· ἐάν δέ εὑρεθῶσιν ἐκεῖ δέκα; Καί εἶπεν· οὐ μή ἀπολέσω ἕνεκεν τῶν δέκα. Ἀπῆλθεν δέ Κύριος, ὡς ἐπαύσατο λαλῶν τῷ Ἀβραάμ, καί Ἀβραάμ ἀπέστρεψεν εἰς τόν τόπον αὐτοῦ (Γεν. 18, 22-33).

Στήν περίπτωση αὐτή, ἡ θεοφάνεια ὅπως μᾶς τήν περιγράφει τό βιβλικό κείμενο, δέν εἶναι τοῦ εἴδους τῆς μυστικιστικῆς θεωρίας ἤ μιᾶς ἀτομικῆς θρησκευτικῆς ἐμπειρίας. Εἶναι θεοφάνεια πού συνδέεται μέ τίς τύχες μιᾶς ὁλόκληρης πόλεως, καί μέ τήν περαιτέρω ἱστορία ἑνός λαοῦ. Εἶναι θεοφάνεια στήν ὁποία ἡ ἀνθρώπινη πλευρά δέν εἶναι παθητικός δέκτης, ἀλλά μέσῳ τῆς θεοφανικῆς εὐκαιρίας παρεμβαίνει στό ἱστορικό γίγνεσθαι.

Ἡ περίπτωση τῆς θεοφανείας παρά τήν δρῦν Μαμβρῆ, ἐκφράζει τήν ἀναζήτηση ἀπό τόν ἄνθρωπο ἑνός Θεοῦ ὁ ὁποῖος ἐμφανίζεται ὑπό συνθῆκες ὁρατές καί ἁπτές προκειμένου νά διαλεχθῆ μέ τόν ἄνθρωπο καί νά τοῦ δώση τήν δυνατότητα δραστικῆς συμμετοχῆς στή διαμόρφωση ἱστορικῶν ἐξελίξεων διαφόρου μορφῆς καί ἐντάσεως. Ὁ θεοφανικός διάλογος στό Γεν. 18, 22-33 ἀποτελεῖ λαμπρό δεῖγμα ἀναζητήσεως ἑνός Θεοῦ ὁ ὁποῖος παρέχει στόν ἄνθρωπο τήν εὐκαιρία παρεμβάσεως, ἡ ὁποία μπορεῖ νά τροποποιήση ἀκόμη καί τό σχέδιο τοῦ ἴδιου τοῦ Θεοῦ.

Ἡ παραπάνω ἄποψη ἐπιβεβαιώνεται καί ἀπό τίς θεοφανικές ἐμφανίσεις στόν Μωϋσῆ, ὅπως περιγράφονται στά κεφάλαια 3 καί 32-34 τοῦ βιβλίου τῆς Ἐξόδου. Λόγου χάριν, στό κεφάλαιο 32 τῆς Ἐξόδου ἀναφέρεται ὅτι *ἐλάλησε Κύριος πρός Μωϋσῆν ἐνώπιος ἐνωπίῳ, ὡς εἴ τις λαλήσει πρός τόν ἑαυτοῦ φίλον* (Ἐξοδ. 32, 11). Ἐν τούτοις ὁ Μωϋσῆς ζητεῖ ἀπό τόν Θεό μιά πλήρως ὁρατή θεοφάνεια *εἰ οὖν εὕρηκα χάριν ἐναντίον σου, ἐμφάνισόν μοι σεαυτόν· γνωστῶς ἵνα ἴδω σε, ὅπως ἄν εὑρηκώς χάριν ἐναντίον σου, καί ἵνα γνῶ ὅτι λαός σου τό ἔθνος τοῦτο* (Ἐξοδ. 32, 13). Ὁ Μωϋσῆς ζητεῖ τήν θεοφάνεια ὡς στοιχεῖο ἀπαραίτητο γιά τήν ἐπιτυχία τῆς ἀποστολῆς του καί τῆς εὐθύνης του ἔναντι τοῦ λαοῦ. Ζητεῖ τήν θεοφάνεια ὡς δυνατότητα γιά τόν ἴδιο, παρεμβάσεως στήν ἐξέλιξη τῆς ἱστορίας τοῦ Ἰσραήλ, δηλαδή παρεμβάσεως στό σχέδιο τοῦ Θεοῦ γιά τόν λαό Ἰσραήλ.

Παρόμοιες παρατηρήσεις ἰσχύουν καί γιά τήν περίφημη θεοφανική περικοπή τοῦ ἕκτου κεφαλαίου τοῦ βιβλίου τοῦ Ἠσαΐου. Ἡ θεοφάνεια ἐν προκειμένῳ συνδέεται ἄμεσα μέ τήν ἀνάθεση προφητικῆς ἀποστολῆς στόν Ἠσαΐα, δηλαδή συνιστᾶ φαινόμενο δυνατότητος παρεμβάσεως ἀπό πλευρᾶς ἀνθρώπου στή ζωή γενικωτέρων ἀνθρωπίνων συνόλων.

Ἀσφαλῶς οἱ θεοφάνειες τῆς Παλαιᾶς Διαθήκης ἀποτελοῦν πολύμορφα καί πολυσήμαντα φαινόμενα. Νομίζουμε ὅμως ὅτι, μεταξύ ἄλλων, ἀποκαλύπτουν τήν τάση ἀπό πλευρᾶς ἀνθρώπου, ἀναζητήσεως ἑνός Θεοῦ ὁ ὁποῖος νά προσφέρη τήν δυνατότητα θεοφανικῶν ἐμφανίσεων τοῦ βιβλικοῦ τύπου τόν ὁποῖο ἁδρομερέστατα παρουσιάσαμε, δηλ. θεοφανικῶν ἐμφανίσεων κατά τίς ὁποῖες ὁ Θεός καθίσταται ἀντιληπτός διά τῶν αἰσθήσεων, διαλέγεται εὐθέως μέ τόν ἄνθρωπο καί τοῦ προσφέρει τήν εὐκαιρία δράσεως ἡ ὁποία ἔχει οὐσιαστικές ἐπιπτώσεις καί δραστικές συνέπειες πέραν τοῦ ἀτόμου τοῦ δεχομένου τήν θεοφάνεια. Ἡ κοινωνία τοῦ 21^{ου} αἰῶνος παρέχει πολλά παραδείγματα μιᾶς ἀναζητήσεως τοῦ Θεοῦ ἡ ὁποία συνδέεται μέ θεοφανικές δυνατότητες.

Τέταρτη Παραλλαγή: Ἡ ἀναζήτηση ἑνός Θεοῦ δικαιοσύνης

Ἡ τέταρτη βιβλική παραλλαγή στό ὑπό μελέτην θέμα, ἀναφαίνεται σχεδόν σέ ὅλα τά βιβλικά κείμενα ἀλλά προσφέρεται μέ ἔνταση γραφῆς καί περιεχομένου κυρίως στό βιβλίο τῶν Ψαλμῶν καί στά προφητικά βιβλία τῆς Παλαιᾶς Διαθήκης. Πρόκειται γιά τήν ἀναζήτηση τοῦ Θεοῦ ὡς Θεοῦ δικαιοσύνης, ὡς ἀμεροληπτου κριτοῦ τῶν ἀνθρώπων, καί ὡς ἐγγυητοῦ ἄρσεως τῆς πάσης μορφῆς ἐνδοκόσμιας ἀδικίας. Εἶναι χαρακτηριστικό ὅτι ἡ λέξη δικαιοσύνη ἀπαντᾶ περισσότερο ἀπό 80 φορές στούς Ψαλμούς καί 60 περίπου φορές στόν προφήτη Ἠσαΐα. Ἀξίζει νά παραθέσουμε μερικά χαρακτηριστικά χωρία, πρωτίστως ἀπό τούς Ψαλμούς:

Ψ. 10, 7 *Δίκαιος Κύριος καί δικαιοσύνας ἠγάπησε.*

Ψ. 30, 1 *Ἐπί σοί, Κύριε ἤλπισα...ἐν τῇ δικαιοσύνῃ σου ρῦσαί με καί ἐξελοῦ με.*

Ψ. 47, 11 *Δικαιοσύνης πλήρης ἡ δεξιά Σου.*

Ψ. 70, 16-24 *Κύριε, μνησθήσομαι τῆς δικαιοσύνης σου μόνου...ἔτι δε καί ἡ γλῶσσα μου ὅλην τήν ἡμέραν μελετήσει τήν δικαιοσύνην σου.*

Ψ. 96, 6 *Ἀνήγγειλαν οἱ οὐρανοί τήν δικαιοσύνην Αὐτοῦ.*

Ψ. 97, 2 *Ἐγνώρισε Κύριος τό σωτήριον αὐτοῦ, ἐναντίον τῶν ἐθνῶν ἀπεκάλυψε τήν δικαιοσύνην αὐτοῦ.*

Ψ. 118, 40 *Ἐν τῇ δικαιοσύνῃ σου ζῆσόν με.*

Ψ. 118, 172 *Φθέγξαιτο ἡ γλῶσσα μου τό λόγιόν σου, ὅτι πᾶσαι αἱ ἐντολαί σου δικαιοσύνη.*

Στόν προφήτη Ἠσαΐα πλήν ἐκφράσεων ὅπως οἱ παραπάνω τῶν Ψαλμῶν, συναντοῦμε καί ὡραιότατες διατυπώσεις ἀσυνήθους ὑποβλητικότητος μέ ἀναφορά στό θέμα τῆς δικαιοσύνης ὡς κατ' ἐξοχήν ἰδιότητος τοῦ Θεοῦ:

Ἠσ. 11, 5 (ὁ ἀναμενόμενος Μεσσίας) ἔσται δικαιοσύνη ἐζωσμένος τήν ὀσφύν αὐτοῦ.

Ἠσ. 38, 19 *Οἱ ζῶντες εὐλογήσουσίν Σε ὃν τρόπον κἀγώ. Ἀπό γάρ τῆς σήμερον παιδία ποιήσω, ἃ ἀναγγελοῦσι τήν δικαιοσύνην σου, Κύριε τῆς σωτηρίας μου.*

Ἠσ. 45, 8 *Εὐφρανθήτω ὁ οὐρανός ἄνωθεν, καί αἱ νεφέλαι ρανάτωσαν δικαιοσύνην· ἀνατειλάτω ἡ γῆ ἔλεος καί δικαιοσύνην ἀνατειλάτω ἅμα· ἐγώ εἰμι Κύριος ὁ κτίσας σε.*

Ἠσ. 51, 6-8 *Ὁ οὐρανός ὡς καπνός ἐστερεώθη, ἡ δέ γῆ ὡς ἱμάτιον παλαιωθήσεται...τό δέ σωτήριόν μου εἰς τόν αἰῶνα ἔσται, ἡ δέ δικαιοσύνη μου οὐ μή ἐκλίπῃ... Ἡ δέ δικαιοσύνη μου εἰς τόν αἰῶνα ἔσται, τό δέ σωτήριόν μου εἰς γενεάν γενεῶν.*

Τό πάθος τῆς δικαιοσύνης συνδέεται ἄμεσα μέ τήν ἀναζήτηση τοῦ Θεοῦ. Οἱ ἐντονώτατες περί δικαιοσύνης καί ἀδικίας περικοπές προφητῶν, ὅπως ὁ Ἠσαΐας, ὁ Ἱερεμίας, ὁ Ἀμώς, καί ὁ Ὠσηέ, φανερώνουν τήν ἀναζήτηση ἑνός Θεοῦ ὁ ὁποῖος εἶναι πρωτίστως Θεός δικαιοσύνης. Χωρίς ἀμφιβολία, ἕνας σημαντικός ἀριθμός ἀνθρώπων πού ἀναζητοῦν τόν Θεό, ἀναζητοῦν στήν οὐσία ἕνα Θεό πού ἐγγυᾶται καί προσφέρει τήν δικαιοσύνη στήν γνησιότερη καί καθαρότερή της μορφή.

Τά βιβλικά κείμενα μέ τήν ἔντονη φωνή τοῦ Θεοῦ γιά τήν ἐπιδίωξη τῆς δικαιοσύνης στόν κόσμο εἶναι ταυτοχρόνως κείμενα στά ὁποῖα ἡ ἀνθρώπινη φωνή ἐκφράζει μέ πάθος τήν δίψα γιά ἕνα Θεό δικαιοσύνης. Ἰδιαίτερα σήμερα, σέ ἡμέρες καί χρόνους πού ἐπληθύνθη ἡ ἀδικία.

Πέμπτη Παραλλαγή: ***Εἰς ἀναζήτησιν τοῦ Θεοῦ τῆς σοφίας καί τῆς γνώσεως***

Μέ τήν πέμπτη βιβλική παραλλαγή περνοῦμε σέ μιάν ἄλλη οὐσιώδη ἔκφραση τῆς ἀναζητήσεως τοῦ Θεοῦ. Πρόκειται γιά τήν ἀναζήτηση ἑνός Θεοῦ χορηγοῦ τῆς γνώσεως καί τῆς σοφίας. Στά βιβλικά κείμενα ἡ τάση αὐτή ἐκπροσωπεῖται ἀπό βασικά σοφιολογικά κείμενα ὅπως οἱ Παροιμίες Σολομῶντος, ἡ Σοφία Σολομῶντος καί ἡ Σοφία Σειράχ.

Στά ἀνωτέρω κείμενα γίνεται συνεχής καί ἐντυπωσιακή ἀναφορά στή σοφία καί σέ συναφεῖς ἔννοιες συνδεόμενες πάντοτε μέ τόν Θεό. Θά παραθέσω ἀμέσως δύο πολύ σημαντικές σχετικές περικοπές.

Ἡ πρώτη προέρχεται ἀπό τό βιβλίο τῶν Παροιμιῶν τοῦ Σολομῶντος καί συγκεκριμένα ἀπό τό περίφημο κεφάλαιο 8 τοῦ βιβλίου αὐτοῦ:

> *Ἐγώ ἡ σοφία κατεσκήνωσα βουλήν καί γνῶσιν καί ἔννοιαν ἐγώ ἐπεκαλεσάμην. Ἐμή βουλή καί ἀσφάλεια, ἐμή φρόνησις, ἐμή δέ ἰσχύς· ἐγώ τούς ἐμέ φιλοῦντας ἀγαπῶ, οἱ δέ ἐμέ ζητοῦντες εὑρήσουσιν. Πλοῦτος καί δόξα ἐμοί ὑπάρχει καί κτῆσις πολλῶν καί δικαιοσύνη· βέλτιον ἐμέ καρπίζεσθαι ὑπέρ χρυσίον καί λίθον τίμιον, τά δέ ἐμά γεννήματα κρείσσω ἀργυρίου ἐκλεκτοῦ.*

Ἡνίκα ἡτοίμαζεν (ἐνν. ὁ Θεός) τόν οὐρανόν, συμπαρήμην αὐτῷ, καί ὅτε ἀφώριζεν τόν ἑαυτοῦ θρόνον ἐπ' ἀνέμων. Ἡνίκα ἰσχυρά ἐποίει τά ἄνω...καί ἰσχυρά ἐποίει τά θεμέλια τῆς γῆς, ἤμην παρ' αὐτῷ ἁρμόζουσα, ἐγώ ἤμην ᾗ προσέχαιρεν. Καθ' ἡμέραν δέ εὐφραινόμην ἐν προσώπῳ αὐτοῦ ἐν παντί καιρῷ, ὅτε εὐφραίνετο τήν οἰκουμένην συντελέσας καί ἐνευφραίνετο ἐν υἱοῖς ἀνθρώπων (Παροιμ. 8, 12-31).

Ἡ δεύτερη περικοπή προέρχεται ἀπό τό βιβλικό κείμενο τῆς Σοφίας Σολομῶντος. Ἐδῶ ἡ σοφία ἐμφανίζεται μέ ἕνα σύνολο θαυμαστῶν ἰδιοτήτων:

Ἔστι γάρ ἐν αὐτῇ (δηλ. τῇ σοφίᾳ) πνεῦμα νοερόν, ἅγιον, μονογενές, πολυμερές, λεπτόν, εὐκίνητον, τρανόν, ἀμόλυντον, σαφές ἀπήμαντον, φιλάγαθον, ὀξύ, ἀκώλυτον, εὐεργετικόν, φιλάνθρωπον, βέβαιον, ἀσφαλές, ἀμέριμνον, παντοδύναμον, πανεπίσκοπον καί διά πάντων χωροῦν πνευμάτων νοερῶν καθαρῶν λεπτοτάτων. Πάσης γάρ κινήσεως κινητικώτερον σοφία, διήκει δέ καί χωρεῖ διά πάντων διά τήν καθαρότητα· ἀτμίς γάρ ἐστιν τῆς τοῦ Θεοῦ δυνάμεως καί ἀπόρροια τῆς τοῦ παντοκράτορος δόξης εἰλικρινής· διά τοῦτο οὐδέν μεμιαμμένον εἰς αὐτήν παρεμπίπτει. ἀπαύγασμα γάρ ἐστιν φωτός ἀϊδίου καί ἔσοπτρον ἀκηλίδωτον τῆς τοῦ θεοῦ ἐνεργείας καί εἰκών τῆς ἀγαθότητος αὐτοῦ. μία δέ οὖσα πάντα δύναται καί μένουσα ἐν αὐτῇ τά πάντα καινίζει καί κατά γενεάς εἰς ψυχάς ὁσίας μεταβαίνουσα φίλους θεοῦ καί προφήτας κατασκευάζει· οὐθέν γάρ ἀγαπᾷ ὁ θεός εἰ μή τόν σοφίᾳ συνοικοῦντα. ἔστιν γάρ αὕτη εὐπρεπεστέρα ἡλίου καί ὑπέρ πᾶσαν ἄστρων θέσιν (Σοφ. Σολομ. 7, 22-29).

Ταύτην ἐφίλησα καί ἐξεζήτησα ἐκ νεότητός μου

καί ἐζήτησα νύμφην ἀγαγέσθαι ἐμαυτῷ καί ἐραστής ἐγενόμην τοῦ κάλλους αὐτῆς (Σοφ. Σολομ. 8, 2).

Τό πάθος τῶν περικοπῶν αὐτῶν εἶναι ἐμφανέστατο. Ἡ σοφία, ἡ ἀπόλυτη γνώση, δέν προσωποιεῖται ἁπλῶς κατά μεταφορικό τρόπο, ἀλλά κυριολεκτικά ὑποστασιοποιεῖται, σχεδόν ταυτίζεται μέ τόν Θεό. Τά κείμενα αὐτά εἶναι ἐνδεικτικά μιᾶς ἀναζητήσεως τοῦ Θεοῦ ὡς κέντρου καί πηγῆς σοφίας καί ἐν τελικῇ ἀναλύσει ὡς πηγῆς τῆς ἀπόλυτης γνώσεως καί τῆς τέλειας ἐπιστήμης. Ὁ προβαλλόμενος καί ἀναζητούμενος Θεός στίς παραπάνω περιπτώσεις τῆς λεγομένης σοφιολογικῆς βιβλικῆς γραμματείας εἶναι ἕνας Θεός τῆς σοφίας καί γνώσεως, ὁ Ὁποῖος γίνεται ἀντικείμενο μιᾶς ὁλοκληρωτικῆς ἀφοσιώσεως, μιᾶς χωρίς ἀνάπαυση προσπαθείας κατακτήσεως. Στά παραπάνω ὅμως κείμενα ἡ σύνδεση τῆς ἀπόλυτης σοφίας μέ τόν Θεό εἶναι ἄμεση καί ὀργανική, γι᾽ αὐτό καί μποροῦν ἄνετα νά ἑρμηνευθοῦν ὡς βιβλικά κείμενα ἐκφραστικά τῆς ἀναζητήσεως ἀπό τόν ἄνθρωπο ἑνός Θεοῦ πού εἶναι τό κέντρο καί ἡ πηγή τῆς τέλειας σοφίας καί τῆς ἀπολύτου γνώσεως.

Ἐπίλογος

Μετά τήν πέμπτη παραλλαγή θά μποροῦσαν νά ἀναφερθοῦν ἀκόμη πολλές ἄλλες. Τά βιβλικά κείμενα τῆς Παλαιᾶς Διαθήκης προσφέρουν ἄφθονο ὑλικό πού ὑποβάλλει τήν ἰδέα τῆς ἀναζητήσεως τοῦ Θεοῦ σέ ποικίλες μορφές, πού μιλοῦν γιά ἀναζήτηση ἑνός Θεοῦ ἐλέους, οἰκτιρμῶν καί παρακλήσεως, γιά ἀναζήτηση ἑνός Θεοῦ ἁγνότητος καί ἁγιότητος, γιά ἀναζήτηση ἑνός Θεοῦ δυνάμεως, γιά ἀναζήτηση ἑνός Θεοῦ ἐλευθερίας, γιά ἀναζήτηση ἑνός Θεοῦ ἀληθείας. Ἡ ἀναφορά παραλλαγῶν στό θέμα αὐτό θά μποροῦσε νά συνεχισθῆ ἐπ' ἄπειρον. Τό βάθος τῆς ἀνθρωπίνης ψυχῆς, οἱ δυνατότητες τοῦ ἀνθρωπίνου πνεύματος, καί τά ἀπίθανα ὑπαρξιακά βιώματα τοῦ ἀνθρώπου θά δημιουργοῦν ἀδιάκοπα διόδους προσβάσεως πρός τόν Θεό, θά συνθέτουν νέες παραλλαγές ἤ θά ἐπαναλαμβάνουν παληές.

Ἐάν περάσουμε ἀπό τήν Παλαιά στήν Καινή Διαθήκη θά ἀνακαλύψουμε μιά ριζική ἀλλαγή. Ἐδῶ ὁ ἀναζητούμενος Θεός γίνεται ὁ ἀναζητῶν Θεός. Ἐδῶ ὁ Θεός δέν ἀναζητεῖ ἁπλῶς τόν ἄνθρωπο. Γίνεται ἄνθρωπος: *Ἐν ἀρχῇ ἦν ὁ Λόγος...πάντα δι' αὐτοῦ ἐγένετο...Καί ὁ Λόγος σάρξ ἐγένετο καί ἐσκήνωσεν ἐν ἡμῖν* (Ἰωάν. 1, 1-14).

Στήν Καινή Διαθήκη οἱ παραλλαγές πού ἀναπτύξαμε ἐναρμονίζονται καί συνυφαίνονται σέ μιάν ἀδιαίρετη ἑνότητα μέ κέντρο τό πρόσωπο τοῦ Ἰησοῦ Χριστοῦ. Ὁ Χριστός γίνεται ἡ ἄρση τοῦ τραύματος τῶν πρωτοπλάστων καί ἡ ὑπέρβαση τῆς ἐνοχῆς καί τῆς ἁμαρτίας. Αὐτός γίνεται ἡ τέλεια καί ἀπόλυτη θεοφάνεια, ἡ πλήρης δικαιοσύνη, τό μοναδικό καί ὑπέροχο Σύ, καί ὁ τέλειος Ἄλλος. Αὐτός γίνεται ἡ *Θεοῦ σοφία* (Α' Κορ. 1, 24), ὁ πληρώσας πᾶσαν δικαιοσύνην καί ὁ *δικαιῶν* ἀκόμη καί τόν *ἀσεβῆ* (Ρωμ. 4, 5).

Ὁ Χριστός ἐν τέλει ἀποβαίνει ἡ ὑπέροχη δυνατότης ἀπαντήσεως στό ἐρώτημα τῆς ἀναζητήσεως τοῦ Θεοῦ. Ἀποβαίνει ἡ βεβαιότης μετατροπῆς τῆς ἀναζητήσεως τοῦ Θεοῦ σέ συνάντηση μαζύ Του, σέ μόνιμη θεοφανική ἐμπειρία, σέ διαρκῆ ἕνωση.

Ἐν τελευταίᾳ ἀναλύσει ὁ Ἰησοῦς Χριστός συνιστᾶ τήν ὁριστική λύση στό πρόβλημα τῆς ἀναζητήσεως τοῦ Θεοῦ, μιά λύση πού καλύπτει ὅλες τίς πιθανές καί ἀπίθανες παραλλαγές τοῦ προβλήματος σήμερα καί στό ἄμεσο καί τό ἀπώτερο μέλλον, στήν παροῦσα καί στίς μέλλουσες γενεές.

"I Have Sought Your Face" (Psalm 27:8): Biblical Variations on the Theme of the Quest for God

Academy of Athens

Athens, Greece
November 14, 2003

Your Beatitude,
Your Eminence, Most Reverend Representative of
His All Holiness, the Ecumenical Patriarch,
Most Esteemed President of the Academy of Athens,
Your Excellency, the President of the Parliament
of the Hellenes,
Most Esteemed Ladies and Gentlemen Members
of the Academy,
Distinguished Guests,
Ladies and Gentlemen,

Unto the Lord my God do I give thanks for this official ceremony.

May I express my warmest thanks for this truly extraordinary honor, my election as a Residing Abroad Member of the Academy of Athens and today's official induction. I am deeply moved by my accession to this august and renowned domain, a sacred grove of science, philosophy and art. Indeed it has filled me to repletion with grateful esteem, as much for the elect Members of the Academy, as it has for our God, the God of Wisdom and the Father of Lights.

Most especially, I should like to thank the highly esteemed and beloved President of the Academy of Athens, Professor Gregorios Skalkeas, for his gracious opening address, which was so indicative of his noble, insightful, and generous spirit. May I also express particular thanks to my brother in Christ, His Eminence Metropolitan John of Pergamum, for his introductory presentation; a revelatory exposition of his remarkable theological learning, brilliant acumen, and deep spirituality. My heartfelt thanks are due as well to those select and beloved members of the *Omogenia* for their considerable graciousness in traveling from America to be present at today's official ceremony.

And now, I have the extraordinary honor, in these few moments, to present my brief remarks, certain fundamental points on my stated theme, "'I Have Sought Your Face' (Psalm 27:8): Biblical Variations on the Theme of the Quest for God."

Introduction

The quest for God by humankind in every age, every civilization and every quarter of the globe, constitutes a fundamental religious phenomenon. It is a phenomenon that presents itself in various forms and is frequently expressed in diametrically opposed ways. These have direct impact on language, art, science, politics, economics and the life of the mind in general. This is as true of the progressive intellectual climate of the present age, as it was in the beginning stages of human history.

The quest for God, an elemental religious phenomenon, can, in the final analysis, be reduced to the following: a simple but substantive movement of the human "I" toward the divine "Thou." It is nothing less than the powerful impetus of the human person, existing in the world, propelled toward the surpassing existence of God. But this single, incomplete reference ought not give the impression that this phenomenon is so simple and easily understood. There is a seemingly endless and constantly expanding bibliography on this subject that highlights the complicated and multifaceted nature of the phenomenon of the quest for God by humankind. The texts of the Bible offer a wonderful illustration of this point. These texts, while they reveal the word of God, simultaneously reveal the human word concerning God. Although they manifest essentially the will of a God Who seeks out humanity, they also manifest the restless desire of the human person who is existentially in a condition of a quest for God. In this regard, verse 8 of Psalm 26 of the Old Testament is characteristic: *"My heart said unto You: I have sought Your face, O Lord, Your countenance will I seek."* This verse, which constitutes a portion of the title of the present address, is an organic part of the God-inspired text that naturally belongs to the wider sphere of God's revelation. But certainly it is clear that the same text expresses the human inclination toward the Divine with absolute clarity and indubitable intensity. Consequently, this verse could be studied as a text indicative of humankind's quest for God.

Indeed, the theme is expressed, with an eloquent and stimulating manner, in many other biblical texts. At times directly and at times indirectly, this theme of humankind's quest for God arises in different and interesting ways. The differences highlight who this sought-after God is and describe His distinguishing characteristics. I would now present in a summary fashion a few of these abovementioned ways that constitute basic biblical variations on the vital existential phenomenon of humankind's quest for God.

First Variation:
From nothingness, chaos and formlessness to order and the reasoned governance of the universe

This first variation appears in the first chapter of Genesis, the first book of the Old Testament. Let us listen to some select verses:

> *In the beginning God created the heavens and the earth. The earth was without form and void, and darkness was upon the face of the deep; and the Spirit of God was moving over the face of the waters* (Genesis 1:1-2).
> *And God said, "Let there be light;" and there was light* (Genesis 1:3).
> *And God said, "Let there be a firmament in the midst of the waters, and let it separate the waters from the waters." And it was so* (Genesis 1:6).
> *And God said, "Let the waters under the heavens be gathered together into one place, and let the dry land appear." And it was so* (Genesis 1:9).
> *And God said, "Let the earth put forth vegetation, plants yielding seed, and fruit trees bearing fruit in which is their seed, each according to its kind, upon the earth." And it was so* (Genesis 1:11).
> *And God said, "Let there be lights in the firmament of the heavens to separate the day from the night; and let them be for signs and for seasons and for days and years, and let them be lights in the firmament of the heavens to give light upon the earth." And it was so* (Genesis 1:14,15).
> *And God said, "Let the waters bring forth swarms of living creatures, and let birds fly above the earth across*

> *the firmament of the heavens." And it was so* (Genesis 1:20).
>
> *And God said, "Let the earth bring forth living creatures according to their kinds: cattle and creeping things and beasts of the earth according to their kinds." And it was so* (Genesis 1:24).
>
> *Then God said, "Let us make man in our image, after our likeness; and let them have dominion over the fish of the sea, and over the birds of the air, and over the cattle, and over all the earth, and over every creeping thing that creeps upon the earth." So God created man in his own image, in the image of God he created him; male and female he created them* (Genesis 1:26,27).
>
> *And God saw everything that he had made, and behold, it was very good* (Genesis 1:31).

What is it that we observe in this instance? Here we have a description of the creation of all that is, with particular emphasis on the planet Earth, our planet. The description advances through successive phases defined by repeated basic terms (e.g., *"and God said," "and it was so," "first day," "second day,"* etc.). This is to demonstrate the systematic and balanced procession of the most important aspects of the creation. These aspects cover a wide range of the creative activities that come to their actualization through the almighty word of the Creator God. At the conclusion of the six time periods, during which the most important aspects of the created order come to being, the picture that emerges is as follows: from a primal condition of nothingness and nonexistence a universe is created, viewed from a human perspective as geocentric. Accordingly, *the earth was without form and void, and darkness was upon the face of the deep*. The terminology is a terminology of chaos, formlessness and darkness. But as we proceed, the darkness recedes, the earth takes on a distinct shape and form with the separation of land and sea. The vegetal, animal and stellar worlds emerge, and, lastly, humankind is created. The human race is created *in the image and according to the likeness of God,* with the commandment, *increase, multiply, fill and have dominion over the earth* (Genesis 1:28).

This extraordinary text can be read and interpreted not only as a theological, biblical description of the creation of the world, but as an expression of the specific quest for God. In this instance, the quest aims at a God Who takes away the nonexistence of the world, that is, Who creates the universe out of nothingness. Furthermore, He successively transforms the primal chaos into cosmos. He introduces light into the primordial darkness. He establishes the properties of the oceans and the dry land, bringing forth life. Finally, He creates the human being, to whom He grants the control of all things. Here the quest for God is connected with the surmounting of cosmic fear. On the one hand, this is the transcending of the existential dread that comes from the chaos and disorder at the elemental level of nature. On the other hand, it exceeds the threat of being overwhelmed by the animal and vegetal kingdom. Moreover, the creation of the cosmos is achieved through the spoken word alone, through the successive *and God said,* which punctuate the relevant descriptions. This projects the almighty power and mindful purpose of God inasmuch as the sought-after God grants to humankind the dominion of planet earth.

The sought-after God of the first chapter of Genesis is a Creator God. He is a Maker of substantial reality in opposition to nihilistic nonexistence. He fashions order in opposition to chaos, and logical forethought and providence in opposition to illogic and chance occurrence. There can be no doubt that such a God is the God that contemporary humankind eagerly seeks after.

Second Variation:
From the mortal injury and the Fall to restoration

The second biblical variation on the theme of the quest for God comes from another most important Old Testament text, from the third chapter of the book of Genesis. It concerns the description of the Fall of the first-formed Adam and Eve, the ancestral sin of the first human couple. Again we present a few verses from the third chapter of Genesis describing this tragic fall:

> *Now the serpent was more subtle than any other wild creature that the Lord God had made. He said to the woman, "Did God say, 'You shall not eat of any tree of the garden'?" And the woman said to the serpent, "We may eat of the fruit of the trees of the garden; but God said, 'You shall not eat of the fruit of the tree which is in the midst of the garden, neither shall you touch it, lest you die.'" But the serpent said to the woman, "You will not die. For God knows that when you eat of it your eyes will be opened, and you will be like God, knowing good and evil." So when the woman saw that the tree was good for food, and that it was a delight to the eyes, and that the tree was to be desired to make one wise, she took of its fruit and ate; and she also gave some to her husband, and he ate. Then the eyes of both were opened, and they knew that they were naked; and they sewed fig leaves together and made themselves aprons.*
>
> *And they heard the sound of the Lord God walking in the garden in the cool of the day, and the man and his wife hid themselves from the presence of the Lord God among the trees of the garden. But the Lord God called to the man, and said to him, "Where are you?" And he said, "I heard the sound of You in the garden, and I was afraid, be-*

> *cause I was naked; and I hid myself." He said, "Who told you that you were naked? Have you eaten of the tree of which I commanded you not to eat?" The man said, "The woman whom You granted to be with me, she gave me fruit of the tree, and I ate." Then the Lord God said to the woman, "What is this that you have done?" The woman said, "The serpent beguiled me, and I ate." The Lord God said to the serpent, "Because you have done this, cursed are you above all cattle..." To the woman He said, "I will greatly multiply your pain in childbearing; in pain you shall bring forth children..." And to Adam he said, "Because you have listened to the voice of your wife, and have eaten of the tree of which I commanded you, 'You shall not eat of it,' cursed is the ground because of you; in toil you shall eat of it all the days of your life..."* (Genesis 3:1-17).

The above basic description of the fall of the "Protoplasts," the first-created, a deeply traumatic event, refers to the breaking of the relationship between God and man. This relationship was characterized by intimacy, immediacy, full communion, a primeval innocence and purity, and the total freedom to choose from the human side, to follow the guidance of God.

The above description, a classic in its kind, reveals crucial elements that relate to the quest for God. Without a doubt, there is a limitless grief for the human failing, the "Fall." There is a deep yearning and ardent longing for a restoration of the original relationship, as a relationship of precisely the intimacy and complete communion. There is a desire to retrieve the lost innocence and the possibility of the proper operation of human freedom to choose the good.

The building blocks of this description of the "Fall of the Protoplasts" reveal a form of the quest for God as a quest for the Absolute "Thou": a "Thou" with Whom there exists immediate access; a "Thou" Who is able to heal even fatal human faults; a "Thou" who can wipe away the aboriginal guilt. Here the quest for God is a search for the holistic relationship that existed between God and humankind before the Fall. This relationship would exceed the traumatic rupture that occurred after the Fall. This relationship would satisfy the deepest human yearning for the Perfect "Thou," for the Absolute "Other" with Whom there is intimate communion. Such a human longing, such a quest for God is easily discernible in the world of 2003.

Third Variation: The experience of Theophany

We encounter the third biblical variation in the topic of the quest for God in a series of excerpts in the books of Genesis and Exodus. These excerpts describe certain manifestations of God to important biblical personages: Abraham, Jacob, Moses and others. We meet these "Theophanic" appearances in chapter 18 of Genesis (Abraham by the Oak of Mamre), chapters 28 and 32 of Genesis (Jacob at Bethel and Peniel), and chapters 3, and 32-34 of the book of Exodus (Moses before the burning bush and at Mount Sinai).

The events surrounding Abraham in chapter 18 of Genesis are introduced with the characteristic phrase: *And God appeared to him* (i.e. Abraham) *by the oaks of Mamre, as he sat at the door of his tent in the heat of the day* (Genesis 18:1). The following portrayal leaves no doubt that this is a Theophany of a special type. This Theophany is no mere momentary manifestation. Rather it encompasses an announcement of serious developments in the life of Abraham and in the immanent destruction of Sodom. The essential portion of this Theophany is the surprising dialogue between Abraham and God. To hallmark its significance, we shall cite it in its entirety. Here is Abraham intervening for the salvation of the people of Sodom:

> *But Abraham still stood before the Lord. Then Abraham drew near, and said, "Will You indeed destroy* [in Sodom] *the righteous with the wicked? Suppose there are fifty righteous within the city; will You then destroy the place and not spare it for the fifty righteous who are in it? Far be it from You to do such a thing, to slay the righteous with the wicked, so that the righteous fare as the wicked! Far be it from You! Shall not the Judge of all the earth do right?" And the Lord said, "If I find at Sodom fifty righteous in the city, I will spare the whole place for their sake." Abraham answered, "Behold, I have taken upon myself to speak to the Lord, I who am but dust and ashes. Suppose five of the fifty righteous are lacking? Will You destroy the whole city for lack of five?" And He said, "I will not destroy it if I find forty-five there." Again he spoke to Him, and said, "Suppose forty are found there." He answered, "For the sake of forty I will not do it." Then he said, "Oh let not the Lord be angry, and I will speak. Suppose thirty are found there." He answered, "I will not do it, if I find thirty there." He said, "Behold, I have taken upon myself to speak to the Lord. Suppose twenty are found there." He answered, "For the sake of twenty I will not destroy it." Then he said, "Oh let not the Lord be angry, and I will speak again but this once. Suppose ten are found there." He answered, "For the sake of ten I will not destroy it." And the Lord went his way, when he had finished speaking to Abraham; and Abraham returned to his place* (Genesis 18:22-33).

In this excerpt, the Theophany is neither a mystical vision nor the religious experience of an individual. It is a Theophany that is connected with the fortune of an entire city, and the further history of a people. It is a Theophany where the human component is no mere passive recipient. Rather, the human component seizes the opportunity of the Theophany to intervene in history.

The incident of the Theophany by the Oak of Mamre expresses the human quest for a God Who is manifest through visible, tangible conditions in order to dialog with humankind and give us the ability to be active participants in the formation of history, to make a difference in the shape and intensity of our own evolution. The Theophanic dialog in Genesis 18:22-33 represents a shining example of the quest for a God Who grants humankind the opportunity for intervention, an opportunity that can modify even the plan of the very God!

This aspect is confirmed by the Theophanies manifested to Moses, especially those mentioned in chapters 3 and 32-34 of the book of Exodus. For example, in chapter 33 of Exodus we read that: *the Lord used to speak to Moses face to face, as a person would speak to his friend* (Exodus 33:11). In this instance, Moses seeks from God a complete visible Theophany: *If I have found favor in Your sight, show me now Your ways, that I may know You and find favor in Your sight. Consider too that this nation is Your people* (Exodus 33:13). Moses seeks the Theophany as a necessary element for the success of his mission and his responsibility for the people. He seeks the Theophany in order to become able to intervene in the developing history of Israel, which is intervention in the plans of God for the people of Israel.

Similar observations are present in the famous Theophany in the sixth chapter of the book of Isaiah. The Theophany is associated with the appointment of Isaiah's prophetic mission. Again, we see the phenomenon of the human capacity to intervene in the life of humankind in general.

The Theophanies of the Old Testament surely comprise polymorphous and polysemantic phenomena. Moreover, they reveal the tendency of humankind to search for God, the God Who has offered Theophanies of the biblical type we have described above, the God, Who through these Theophanies makes Himself accessible through a sensory experience, Who dialogs directly with the human person, and Who offers the human person the opportunity for action that has substantive results and dynamic consequences that reach well beyond the individual who received the Theophany. Twenty-first century society provides many examples of the quest for a God that offer Theophanic possibilities.

Fourth Variation: The quest for a God of righteousness

The fourth biblical variation in our study appears in nearly every biblical text, but with particular emphasis in the book of the Psalms and the prophetic books of the Old Testament. Here we have the quest for God as the search for the God of righteousness, the impartial judge of humanity, the guarantor that every type of injustice in this world will pass away. Most notable is the frequency of the word "righteousness" in the book of Psalms, which occurs in more than 80 passages and in approximately 60 passages in the Book of the Prophet Isaiah. It is certainly worth looking at a few of these passages, beginning with the Psalms:

Psalm 11:7 *For the Lord is righteous and loves righteousness.*

Psalm 31:1 *In You, O Lord, have I hoped ... in Your righteousness deliver me, and rescue me.*

Psalm 48:10 *Your right hand is full of righteousness.*

Psalm 71:16,24 *O Lord, I will make mention of the righteousness which is Yours alone... Moreover my tongue will meditate on Your righteousness all the day long.*

Psalm 97:6 *The heavens declared His righteousness...*

Psalm 98:2 *The Lord has made known His salvation, in the sight of the nations He has revealed His righteousness.*

Psalm 119:40 *In Your righteousness enliven me.*

Psalm 119:172 *My tongue shall speak of Your sayings, for all Your commandments are righteousness.*

In the Book of the Prophet Isaiah, we encounter, in addition to a language similar to the Psalms, expressions of superb beauty and strong suggestiveness projecting righteousness as the quality *par excellence* of God:

Isaiah 11:5 (of the coming Messiah) *Righteousness shall be the girdle of His waist.*

Isaiah 38:19 *The living shall bless You, as I do.*
For from this day I shall father children
who will declare Your righteousness,
O Lord of my salvation!

Isaiah 45:8 *Let the heavens above rejoice,*
and let the clouds rain down righteousness;
let the earth bring forth mercy and
let it bring forth righteousness;
I Am the Lord Who has created you.

Isaiah 51:6-8 *The heavens are only as firm as smoke,*
and the earth will wear out like a garment...
but My salvation will be for ever,
and My righteousness will never be ended...
My righteousness will be for ever,
and My salvation to all generations.

The passion for righteousness is intimately linked to the quest for God. The very vivid citations from the prophets on justice and injustice, such as Isaiah, Jeremiah, Amos and Hosea, reveal the quest for a God Who, above all else, is a God of righteousness. Doubtless, the vast majority of humankind who seek God essentially seek a God who would not only offer humanity righteousness, but indeed guarantee the most genuine and pure form of justice.

The biblical texts that manifest the intense voice of God for the pursuit of justice in the world are simultaneously texts that bear witness to the intense cry of the human person who thirsts for a God of righteousness. This is all the more so today, when the current conditions of the world are so full of injustice.

Fifth Variation:
The quest for the God of wisdom and knowledge

In this fifth biblical variation, we pass on to another substantial expression of the quest for God. Here we see the search for a God Who is the source of knowledge and wisdom. This tendency is represented in the wisdom literature of the Bible, the Proverbs of Solomon, the Wisdom of Solomon and the Wisdom of Sirach.

In the above texts, we encounter an impressive and continuous reference to wisdom and similar concepts always connected to God. Let me offer two very significant, pertinent examples.

The first is from the Proverbs of Solomon, specifically from the famous eighth chapter of this book:

> *I, wisdom, dwell in counsel, and I find knowledge and discretion. Mine is counsel and mine the sound wisdom. I love those who love me, and those who seek me diligently find me. Riches and honor are with me, righteousness and the possession of abundance. My fruit is better than gold, better than precious stones, and my yield than choice silver.*
>
> *When He established the heavens, I was there, when He delimited His throne upon the winds. When He made firm the skies above, when He marked out the foundations of the earth, then I was beside Him and I rejoiced before Him. I was daily His delight, rejoicing before Him always, rejoicing in His inhabited world and delighting in the sons of men* (Proverbs 8:12-31).

The second passage comes from the Book of the Wisdom of Solomon. Here, wisdom is presented in a sum of marvelous qualities:

> *For in her* [i.e. wisdom] *there is a spirit that is intelligent, holy, unique, manifold, subtle, mobile, clear, unpolluted, distinct, invulnerable, loving the good, keen, irresistible, beneficent, humane, steadfast, sure, free from anxiety, all-powerful, overseeing all, and penetrating through all spirits that are intelligent and pure and most subtle.*

For wisdom is more mobile than any motion; because of her pureness she pervades and penetrates all. For she is a breath of the power of God, and a pure emanation of the glory of the Almighty; therefore nothing defiled gains entrance into her. For she is a reflection of eternal light, a spotless mirror of the working of God, and an image of his goodness. Though she is but one, she can do all things, and while remaining in herself, she renews all things; and in every generation she passes into holy souls, and makes them friends of God, and prophets; for God loves nothing so much as the man who lives with wisdom. For she is more beautiful than the sun, and excels every constellation of the stars (Wisdom of Solomon 7:22-29).

I loved her, and sought her from my youth, and I desired to take her for my bride, and I became enamored of her beauty (Wisdom of Solomon 8:2).

The intensity of these passages is obvious. Wisdom, absolute knowledge, is not presented in a metaphorical style. Rather, there is a literal personification, nearly identifying her with God. The texts are indicative of a quest for God Who is the center and source of wisdom, and Who is, in the final analysis, the source of absolute knowledge and perfect science. The God Who is projected and is sought-after in the above passages of this sophiological biblical literature is a God of wisdom and knowledge. He is the object of an all-encompassing devotion and a relentless, ceaseless striving. In the abovementioned texts the connection of absolute wisdom and God is immediate and organic. For this reason, these biblical texts can be easily interpreted as expressive of the human quest for God that is the center and source of perfect wisdom and absolute knowledge.

Epilogue

After the fifth variation, we could mention many more. We could offer many other variations because the texts of the Old Testament present abundant material. They suggest the idea of the quest for God in an abundance of forms: as a search for a God of mercy, of compassion, and of consolation, a quest for a God of innocence, purity and holiness, the pursuit of a God of power, of freedom, of truth. The variations are endless. The depth of the human soul, the potentialities of the human spirit, and the incredible existential realities of humanity create ceaseless incursions and opportunities to enter into dialog with God, and these will surely bring about new variations or repeat the former ones.

If we pass from the Old Testament to the New, we will discover a radical change. Here, the sought-after God becomes the God Who seeks after us! And God does not simply seek us; He becomes One of us! *In the Beginning was the Word, the Logos ... all things came into being through Him .. and the Logos became flesh, and dwelt among us* (John 1:1-14).

In the New Testament, the five variations that we presented from the Old Testament are interwoven and conform in a total and absolute way with the person of Jesus Christ. It is Christ Who takes away the traumatic bruise of the sins of the Protoplasts, and it is Christ Who overcomes the guilt of their sin. He is the perfect and absolute Theophany, the fullness of righteousness, the unique and highest "Thou," the perfect "Other." He is the *Wisdom of God* (I Corinthians 1:24), Who fulfills all righteousness and even more, *justifies the ungodly* (Romans 4:5).

In the end, Christ proves to be an exceedingly compelling answer to the question of man's quest for God. Here we have the confirmation that the quest for God is to be transformative through the encounter with Christ, a unique Theophanic experience of continuous union.

In the final analysis, Jesus Christ is the decisive solution to man's quest for God. He is the resolution that solves both the probable and improbable variations on this search, both for today and for the future, in our present generation and in those yet to come.

Index of Subjects

C

D

E

F

G

I

J

K

P

R

S

T

U

V

W

Y

Index of Biblical Citations

Old Testament